DOWN EASTER CAPTAIN

DOWN EASTER CAPTAIN

by

CAPT. W. J. MOORE, D.S.C., R.D.

ARTHUR H. STOCKWELL, LTD.
Ilfracombe   Devon

PRINTED IN GREAT BRITAIN BY
BRISTOL TYPESETTING CO. LTD.
BARTON MANOR - ST. PHILIPS
BRISTOL 2

CONTENTS

MAPS AND ILLUSTRATIONS

INTRODUCTION

CAPTAIN WALTER LYMAN JOSSELYN was one of the last of the shipmasters serving in that great fleet of American sailing vessels known to the international brotherhood of seamen as Down Easters because they were built and owned in the seaport towns 'down east' in Maine, New Hampshire, Massachusetts, and Connecticut. Born at Duxbury, Mass., in 1841, he was at sea from 1856 until his death in 1913, spending forty of those fifty-seven years in command of deepwater sailing ships and rounding Cape Horn some fifty times. Only his last ship, the *Nuuanu*, was not a true Down Easter, being a Clyde-built iron vessel. He was my grandfather.

Like many a voyager before and since his time, he kept some record of his adventures. His manuscripts of reminiscence which are in my possession make a considerable addition to the story of the sailing ship, and they contain a unique view of world history and of sea life in the second half of the last century and the early years of this. Some of them were apparently written as articles for newspapers or magazines and a few of them may have been published. Others were in a rough unfinished state. All throw light on the character of the man and the life of his era. As a shipmaster myself, though of another age, having a long personal acquaintance with most of the seas he sailed, I have tried to dovetail his yarns into a continuous narrative, preserving as far as possible the original words and style. This is his story.

It is a tale for sailors and lovers of ships and the sea. The lessons of the past help us to understand the present, and I feel sure that any of the younger generation of seafarers who may read it will agree with me that though the places, the ships, and the techniques have changed, our basic problems remain unaltered.

W. J. Moore

Penzance 1967

CHAPTER ONE

Early days of Captain Josselyn—Five voyages in barque
Sicilian—*First voyage (Boy) to Ocoa, St. Domingo—Second*
voyage (O.S.) to Malaga—Third voyage (O.S.) to Gibraltar,
Cadiz, and Messina—Fourth Voyage (O.S.) to Malaga—Fifth
voyage (A.B.) to Malta and Messina.

THIS ACCOUNT of my life from my earliest recollections to the
present time includes more than fifty-four years at sea, during
which period I remained at home once nearly two years at the
time of my marriage, and once for about nine months when I
had double pneumonia. I was in the barque *Sicilian* two years,
the ship *Reynard* eight years, ship *Nevada* one year, ship *Matchless* four years, barque *Coringa* eight years, barque *John D.
Brewer* fourteen years, and now I am in the barque *Nuuanu*
thirteen years already, making my twelfth voyage around Cape
Horn to Honolulu in her. I suppose that three-fourths of this
time I have been actually at sea, out of sight of land.

From memory I have written every voyage separately. One
of the beauties of sea life is that you have so much time to read
and think. During the two years I was ashore I scarcely looked
into a book, and I remember to this day my delight, when I went
to sea again as Chief Mate of the *Matchless,* and had the whole
four hours of my first watch below in which to read anything I
wished.

When I was a schoolboy almost every speaker who addressed
us would say " Set your mark high." I was determined to set mine

high enough, so decided I would be a sea captain. I thought that was about as high as anything. My sisters wanted me to go to College, but usually a child can only understand its own environment and I was no exception. An everyday remark by grown-up people at that time in our town was " What's the use of all this studying. I only went to school for a short time, and old King Cæsar (the richest man in town) can hardly write his own name." Yes, that was high, to be rich, and the richest man was the highest. As most of the well-to-do men in the town were sea captains it was but natural that most of the boys took to the sea, not for love of the occupation but because it seemed to be the quickest way to get an independence. I think most of my teachers thought me a nuisance, but I wish they were living now so that I might tell them their trouble over me bore fruit.

How little I expected to spend half a century on the ocean, in all climates and among all kinds of people. And what changes there have since been in our town and district. In those days our ships were not only manned from home, many of them were built at our own doors and from our own forests. Practically everyone in town was in some way connected with a ship, and in the country every oak tree that was of size and shape was marked for a ship, either for a knee, a rib, a beam, a mast or some other part of the vessel. During spells at home between my early voyages I would often meet farmers in the country twenty miles from salt water who, on learning that I was a sailor, would leave their yoke of oxen in the furrow and spend all the time I would give them talking about the sea life. Some would say " I went to sea with Captain So-and-so, then took my money and bought this land." Others would show me the old marline spikes and palms, or other relics of sea life, which they had kept and still found a use for on occasion.

In the now quiet little town of Duxbury, Mass. nearly every house had been built by a sea captain, and in 1850 these men were still masters of vessels trading to all parts of the world. Today I am the only shipmaster in town in active service. When Corner Stone Lodge was founded over one hundred years ago all its members were shipmasters. I am now its only member still at sea. Fifty years ago it was heavy sarcasm to address the skipper of a fisherman as Captain, for to his men he was always and only the Skipper. Nowadays men who have scarcely been outside the Gurnet Light, if they own their own boat and can pull a pair of

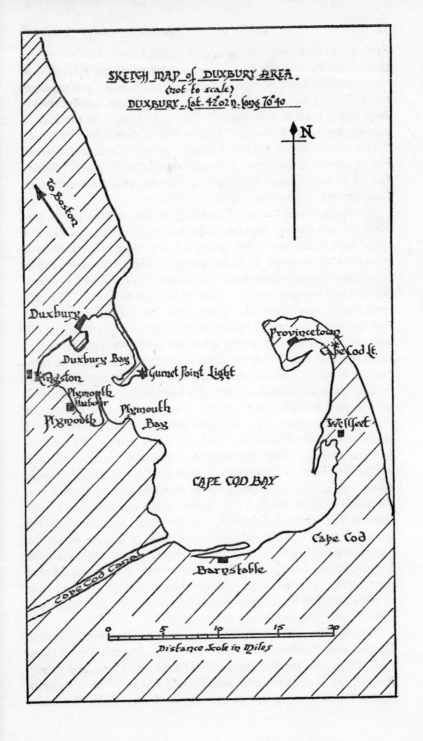

SKETCH MAP of DUXBURY AREA.
(not to scale)
DUXBURY. Lat. 42°02'N. long 70°40

N

to Boston

Duxbury

Duxbury Bay

Kingston

Plymouth Harbour

Plymouth

Plymouth Bay

Gurnet Point Light

Provincetown

Cape Cod Lt.

Wellfleet

CAPE COD BAY

Cape Cod

Cape Cod Canal

Barnstable

0   5   10   15   20
Distance Scale in Miles

oars, have their mail addressed to Captain —. And of course there have been as great changes on board ships, not only in their construction but also in their discipline, food, and management. Fifty years ago the Laws of Storms were hardly known. As a boy I used to hear captains and mates laugh at the idea of anyone knowing a law for storms, for did not the Bible say " The wind bloweth where it listeth, ye hear the sound thereof, but ye cannot tell whence it cometh or whither it goeth." Today failure to understand the Laws of Storms would prevent men from getting Masters' or Mates' Certificates.

My earliest memory is of standing on the lounge in the east room of our house, just one hundred yards from the shore. I could have been only a few years old, my head being then only level with the window. I can see now the fishing schooners, pitching at their anchors in a violent north-east storm. Of course everyone in Duxbury was weather-wise, or thought they were. We kept cows and a good many old sailors came for milk. They foretold that the weather would improve when the moon quartered. It did not, nor did it get much better when the moon was full. So at this early age I already began to doubt the moon as a means of forecasting weather, a doubt since confirmed by a lifetime of observation. Naturally I took charge of a boat as soon as I could pull an oar, and at eight years of age went anywhere in a dory. At eleven I took charge of a sail boat alone, and from then until I was fifteen I sailed boats, lost and won races. How well I remember that first sail alone. My brother told me to bring the *Queen of the Bay* from her moorings at Harden Hill to Hunt's Creek, about a mile. No naval captain ever assumed command of a new ship with more pride than I took over that boat. She was a large boat of her class, a Spritsail, the foremast being always left standing as it was too large for one man to handle when the boat was pitching. With my brother directing me from the bank I brought her alongside without scratching the paint. At that time anyone who failed to pick up their moorings the first time or who bumped a boat was proclaimed a lubber, and there was always some Argus-eye on you.

The *Sicilian*, a barque of 320 tons, built at Kingston by Joseph Holmes, was the first vessel I went to sea in. Captain Allen Dawes was Master, his brother James H. Dawes was Mate, and Henry Parsons, of Newfoundland, was Second Mate. What wonderful stories Parsons could tell of catching seal in the ice. We had a coloured cook and a crew of six men—Long Jim, from Maine; Big Bob from Vermont, a giant in size and weight who had been a boat-steerer in whalers for years; Little Jack from New York State; Jim, an Englishman, who was a Boston rigger; and a Dutchman we called Honch. Of course I was in the forecastle with the men and they took as good care of me as if I had been their own child. For some reason or other they called me Philip, and I went by that name for the two years I was in the ship. When I compared my first experience at sea with that of others I cannot help thinking that I was very fortunate. They were all certainly good-hearted men. But I am going too fast.

When it was decided that I was to go to sea, against the wishes of the family, I began to get ready. The first thing was to get a sea-chest, then my clothes. Many tears were sewn into those garments, and though I was not meant to see them, I did, and realised their value. When I started for Boston in the afternoon of May 9th, 1856, all said goodbye as though I were coming back in a day or two. I had never been in a city before, the noise seemed terrific. We found the barque at the Eastern Steamboat Wharf, but as it was late there was no one on board but Mr. Parsons, the Second Mate, who received us very cordially. My father, being a ship carpenter, was supposed to know about ships, but really he did not know a rope. First he and Mr. Parsons sent me aloft to see if I could climb, but I had always been a good climber and soon satisfied them on that point. Next they tested my knowledge of the rigging and ropes. I was able to make a good impression there too, for I had built and rigged a small ship with my next door neighbour and chum, Frank Wadsworth, and knew every piece of standing rigging. The Second Mate was pleased to find I knew so much, and the next day he took me aloft and showed me how to loose and furl a sail and to make up gaskets, all of which I found so interesting that I had no time to feel homesick.

Looking back over all these years there is no voyage that seems quite as fresh as the first. The next day we were to sail, and all the crew came aboard sober except the Englishman, Jim. He would not come on board for a long time, but remained on the wharf saying " The understanding was there were to be six Able Seamen," and pointing aloft to where I was working, " Do you call that thing an Able Seaman?" However, he was finally coaxed on board, we let go the mooring ropes, and with a fair wind sailed down the harbour, instead of towing down as we would nowadays. I loosed all the sails on the Main, but in making up the gaskets on the royal yard made them up as I had been shown on the other yards instead of bringing them into the bunt. That night, when they had to furl the royal, I heard a great enquiry as to who had loosed that sail! I believe that more than half I know about ships I have learned through making mistakes instead of being taught. Most Mates prefer finding fault with greenhorns to taking pains to teach them. Perhaps that is the better way, to let them find out how little they know.

Since I had been on the water from earliest remembrance I did not expect to be seasick, but before we were outside of Cape Cod I was sick unto death. I believe that if I could have got ashore then nothing would have tempted me to go to sea again. The last thing I remember was Jim pointing out to me the Norset Lights, for he had sobered up and was a good friend to me. These three lights I have never forgotten, and whenever I see them, that first night at sea comes into my thoughts again. Soon I was too seasick to care.

A day or so later I began to be of use on board. On a beautiful night with a full moon the Second Mate told me at ten o'clock to go forward and relieve Jim on the lookout. When I went to take over on the topgallant forecastle we were going along at about seven knots with a pleasant breeze on the quarter. Jim said, "Now, Philip, when you see a ship in the night she don't look white as she does in the day, but black." "Is that one there?" I said. Jim looked, and sang out, "Sail ho, right ahead." This sail had been in sight for some time as she was going the same way, neither Jim nor the Second Mate had seen her. The fact probably was, that having been so long in command of boats, I was better able to keep a lookout than any person on board except the captain, or someone who had been in command of something.

One who knows all about boats has little to learn about the handling of ships. There is one thing, however, that I often find lacking in young people who really know how to handle a boat, and that is judgment of the weather. Of course, in a race you must keep sail on as long as possible, but I find so often they cannot judge the wind, and frequently lose a race by carrying away a sail or perhaps a mast. Some men can never estimate the power of the wind by the look of a squall. Sometimes I think one

Barque "Sicillian"

must be born with some instinct or intuition, for with all my experience, after squalls all day, I will see one coming that I know has more wind than the others. It looks the same, and I could not give a reason why I am sure there is more wind in this squall, but I am seldom mistaken.

What I missed more than anything else at first was good water. I could get along well enough with the grub, as sailors call the food, but I had always been accustomed to nice cool water from " the old oaken bucket " and drinking warm water that had been kept in a cask made me feel sick. At the present day ships carry their water in iron tanks below decks and it is very good, in fact I prefer it to the water ashore when I arrive in port.

One day we saw a fine school of sperm whales, with heads as square as a house, and the whalers in our crew told tales of their capture. I have never seen a whale captured, but I believe I know everything about whaling, from the care of the boats and all their gear to the most minute details of Making Fast To, Lancing, Towing To Ship, Cutting In, Trying Out, and Stowing Down. I can sing now a dozen whaling songs, for in my young days at least one half of our crews were whalers. I always took a great interest in the business and expected some day to go whaling.

As we went down through the West Indies we had a reefing match, but only for a few hours and only enough to show me what it was like in warm weather. It takes cold weather, rain, hail, and snow to make reefing interesting. It used to be a pleasure to me and I have spent many happy hours reefing sails and pitting my knowledge against Neptune's. But the romance has gone for me now and just a good whole-sail breeze satisfies me. After a rather long passage of twenty-two days we arrived at Ocoa, a little bay on the south side of St. Domingo, coming to anchor in the evening. There were quite a number of vessels there from various parts of the world, several English barques and one or two Dutch galliots. Everything was of interest to me and I scarcely slept during that night from excitement. Only the sound of crowing roosters in the morning was familiar. Everything else was new. I had never seen a mountain before and never tired of looking at them while at Ocoa.

Next morning we had to move the barque and had to run the lines with our own boat. It took two men to handle her, but happening to be alone in her I took both oars and managed her myself in the way all our fishermen at home handled a dory. This excited some curiosity, but Captain Dawes, being an old fisherman himself, was very proud of his Yankee boy who handled his boat alone while the English vessels had six or eight apprentices to a boat. He had the oars shortened for me and from that time I was made boatman, sometimes having to wait ashore till late at night for him. It was great fun to compare notes with the English boys and we became great chums while we waited, often until midnight, for our captains.

Captain Dawes was a dear old man, though a better fisherman than sailor. The long passage from Boston had driven him nearly crazy, and in fact he did die insane in less than two years. And that reminds me, I believe more sea captains become insane than any other class of people. I went to sea with only five different masters before I was Master myself and three of them died insane. I think the reason was that they had no work to do, only worry. From the time they started at sea until they were masters they did a lot of hard physical work, but the Master of a ship was never supposed to lift a finger. If he coiled up a rope that was lying under foot, the Officer of the Watch would think he had not done his duty and would tell his watch never to leave a rope for the Captain to coil up. So most captains would do nothing but worry about the winds till their nerves were all gone. I know of no other reason, for the life at sea is the healthiest possible.

One morning I was sent ashore with the boat to bring off some Negroes to help discharge the cargo. Among them was a soldier who had insisted on getting into the boat. As they all spoke French I did not know who was who, but the other soldiers on the wharf laughed a good deal, and when we reached the barque the Mate scolded me, making me row this man ashore again. On the way back he seized the oars from me and pulled alongside the brig *General Foster* to see if he could get some work there. Not succeeding, he allowed me to pull him ashore. Instead of taking him to the Boat Landing I backed up to the end of the wharf, and as soon as he got his handhold, for he could just reach the top of the wharf, I pulled away and left him clinging, for I was mad with him. As none of his chums would help him up, but made fun of him, he had to drop into the water and swim to the steps. Luckily he could swim. These soldiers

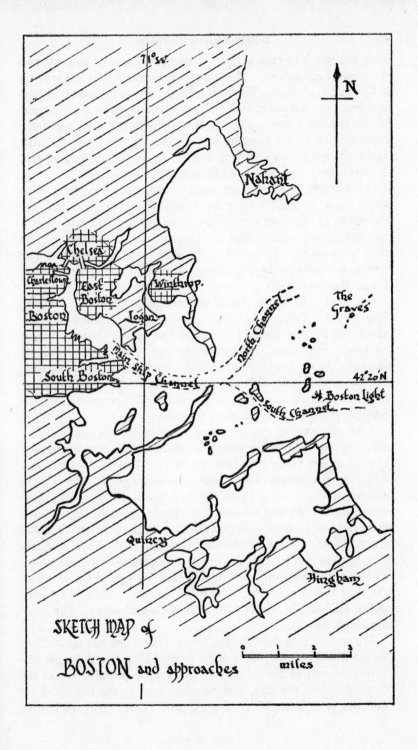

71°W.

N

Nahant

Chelsea

Charlestown

East
Boston

Winthrop.

Boston

Logan

The
Graves

North Channel

South Boston

Main Ship Channel

42°20′N

Boston Light

South Channel

Quincy

Hingham

SKETCH MAP of

BOSTON and approaches

0   1   2   3
                miles

were not much to look at. St. Domingo was a poor country and we used to say one suit of clothes was as much as there was on a Company of them. When I told the men on board of this incident they warned me to look out for the fellow as he would lay for me. So I went up the wharf only with Big Bob. I thought he could lick all the Negroes in the place! I never saw the man again, though it was annoying to have to watch out for him and I went ashore less than I might have otherwise done.

On Sunday mornings we used to take the long-boat with water casks up a little river for water. That was great fun, for the banks of the river were surrounded by coloured girls, washing clothes and bathing and cracking jokes with the sailors. The trees grew down to the water and were full of tropical birds. The people seemed very happy, singing at their work. We used to go far up the river to get good water above the town.

One night the Trade Wind was exceptionally strong and the brig *General Foster,* whose bow ports were open, filled and capsized. We were awakened by the shouting of the Customs Officer on board, each vessel in port having one to see that we did not smuggle. As the brig was loaded with lumber she could not sink, but lay on her side with her masts in the water. Our boat was the first to their assistance and rescued all her crew from the waterlogged hull to which they were clinging.

After discharging our cargo of flour in barrels we loaded a cargo of logwood, being about a month in the port altogether. On the return voyage we had one of the *General Foster's* crew with us, a coloured boy about my own age. I have always remembered the name of that brig because the gang of Negro stevedores would sing all kinds of chanties, as only the coloured men can, as I carried them back and forth between ship and shore. Their voices made an unforgettable impression, on those delightful mornings with the sun creeping up over the mountains and everything so still and quiet. When we passed the wreck of the brig they would sing "The old *General Foster* she's gone down, Hi-Lo. The old *Gen'l Foster* she's gone down, why don't somebody Hi-Lo?"

We were fifteen days coming home. Had a fine run up to Nantucket Shoals, then spent a week in fog. This was the most disagreeable part of the whole voyage, but we sounded round the Cape and into the Bay, and one forenoon as the fog lifted we saw the pilot boat. When the fog shut down again we backed the main yard, waiting for the pilot to find us and come on board. Then we squared away for Boston Light with a fresh S.E. wind.

It happened that Jim, the Englishman, was at the wheel. The pilot was very anxious in the thick fog, and after complaining several times he turned to the Captain and said, " Captain Dawes, haven't you got anybody that can steer straight? I can't run for Boston Light with this man." " I guess so, come here Walter," and the man who would not come on board two months before because I was not an Able Seaman was turned away from the wheel and I took his place. Steering was my boyhood pride, and if a sailor is a good helmsman the captain will forgive him other faults. The *Sicilian* was a splendid vessel to steer, and without any helm at all or only an occasional spoke, went as straight as an arrow.

After running as long as the pilot dared we came to with both anchors down. It was blowing fresh, with quite a sea running. Today in such a fog the whistle or siren at the lighthouse would tell the pilot his whereabouts. After we came to anchor several vessels passed so close you could hear their men talking on deck. During my watch in the night one of these thought our riding light was Boston Light and came so close that I heard them say, " That ain't Boston Light, 'tis a vessel to anchor " as they sheered clear of us. Speaking of lights reminds me—we carried no side lights in those days, and some time later had only a Bowsprit lantern. Before morning the fog cleared away, and when all hands were called at 4.0 a.m. to weigh the anchors we were so near Boston Light we could almost throw a stone to it, and one vessel was ashore on the Graves. It was hard work getting the anchors aweigh, but afterwards it was fine. With square yards we sailed to Fisk's Wharf, made fast, and furled the sails. The voyage was over.

All the sailors went ashore to their respective boarding houses, but I had to remain on board with only the Second Mate and the cat, to be paid off next day. This was the most homesick part of the voyage, as I knew no one in Boston. I was paid off with twenty-three dollars, besides two dollars the Captain gave me for helping to get the anchors from the *General Foster* which he had bought. Then I made my way home, by hack to the Old Colony Depot, where I bought my ticket for Kingston. When the Conductor called out " North Hanson " my homesickness suddenly vanished, for I had relatives there and could have

walked home on foot. I was now as happy as possible. I was
the only passenger on the Stage Coach from Kingston to Duxbury. How nice the woods smelled, and the huckleberries were
just coming on. Whenever I have passed that way since all that
has come back to me. I reached home at 3 p.m., having been
away two months and nine days. Though I have since made
two voyages of forty-four months each, that first voyage
still seems the longest if not the most eventful I have ever
made.

After a short time ashore I again joined the *Sicilian* for a
voyage to Malaga in Spain. Of the old crew we had only little
Jack, and the same officers. This time I was shipped as an O.S.
(Ordinary Seaman) and another Duxbury boy, Pelham Freeman,
was also an O.S. He had been one voyage around the Horn in
the clipper ship *Witchcraft*, but as he was only her cabin boy
he had very little experience in working a ship. Incidentally, the
Witchcraft carried a crew of forty men in addition to the master,
four mates, carpenter, cook, steward, and cabin boy—a total of
forty-nine. My vessel today, which is about the same size, has
only sixteen men all told, illustrating one of the greatest changes
made at sea in fifty years.

We had another boy, Richard Cole from Plymouth, who was
afterwards an apprentice in the Boston pilot boats. Two men
from Newfoundland completed the crew, so we were mostly from
our own county. There were four passengers—a young man from
Abington, the Captain's son aged ten, the Mate's son aged five,
and a Mr. Lane, whom I met again a few years ago. We had not
the least idea we had ever met before until, in the course of
conversation, we discovered we had made a voyage together forty
years previously. But I am now so used to meeting old associates
that it seems any man old enough is liable to have been in some
way associated with me, as anyone who follows this narrative
will notice. The younger of the two boys, who sailed with me
several voyages, became Captain John C. Dawes, of Kingston,
Mass., and died on 10th August, 1908, very suddenly of heart
disease.

Leaving Boston in August we had a pleasant passage to Malaga,
where we were put in quarantine for ten days or more to see
that no sickness developed on board. Every morning the doctor's
boat came alongside to count the crew, and if anyone was laid up

we should have to go to Port Mahone and remain there until all hands were on deck. I imagine a few dollars would have made it all right, for in later years, when master of a vessel with cholera on board, one hundred dollars saved me from going a month's trip. We were, however, allowed to discharge any cargo that could go into the water. They would bring us a lighter from shore which we filled with oak staves. This we would tow towards the beach outside the harbour, anchoring it just beyond the breakers and there throwing the staves overboard for the Spaniards to pick up on the shore. As soon as our quarantine period expired we discharged the balance of the cargo, consisting of flour, and then had to wait till the season for loading raisins. We waited several weeks, during which time we fixed the barque all up, overhauling rigging and painting inside and out. We lay in tiers, whole rows of vessels moored head and stern. We could go from one to another by throwing a rope across, very easy for a sailor, and since most of the American vessels had some boys in their crews we did quite a lot of visiting. There was quite a fleet bound to Boston with raisins.

Here I first made the acquaintance of the bumboat—not *Little Buttercup*, but men who had grapes, wine, and all kinds of fruit for sale. From morning to night they were drawling out " Grapes Johnnie, grapes Johnnie, vien tru gar." I don't know what the last words meant. I always thought it must be something about wine, but the Spanish for wine is vino. Of course, as in all hot climates, we had awnings spread to protect the decks, as well as the crew, from the sun, and we usually slept on deck under the awning. Only one of our men had been across the Line and he had been as far south as Buenos Aires. We all regarded him as an oracle, until one day as we reclined under the awning he told us, " When I was in Buenos Aires we were so near the sun you could hear it roar when it rose." This was too much for Dick Cole and myself and we roared with laughter, but he actually believed it and wanted to fight us for laughing at his statement. I wonder what became of Dick. The last I heard of him he was boat-keeper on the Boston Pilot Cutter and, as I understood it, when the small row-boat had put a pilot on some vessel he did not wait for it to return, or did not wait long enough to find out what had become of it, but returned to Boston without it and the boat and the two men were never heard of again. It was probably one of those terrible mistakes men sometimes make, for he was a goodhearted fellow. Anyhow, Dick was dismissed from the pilot service.

Our cargo of raisins came in small boxes of thirty pounds, also in half and quarter boxes. They were stowed by stevedores and it was quite an art, we sailors merely passing the boxes from the lighter to the stevedores. In this port I learned my first chanty (sailors call them shanties). A small English steamer that lay close to us used to hoist her boat every night with a song. Since then I have learned nearly all the shanties of the world. In most ships it was considered the thing to hoist the topsails by a shantie, but a few captains got so smart that they would not let their crews sing at work, because they said they could do it quicker without a song. This was all very true, but it was a great mistake, for there is nothing so good for a man's health as a little fun now and then, and this more than makes up for the few minutes used in setting the sail by a song. In old times singing was the rule, and I remember in Java thirty years ago all the nursemaids used to hum a song which I could not place at first as the words were either Dutch or Javanese. Finally it came to me, it was the old English shantie " Nancy Dawson."

All these fruiters were the best of sailors, for fruit was a perishable cargo, especially oranges, and the first to arrive in had all the market. We thought our barque could sail as well as most of the fleet, only there was one hermaphrodite brig that could beat the lot. She could sail fifteen knots. Sometimes I have known a vessel to lose by sailing fast, at least for a short time, though not in the long run. We left Malaga in company with another barque bound for Boston. The wind was West, we sailed much faster than she did and got almost out of sight. However, when the wind hauled to N.W. and let us luff, the other vessel was placed several miles to windward, enabling her to pass Gibraltar before us by sailing slower, so the race is not always to the swift.

On the way home we carried away our fore topmast, and the main topgallant mast went with it. Captain Allen Dawes, as I have remarked, was more of a fisherman than a square-rigger, having been all his life in schooners. The story was told that when he first took charge of the *Sicilian* the pilot tacked her and he said, " Now Pilot, let me see you do that once more and then I think I can do it." He sailed a square-rigger as he would a schooner, carrying sail till all was blue when on the wind, but when off the wind he would reduce sail. Of course in a square-rigged vessel the custom is quite the reverse. One morning near the Western Islands he was driving into a head sea when the fore topmast went over the bow. It was the Mate's watch on deck, and he blamed it on the poor steering of the boy at the wheel, who was Pelham Freeman, the O.S. from Duxbury. But the boy had a different story to tell. He said the Mate was yarning to him about Sally Faunce, and I guess the boy had the rights of it, for the Mate, even after he was Master, could not keep from yarning with the man at the wheel, and that is contrary to all rules on board ship. Many years later, when he was in command of the fine ship *Matchless* and I was his Mate, I remarked that I had never seen a squall strike a vessel without some sign in the sky or water, unless she was under a high bluff or a mountain. " Oh, yes, I have," he said, and he related this incident of carrying away our fore topmast, saying the squall came right out of the air without a sign. He had forgotten I was there at the time. Of course I made no answer, for you never contradict the Captain, even if he says the sun rises in the West. I had not forgotten how we pitched into a head sea all night so that no one could go on the forecastle to keep a lookout, and what was worse, that the rigging was as slack as possible fore and aft. I have always called that squall a " Sally Faunce squall "!

In a few days we had another topmast up and made a fair passage to Boston, in spite of a long time in the Gulf Stream with head winds and falling in with a sinking brig, the *Cuedad Bolliver*. We took her crew off and brought them home with us. Her six sailors were Filipinos from Manila. At that time, in 1856, we had a great many sailors from Manila. Ships from San Francisco, bound for China and India, would call at Manila for sailors as they were hard to get at 'Frisco and demanded high wages. Then the captains would, if without any conscience, contrive to get rid of their crew and hire a cheap crew of Manila men.

Here is an actual happening on a famous American clipper ship. She was bound for Calcutta and could not get a crew. The captain made an agreement with some longshoremen to come on board and work the ship outside the harbour. He also hired another gang to trim down the ballast, and while they were down the hold he worked the ship to sea (there were no tugboats in those days). When the crowd down the hold came up they found they were at sea and were forced by the captain and officers to go on the trip. There was no help for them then, but they made up their minds they would get paid for being kidnapped when they reached Calcutta. The captain made a southern passage through Ombay Pass, south of Java, and anchored at Timor Island. There he went ashore and engaged some natives to ship for Calcutta. When he returned on board he called the men he had shanghaied, complimented them on their good behaviour, and told them they might go ashore for the day if they liked. Thinking they would like a run ashore they took the few dollars the captain gave them and went for the day. No sooner had they reached the shore than they saw the ship making sail, leaving them in that wild and isolated country. Eventually they reached home, I believe, and it cost the ship and owners a lot of money. I would hardly credit this story if I had not seen things as bad, which I will relate, on the celebrated ship *Great Republic*, which came under my observation a few years later. So at that time there were all kinds of natives sailing in our American vessels. These six Filipinos were a pretty good lot. Most of them could talk English and I learned considerable Spanish from them.

When we reached Boston I thought I'd had enough of the sea and had made up my mind to try something ashore. But when I told the folks of it, to my surprise instead of being pleased they encouraged me to go away again, so I continued. Anyway it is doubtful if I could have been contented ashore after this taste of salt water.

I was still an O.S., though I deviate so much from the narrative of the voyage that you might imagine I had been going to sea for more than six months. It was cold weather now, in December, and things were very different from the summer yachting weather. There was ice all about the decks, our water casks were frozen, and I had to go ashore to get a drink of water. I was all alone in the forecastle, except for the bed bugs (there were plenty of them). There was no fire in the forecastle, nor was there one aft in the cabin. In those days it was thought to spoil a sailor to give him a fire. Nowadays the law of the U.S. obliges ships to have a fire, either in the forecastle or somewhere the seaman can have access to it. I wonder I did not freeze to death, but I had been brought up to do without a fire. The day we left Boston the thermometer was sixteen degrees below zero.

We had the same Captain, Mate, and Cook, but Mr. Parsons

had a fight with the cook and would not sail with him again. The cook had been rather impudent to him, would not bring him his coffee in the mornings but made him come to the galley for it or go without. So we had a new Second Mate, a Mr. Pert of Nova Scotia. Little Jack and the two Newfoundlanders joined again, and two regular sailors, both American. Allen was from Connecticut, had been in both English and American men-of-war, and was as neat as wax. Jim was from Maine and, though a good sailor, he was also the dirtiest sailor I ever saw. They were the first real sailors who knew their business I had seen. Our new Second Mate was a rather elderly man, about fifty and not very large, but he knew his business too.

I was awful glad when we sailed, it was so cold any change was welcome. We started in a screaming North Wester, with reefed topsails as we went down the bay. The wind hauled to the Eastward and we passed through the South Channel in a North-East snow storm. I had the first wheel from eight to ten p.m. As the wind kept heading us the Second Mate would keep looking at the compass, but I held her to her course and he said, "Well, boy, you know how to steer." I had one hour's lookout from eleven to midnight and I spent it in kicking the foremast to keep my feet warm. We had leather boots in those days, rubber boots had not been invented. In the morning it was warmer but still snowing.

I shall never forget when coffee time came. We got our coffee, and the cook sang out to the Second Mate, " Car-fee." As he took no notice of the call, a little later he sang out " Car-fee ready, Sir." Still the Second Mate took no notice, but walked back and forth in the snow on our long poop deck that went to the main hatch. Again he sang out, " Mr. Pert, Car-fee ready, Sir." The Second Mate walked deliberately to the rail, took out an iron belaying pin, went to the weather door of the galley, banged it open letting the snow and wind into the galley, and said quietly, " You damned black son-of-a-bitch, do you think you are going to fool with me as you did with Parsons? Bring my coffee on the poop and be quick about it, or I will see which is the hardest, this pin or your head." And the cook trotted up with the coffee quickly. Not only that, he was made to pull and haul on the braces like a sailor all the trip. The cook was the one to leave the ship the next voyage.

We had a good passage of twenty-two days to Gibraltar, where we were sent for orders, during which time I learned more seamanship than in any previous voyage. It was winter and rough weather prevailed. There was not a day on which we did not have to take in sail, and make it, and we were days under reefs. Above all, we had a Second Mate and two sailors who really knew their business. On the evening that we arrived at Gibraltar there was a gale blowing. We had to let go both anchors and a lot of chain to hold her. After we had furled the sails and got below into our cosy forecastle Jim, the Down Easter, after sitting on his chest a while and having a comfortable smoke, said, " Well, I believe I will take off my boots tonight." Someone asked, " When did you have them off last?" " Not since we left Boston." For twenty-two days he had not taken his boots off, even to sleep, and his feet wet almost every day. When he removed them there was just a little rim of stocking round his ankle, the rest was black mud. I could never have believed a man could be so filthy and so lazy if I had not seen it. Is it any wonder that sailors become sick when they live in such a way? But most of them are like children, they become so used to being told what to do that they lose all sense of responsibility. I always make a practice of having all beds and bedding on deck in the sun once a week. My own bed goes on deck and the men cannot complain at having to do what the Master does himself. Many old sailors think it is a foolish piece of business, but after a time they seem to like it and complain if the weather will not permit it. But for this rule many sailors, and many mates, would not take their beds on deck once during a voyage of five months. I think this is one of the reasons I have never had any outbreaks of sickness during my thirty or so years as Master.

After a few days in Gibraltar we were ordered to Cadiz, which was only a short run. We were a long time discharging, and I used to be sent in with a lighter of cargo nearly every day. I enjoyed going in under the old fortifications that seemed as old as Columbus. We took sand ballast, but did not have enough, so took a long time, a whole month, to reach Messina in Sicily. On the way we experienced all kinds of weather, even a thick snow storm, and came near to losing the barque on Cape Bon.

The day we arrived at Messina we had some terrific squalls, which obliged us to clew up all sails to lower topsails. I remember Little Jack saying as he looked at the clouds, " Are those the beautiful Italian skies we read about?" Another barque in company carried away her main yard and had to go back to Faro Point and anchor. She came into the harbour next day. The water was quite smooth as we were so close to the shore. To me it was just like being in Duxbury Bay, I never enjoyed myself more in my life. The current must have been with us, for with so little sail we worked up until we could reach into the harbour. An English man-of-war had a hawser to another vessel we passed and was hauling her off the shore. At last we entered the port which is like a cup, deepest in the middle, and though we let go both anchors and all our ninety fathoms of chain on each, we dragged until the anchors were in the middle of the harbour. I imagine that harbour is the crater of an extinct volcano, for the whole of Sicily and Italy is volcanic.

As soon as we had the sails furled we had to go ashore to the Protest Office and be " smoked," as the men called it. I suppose we were fumigated, but even the Captain had to be " smoked." The next day was fine and we moved to our berth for loading. We hauled stern to the quay, with a staging over the stern on which to walk ashore. I wanted to go tramping up in the mountains, but of course that was out of the question, so I was seldom ashore. After taking some sulphur in the bottom we filled the ship with oranges in boxes for Boston. Each day we had all the oranges we could eat sent to us from ashore, the finest I have ever seen but too ripe to keep all the way home.

Our homeward passage was very long and Captain Dawes was out of his head. First we were a long time getting out of the Mediterranean, then when up to the Grand Banks we had four days dead calm. And all the time our oranges were rotting. Captain Dawes would froth at the mouth, then when we had headwinds he would steer the ship himself for eighteen hours at a stretch, allowing only the Second Mate or me to relieve him for his meals. I believe he had considerable money invested in the cargo. Six days after we reached home he was taken ill at Kingston Depot and only lived a few days. He was a very large man and so goodhearted, it seemed a pity he should die.

As soon as we arrived off Cape Cod we hoisted a signal. A tug was sent from Boston for us with a crowd of stevedores on board. They made all ready and before the barque was fast to the wharf they were putting out boxes of oranges. By three o'clock that afternoon they were all out and sold by auction. The little incidents of this voyage of five months are not so well remembered as those of the first one which, although it was only two months and nine days, seemed much longer.

My fourth voyage was a short trip to Malaga again for raisins, returning to Boston, and being in the summer it was like a yachting cruise. Our old Captain Dawes was dead and his brother James H. Dawes, who had been Mate for the past year, was Master. It was not his first experience as Master, for when he was a young man he had charge of a brig bound to the West Indies, I believe. A few days out he had fallen in with a ship in distress and, with difficulty and at great risk, he had saved the remainder of her passengers and crew, returning to New York, the nearest port, as he had neither room nor provisions for so many. Landing them all safely, he was greatly praised for his courage, skill, and kindness. But he then remained too long in port and, I think, took a run home. The brig was chartered by William F. Weld & Co. who ordered him to proceed on his voyage. Captain Jim went when he was ready but on his return was fined by Weld & Co. He was so ill-advised by his friends as to go to law with Weld & Co. and, of course, lost his case and all the money he had, as well as his position in command. We are allowed to deviate from our voyage to save life but not to stay unnecessarily long in port. So he had to go back to Mate again.

We had a new Mate this time, Mr. Bryant, from Plympton. Mr. Pert was again Second Mate, Little Jack continued with us, and there was a big Irishman, a powerful man measuring forty-eight inches under his arms. Though a quiet man on board and a good sailor, he never went ashore without a fight, and he always won. Three Englishmen and another A.B. from Duxbury called George Josselyn, who afterwards commanded fine ships, made up our crew. We had two passengers, a young Boston man called Potter and one other whose name I forget.

When we were all ready for sea we were detained by a North East storm. Four of us were in the forecastle and, having nothing else to do, went out on the wharf and pitched coppers, as we used to call the old-fashioned cents. At that time playing cards for money was an everyday occurrence. There was no law against it, and boys were always pitching cents. I was quite expert at it, having practised various tricks of pitching and turning coins beside the barn when I was a small boy. In a short time I had won all of the dollar and a half which was all we had between us.

A crowd of longshoremen and loafers were looking on, it being a rainy day with little doing. When they saw I had all the money they wanted to pitch with me, thinking they had an easy mark in a boy of sixteen. When they found that I was winning from them too they soon gave up playing, and never discovered the green country boy was winning by a trick under their eyes. I have never used my trick since, and come to think of it, that was the last time I ever pitched coppers.

Another game I have never played since going to sea is Round Stakes, now called Baseball. The bat was called a Cat Stick and bases were called Gools, the first base being known as Your Grannie. The ball was much softer and we usually made our own out of yarn, wound round some rubber and covered with soft leather. The ball was always thrown at a runner, and dodging the ball was the biggest trick of all. The curved ball was unknown, but the swifter the ball was thrown the harder it was to hit. However, the same qualities that won a game then are needed to win one now.

We were soon in Malaga, going through the same routine with quarantine and cargo as before. I only remember going ashore once, to buy some bottles of wine at a wine-shop. They were filled from a cask by a very pretty black-eyed Spanish girl, and before she put in the stopper she always took a little out with her red lips and gave me a smile. But she could not compare with my old schoolmates.

While in Malaga this time we lay near an American schooner. Several times I took our captain over to her in our boat and used to wait in her forecastle until he was ready to go back, so I got acquainted with her crew. They told me about one of their number whose name was Bill and whom their captain had down the hold in irons. They said he was a wonderful man and their captain was very much afraid of him. I refer to him now because I was shipmates with this same man in the *Reynard* six months later. He certainly was the most remarkable man I ever met in a ship's forecastle.

I scarcely remember the passage home, it was such fine weather, and we had a quick run to Boston. As I had some raisins and wine to carry home I went to the Duxbury Packet, a little sloop that went back and forth twice a week when the weather permitted. Captain John Alden, who was a direct descendant of John and Priscilla of Mayflower times and living in the same house they built in Duxbury, was in command of the packet. My, how he could swear. He beat all I ever heard, and I can swear in all languages. They told me they were going down next day and would call for my packages as they hauled by our ship. Early next morning, about four o'clock, someone woke me in the forecastle and asked for my goods, adding, "Why don't you go down with us?" So I threw everything I had on board and dressed as we went down the harbour. I never enjoyed any sail more than that one, for I was a passenger. Whenever I am a passenger today I remember that first time when I could sit down and let someone else obey the captain's orders. They took in the Gaff Topsail and asked me to furl it. If I had done so they would not have expected me to pay for my passage. No, I was a passenger, and though I could have furled that sail much quicker and snugger than they did, for there was only one sailor in the crew, I preferred to be "A gentleman for a day, Jack" as Lady Hamilton called the coxswain of Lord Nelson's gig. So I paid my passage. It was a delightful sail, going up Duxbury Bay in the early afternoon. As we passed my childhood home my father was working in his garden, almost near enough for me to hail him. Then we went down to Powder Point, to Weston's Wharf, about two miles from home.

I have never tried to make myself appear like a sailor and have never had a dot of Indie Ink tattooed into my skin, but this time I had a new cardigan jacket, such as we should now call a sweater. It was a regular English sailor's rig at that time, so I put it on and walked up through the point and village thinking I would look like a sailor for once, and hoping I would meet all my old friends. For the only time out of the hundreds of times I have walked that way I did not meet one person.

I come now to my first voyage as an A.B. (Able Seaman) and my last in the *Sicilian*. We sailed for Malta some time in the fall of 1857 with a cargo of provisions, mostly salt beef in barrels, and had fine weather. Captain James H. Dawes was in command, Mr. Bryant was Mate again, and Mr. Smith from Chatham, Cape Cod, was the new Second Mate. Big Irish Jim shipped again, also Little Jack, George Josselyn, the Abington fellow, and one of the Englishmen of the last voyage, so we had almost the same crew. We had a new cook, a mulatto who called himself the Rev. Gen. Eli Bradbery, but he was always known on board as Eli.

Ship "Reynard"

Ship "Nevada"

We were all on good terms with him, but the Captain did not like him to visit the forecastle so much. There were three passengers, an Italian returning from exile with his son about my age, and an American named Walker, taking a trip for his health. A few days out someone proposed a game of cards. The five men went to the Captain to draw some tobacco, then began to play Bluff for it, a game I had never heard of. By watching I soon got the idea of the game, which they also called Twenty Deck Poker. One dog-watch a man going to the wheel gave me his hand to play, saying, " Here, Philip, take my hand. Here is a pound of tobacco. If you lose it, no matter, but all you win is mine." So I started to play Bluff, and when he came back from the wheel I had two pounds of tobacco. He gave me one of them and I was never short again. In fact my mind was so completely given to cards that I remember little else that happened on the passage, and I was very successful. The passenger boy got very interested and used to bring his father's fine tobacco until he had lost it all. Then his father forbade him coming into the forecastle.

When we arrived in Malta the British fleet was just returning from the Crimean War, the harbour being full of the largest and finest men-of-war in the world. Here was a chance for our Irishman and he made the most of it, coming on board every night covered with the blood of his mortal enemies. Finally he got arrested, and had to appear in court. I never heard that he was fined. The judge asked him what countryman he was, and he replied, " An American," with such a brogue that everybody laughed.

I thought Malta a beautiful place, surrounded as the harbour is on all sides by cities. I used to take our little boat and pull about the harbour in the evenings and on Sunday, and look into the big stern windows of the men-of-war. On the Saturday night before we sailed we were ashore and bought a lot of things. I never knew who paid for them, if anyone did. The shopkeepers seemed to say, " Pay when you come again." I think this is the only debt I owe in the world that I have never paid. It did not amount to more than two or three dollars and I could not have found the place again if I had tried, but we went to sea the next day. Perhaps somebody else paid for what we got.

From Malta we went to Messina again to load oranges for Boston as before. While there we all had a new suit of clothes

c

made. Eli, the cook, had invested in a new spring hat and a velvet
vest at Malta. We were all well supplied with clothing, for the
English sailors from the men-of-war were trading away their
clothes to the bumboats for fruit and we could buy them very
cheaply.

After leaving Messina for home we played cards for oranges.
Eli used to steal the Captain's oranges and come forward to
play. Of course we all played against him, and when the game
was over and we had all his oranges we divided them up. After
the oranges were gone we played for clothing, any new piece of
clothing would do. We played six-handed Euchre for the lot.
On the day we were passing the Grand Banks with a North East
gale I had won about everything there was in the forecastle. It
was my wheel from eight to ten that night and I began to think
that with this fair wind we should soon be in Boston. What
would I do with so many clothes? I could not deceive Mother,
so I decided to give them all back again. When I was relieved
at ten I took the cards and threw them overboard. Then in the
morning before the cards were missed, I gave everybody their
clothing back. From that time to this I have never played cards
for money.

About two days later we were just back of Cape Cod and were
getting up chains to bend to the anchors, when Eli came and
accused me of stealing his spring hat and velvet jacket. I let him
look in my chest and he seemed satisfied that I had not taken
them. He then went to the Captain with his complaint, who said,
" I told you so, those fellows would steal the hair off your head
if you didn't keep out of that forecastle."

We were signalled off Cape Cod and soon the tug and stevedores were after us and took us to Boston. I had an old school
friend, Henry Ward Loring, who was now living in Charlestown. He came on board to see me and I spent Saturday night
with him. Sunday forenoon we took a walk over to the
Sicilian. I had been in her so long that I was a privileged
character, having also sometimes been ship-keeper when in
Boston, so when I got on board I walked down into the cabin.
Lo and behold, there were all the cook's clothes laid out on the
table and Second Mate Smith was selling them to some of his
chums. He turned all sorts of colours when he saw us, and
brought out a box of oranges for me and my friend to help
ourselves. I ate all I could and then filled my pockets, and tried

to make my friend do the same, but Henry did not understand the position as well as I did. If it had not been for the clothes we would not have got any oranges. I learned afterwards that one of the sailors had stolen the clothes and hidden them down the fore hatch among the cargo. This man owed Smith some money and told him where the clothes were on condition that he would call it square. I did not see Eli again to tell him about this, but I think the man who stole them had told him it was me. Years afterwards I met Smith, then Mate of a barque in Shanghai, and he played a very dirty trick on my captain, showing he had not improved in character.

I had now been two years in the *Sicilian* and this last voyage things did not suit me. I was an A.B. this time and refused to do more than my share of the dirty work, which was a mistake on my part for I was not really old enough or big enough to do an A.B.'s work. Perhaps for that reason I was not asked to go again. I never saw the ship again, or any of the sailors except George Josselyn, but the officers I followed as long as I lived. I was later Mate with Captain Dawes and he gave me my first command. I considered myself an Able Seaman now and went down home like an old traveller. Happening to meet an old schoolmate, she said, " I hear, Walter, you have been a voyage at sea since I saw you." I did not tell her I had been five voyages, but I thought it strange everybody did not know of it. And this was the last of my being called Philip!

CHAPTER TWO

First four voyages in ship Reynard, *1858-1861—Boston to San Francisco (A.B.)—Fourth Mate—Honolulu—Jarvis Island —Philadelphia—Second Voyage (Third Mate)—New York for San Francisco—Dismasted near Bermuda in hurricane—Boston refit—San Francisco—Callao—Home in ballast—Coppered in Boston—Third voyage (Second Mate) New York to Liverpool and return—Fourth voyage (Second Mate)—Captain Seymour New York to London and return in ballast.*

When I left the *Sicilian* I expected to go away in her again, but I had not been too pleased with things the last voyage, so hearing that the ship *Reynard*, Captain Ben Freeman of Duxbury, was loading for 'Frisco I went to Boston to see if I could get a chance on her. The Captain took a fancy to me, and I suppose one reason was that I was careful he should not see me with my hands in my pockets, or "beckets" to use a sailor's term. I had heard he did not like it. When I met him on board the ship he said, "All the hands are shipped, but if you want to go I will give you a chance. You need not sign the Articles. If you are as good as an A.B. I will give you Able Seaman's wages." The ship was to sail the next day, so I hurried home.

My last evening in the old town I was in Harvey Soule's store. As everybody knows a country store is more like a club than any place in town. There I met Pelham Freeman, the boy who was at the wheel in the *Sicilian* when she was struck by the *Sally Faunce* squall. Captain Freeman was his uncle and Pelham was going on the voyage as an A.B. He said to me " You will be lost in the *Reynard* among a crowd of twenty-four." I did not reply but determined I would do my best. John Butler, another Duxbury boy, was also an A.B.

The next morning I reported on board at Lewis' Wharf. She was a fine ship, with single topsails and three skysails and she swung sixteen stunsails. Very few ships carry stunsails today. They were set on booms that were rigged out on the ends of the other yards. Few paintings show them properly drawn, even valuable pictures worth thousands of dollars have the stunsails set in an impossible way that would make an old sailor smile.

The Captain's wife was with him and there were three lady passengers, a woman and her two daughters about fifteen and nineteen. In '58 there was no railroad across the continent, a traveller to California had the choice of going round Cape Horn or across the Isthmus of Panama. The Mate, who was washed overboard off Cape Horn, had a wife living in South Boston. The Second Mate, Mr. Nelson, was Norwegian and a fine sailor. He was newly married then, and for many years now he and his son Jack have been driving and keeping hacks in Boston. Mr. Sargent, from Watertown, was Third Mate and a carpenter, cook, steward, four boys, and twenty Able Seamen made up the crew. Billy Smith, the cabin boy, was Mrs. Freeman's nephew. He had a hard time, with two Negroes (the cook and the steward) over him, as well as four women and all the officers. Better to ship in the forecastle than as a cabin boy. The other boys were Benny Winsor, of Duxbury, and Eugene Coleman and Alvin Falker from Cape Cod. Ben's father had been an old sea captain, Eugene's was captain of a whaler, while Alvin's had been a cooper on a whaler and had been buried off Cape Horn.

We hauled into the stream and then the crew came on board. As was usual in those days they were mostly half full, one man in particular was almost crazy and made a racket all night. In the morning I found it was English Bill, the man who was in irons on board the schooner at Malaga the year before. There were two others of that crew with us, but of course I had not actually seen Bill at Malaga. He was a medium sized man of about forty, and not very dangerous to look at. He had lost one of his eyes and was tattooed all over his body. He had been king of some cannibal island for years, but was one of the most highly educated men I ever met on shipboard. He seemed able to converse in any language and knew the "Epitome of Navigation" from cover to cover. I thought I could draw ships, but after seeing his drawings I never tried again. He did not tell who he was or where he came from. We got an idea that he had been an officer in a British man-of-war. In port he was always drunk, and kept so, but he was a fine sailor. He knew all the stars and had Greek mythology down to a household tale. He only made the voyage to 'Frisco. After our arrival I never heard of him again. I think it was his wish to get back to his cannibals again and away from civilization.

We were towed to sea, for the tugboat had now come into use, and just outside of Boston Light, when we had all sail set, we passed close to one of our Duxbury fishermen. I knew her Skipper, Charles Henry Weston, and every man on board. They were bound to Duxbury and that very evening would anchor within a hundred yards of my home. This did not make me feel homesick, for I was at the wheel, not lost as Pelham said I would be, and was proud to be seen steering a fine ship. They passed close under our stern and all waved to me. When the Captain's back was turned I answered them.

I soon found that life was much easier in a big ship than in a little one, for I only had a wheel once in two days instead of twice in twenty-four hours, also the lookout only came one fourth as often. Then we slept practically all night down in the Trades where there was little to keep us awake. We usually crowded around the main hatch, telling stories or sleeping, but all ready to come should the officer of the watch require us. Of course there is a great difference in ships. Some are so strict that they require all the watch to keep on their feet, others are so slack that some of the men would not turn out of their berths if they did not have a wheel or a lookout. In some ships the officers are asleep themselves! The happy medium seems the best. As long as the men come when they are wanted the officer shuts his eyes to some of them sleeping in their watch on deck.

We crossed the Line twenty-four days out, for the *Reynard* was a fast sailor. It was a pleasure for me to climb about her lofty spars. A boy that does not take pleasure in climbing had better not choose the life of a sailor. One evening when we were in the North East Trades, close-hauled on the port tack with all sail set, we were going at about ten knots. It was cloudy and the Captain and his passengers were on the poop. The man on the lookout sang out " Sail Ho, right ahead, close aboard." I ran aft and repeated the report. " What's that," said the Captain, and to the man at the wheel, " Hard down your wheel." Now that was wrong, for we were on the port tack and should have kept away, but it did not matter. Before the ship felt the wheel the other vessel passed us so close that it was only by good luck we did not collide. " Isn't that beautiful," said one of the ladies. " Almost too close for me," said the Captain. In those days we carried no lights at all. Just a few feet more and both ships would have gone to the bottom, probably never being heard of again, for both were going at full speed.

I caught my first big dolphin as we lay becalmed on the Line. The fish would not bite, because we did not know enough to keep the bait jumping to make them think it was a flying-fish. So I put some hooks below, and when he smelled at the white rag on the hook I pulled up and stole him. He was a fine fellow, but strange to say we did not eat him. We were afraid of being poisoned. After the passengers had admired his changing colours as he was dying he was thrown overboard. I know better now and eat all I can catch. The only danger comes from keeping them too long for fish spoil in twenty-four hours in a hot climate. In those days we had so little to eat, no canned goods, no milk, inferior beef and pork, and only hard bread in the forecastle. Now we have a pound of soft bread every day per man, in fact the hard bread or biscuit is quite a luxury, so the thought of throwing away a fine fish of about fifteen pounds still makes me angry. Again, we used to throw away a porpoise after we had taken off the blubber for the oil in it, eating only the liver. In cold weather porpoise which has been hung for a week is superior to beef-steak. The mistake usually made with a porpoise is hanging it up by its tail. There is just enough blubber in the tail to run down and spoil the taste of the whole fish. Cut off all the blubber, hang it, and you will have fine meat which will keep for weeks in cold weather.

We sighted several vessels on the way down to Cape Horn and the time passed very quickly. Though we were a long way south of Buenos Aires we did not get near enough to the sun to hear it roar when it rose, to quote the Newfoundlander who got so mad with us at Malaga when we refused to believe him. We were a long time " Doubling " the Cape, that is in getting from 50 deg. South latitude in the Atlantic to 50 deg. South latitude in the

Pacific, and finally had worked away down south and west of the Horn. One dog-watch we were all called out to brace round the yards, for we were caught aback by a south-west gale. We finally got the yards round, but several of the men had their hands hurt by the swinging yards as we rolled in the sea. The officers had let go the braces and the main yard swung from side to side, till I took a turn with what slack I could get around one of our guns (we had two twelve pounders lashed amidships). When the yards were secured we headed away for the north with a fair wind.

As we scudded under reefed foresail and double-reefed top-sails lowered down on the caps it was my wheel from eight to ten, and she went fine. But no sooner had I left the wheel than she shipped so much water I was called back, and steered until twelve with a man to help me at the lee wheel. I had not been below half an hour when all hands were called on deck to heave the ship to. There were a lot of provisions lashed on deck, some of which had got adrift. The Mate and his watch were trying to secure them when an enormous wave came over, smashing two boats and washing the Mate and a sailor called Brooks overboard. Allen Witham, a young man from Marblehead, was killed and two more were badly hurt. After the ship was hove to she lay quietly till morning when, the gale having moderated, we kept away again for the north. During the night the boy Alvin Falker was missed, but while we were talking about him and just as some-one was saying " It was just about here that his father was buried," he came crawling out in fear. " I ain't dead," he said. One odd coincidence was remarked. The Mate had found some fault with Brooks the previous afternoon, and while the latter was eating his supper he said, " If that Mate was to fall over-board I would not throw him a rope."

Little did he think that before the morning both he and the Mate would be overboard together, with no possibility of rescue. Of course this loss of life cast a gloom over the ship that lasted till we reached San Francisco. At daylight next morning we buried Allen Witham, my first experience of a funeral at sea. It seemed as though Neptune was satisfied now, for we proceeded with favourable gales to port, arriving in 100 days. The first land sighted was Mas A Fuera in 33° 46′ S. 80° 46′ W., which looks like a solid rock some six thousand feet high.

When we reached port I found letters from home for the

first time in my life. I did not know a letter could be so precious. At that time few vessels loaded in 'Frisco for the East Coast, but most took rock from Telegraph Hill as ballast and went to China, South America, or other places for a return cargo. We were sent to Jarvis Island, via Honolulu, to load phosphate for Hampton Roads for orders. While in 'Frisco Mr. Nelson was promoted to Mate, Mr. Sargent to Second Mate, and a new Third Mate, Mr. Staples, was shipped, as well as an entire new crew except for the boys. As we were to load all our cargo in our own boats, and it was handy to have an officer in each boat, I was made Fourth Mate. Having been brought up in boats I was certainly at home in the job and was glad to have this chance, since a man learns more in a month as an officer than in a year before the mast. It takes responsibility to educate a man and one could go to sea for years and never learn to be an officer. Mrs. Freeman went home by way of Panama.

On the way down to Honolulu we had two deck passengers, both cowboys from Missouri. They knew all about horses and cattle and intended to go into that business in the islands. We took fourteen days on the passage down. As there were no tugboats at Honolulu we were pulled into the harbour by oxen. We had a pilot, luffed up as far as we could shoot into the entrance, a whale-boat took our line and met another from the shore that was fast to the oxen. In the meantime we took in all sail, then the oxen drew the ship into the harbour and we were made fast with both anchors out ahead and our stern to the reef. Here we remained about a week, taking in water in casks for Jarvis Island, also a mule which we lowered into the 'tween deck. When I tried to lead him by the halter he backed and fell down into the lower hold, landing on his back on the stone ballast. It would have killed anything but a mule, but he did not seem to mind it. When we had hoisted him again we put on the 'tween deck hatches and finally got him into his stall. That is my only experience with a mule.

The harbour was full of whalers, while outside a number of them lay off and on, waiting for their crews, who were hard to find away in the hills with their sweethearts. No one went ashore from our ship but the Captain. It was a constant amusement to watch the natives swimming and riding in on top of the breakers on their surf boards. From morning to night the waves were full of men, women and children, even babies with their mothers.

There was only one little wharf for boats to land, called Brewer's Wharf. That was fifty years ago. What will it be like in another fifty years? The Yankees talk of making it a second Gibraltar.

We took ten days on the passage to Jarvis Island. This island is the top or crater of an extinct volcano, and is about twelve miles long. It is only forty feet above the water, with a lagoon in the centre, and the coral insects have built upon it. When we arrived the ship *Mary Howland* was loading and we had to wait for her to finish. There was a buoy for us to lie at, but on calm nights we almost swung ashore. Jarvis Island lies twenty miles south of the Equator in long. 160° W., directly in the S.E. Trades, which was all right when there was a breeze. When it fell calm at nights our stern would swing too close to the shore, and the breakers were enough to frighten anyone. The ship trembled and it was several nights before I could sleep for their noise. After discharging the fresh water and the mule we went to sea, for Captain Freeman would not stay at that buoy, though people ashore told him there was not the least danger. However, the very next ship that came there swung ashore and was lost, so I guess it was well we left. We sailed around for two weeks until the *Mary Howland* went, then we took her place. Her buoy was laid in 90 fathoms of water, and under our stern we could get no bottom with our lead line.

Loading with our three boats took about six weeks, as we could carry only two or three tons each trip of about a mile. Some days there was so much surf we could not work. Then we would catch fish, of which there were plenty. The sharks would take about half of them as we were hauling them up. So clear was the water we could see the fish twenty fathoms down. We also had plenty of birds eggs to eat. One kind laid a very nice egg as good as a hen's but not quite as large. On Sundays we went ashore for a change, finding the birds very tame and so thick over our heads that one could not throw an egg into the air without hitting a bird. None of them were good for eating, which seems extraordinary. We almost lived on eggs and used to shake up two or three of them with a little water and ginger in a large-mouthed bottle we had, making a very nice drink. There were twenty-four Kanakas ashore, digging up the phosphate and drying it. This phosphate is decomposed coral, formed from the droppings of the birds on the coral.

Nobody was sorry when the ship was loaded and we were on

our way home. We found Cape Horn much easier when going East. There was an occasional row with the men. Billy Smith tried to stick me with his knife and in taking it away from him perhaps I used him a little roughly. He went to the Captain and asked him if he allowed his officers to strike the crew. When the Captain called me I gave him the knife Billy tried to cut me with, then the Captain gave Billy a good rope's-ending. Later the Second Mate, Sargent, had a row with a man called Mack, who jabbed a knife into his groin. It was only by accident that he did not kill him, and he was laid up a long time, with Mack in irons. It all seems such foolish business to me now. There was no occasion for it, only Sargent and I did not know our business. We were only boys, anyhow, he was twenty-two and I was eighteen. But all was forgotten when we arrived home in one hundred days.

Off Hampton Roads the pilot boat gave us our orders to proceed to Philadelphia, and we learned later that the Captain also got a letter telling him that he had a daughter. We filled away for Philadelphia, everybody as happy as possible. We towed to the wharf and next day all hands were paid off. I was going to remain by the ship, but Billy Smith went off with the men and got drunk, so the Captain sent me home with him and the other boys. I sewed all my wages inside my vest pocket, only keeping enough out to take me home. We took a deck passage on the steamer from New York to Fall River, thinking it was no worse than we were used to and not caring to spend the money for a berth. I have made many trips in those Sound boats since, but I always remember that first one and I always look at the deck passengers, especially if boys, and wonder if I can assist them. But I caught a bad cold sleeping on a pile of leather that time. Arriving at Boston I bid good-bye to the boys. I saw them off and on for years. Benny Winsor sailed with me in the *Reynard* for four years or more and later died at sea as second mate of the *Shooting Star*, being buried off the River Plate. Billy I never saw again. The last I heard of him he was in New Orleans at the beginning of the Rebellion, and has never been heard of since.

After arriving home I asked my mother where I might borrow a boat in which to practise sailing. She thought I would have had enough of the water after being a year afloat, but this was different. In a boat I could be captain and crew too, and soon I was having a sail. Standing out so far that no one could see what I was doing, I practised with the boat to see how far she would shoot into the wind until I had learned all her points. Later in the day when I returned to the moorings I could make the boat go exactly where I wanted, knowing that many eyes would be watching to see if I was still a boatman. As a rule sailors are the clumsiest boatmen in the world, unless they have been brought up in boats before going to sea. They seem to think they can tumble about in a boat as they can on board a ship. I had a good long summer at home and thought that if I'd had an income of five hundred dollars I would never leave the town, for I was very content to play about in a boat with a gun. I often think now that the worse thing a young man can have is rich parents, which prevents him from having the least anxiety for the future.

One day I called on Captain Freeman, who was in town, and I shall never forget how he got up from his seat and seemed glad to see me, saying, " How are you, Mr. Josselyn." It was the first time I'd heard my title since I left the ship, and the first time anyone in town had addressed me as a man. He said he was not yet sure of going in the *Reynard* this time, but promised me a berth as Third Mate. In a few days I was called to join the ship in New York, where she was loading for San Francisco.

Captain Freeman was still Master and we had a new Mate, Mr. William F. Seymour, of Barrington R.I. I found him a different man from any I had yet seen, not very large, but when he spoke the men had to jump. The second day I was on board he called me down for talking to the boys, giving me to understand that an officer must keep his place away from the crew and, in fact, that he had rather a poor opinion of me. The Second Mate, Mr. Lyman G. Reed, was a little mite of a man from Boston, the smallest man I think, that I ever saw as a ship's officer.

I was on board about a week before we sailed some time in the early Fall. During this rather uneventful week I recollect a fight in the galley between two Negroes. We had a coloured cook and one day our old steward from the previous trip came on board. He had been in the ship since she was built and had fitted her out with all her cooking utensils for the galley as well as the cabin. While he was talking with the new cook the latter, not knowing that this was the man who had fitted her out, made some remarks about some of the gear being useless. One word led to another till they went for each other with carving knives and were well cut up before they were separated. I have seen a good many fights as foolish since.

Nothing particular happened the first week out, except that I found we had a live man for Mate, and one not easily suited. Then we pitched into a hurricane, not far from Bermuda. We were lying under two close-reefed topsails, fore topmast staysail, and main spencer. First the main topsail brace parted and the parral carried away. The sail went to pieces and the yard swung by the lifts and halliards till it battered away the main topmast. The main yard came down on deck, punching a hole in it, the mizzen topgallant mast broke off, and the fore royal and skysail yards were broken in two by the braces. All the rest of the sails blew away, even the main spencer, that will stand almost anything. But for the fact that it moderated in the morning we should have gone to the bottom, for our deck was badly torn up by the main yard.

I can't say that I enjoyed it, but I had enjoyed many a fight in a boat when there was extreme danger, and all my life had heard sailors talking about hurricanes. One has to experience one to know, and I think, though I was frightened, I exerted myself so as to win the approval of the Mate and to hold it ever after. Today a Master Mariner would not have been caught in this hurricane, but in 1859 few masters in the Merchant Marine were familiar with the Laws of Storms. We were hove to on the wrong tack and went into the gale instead of out of it. When it moderated next day we made our way slowly back to Boston, arriving there two weeks later. We discharged a large part of our cargo that was damaged and renewed it, and at the same time changed our single topsails into double topsails, which were then coming into fashion. All the crew left, I was the only one remaining on board during the three weeks we took to get ready again. Benny Winsor, the boy from the previous voyage was still with us, and he went home telling great stories of how I went aloft that morning when the ship was rolling, and cut away the fore royal and skysail yards. I did not know until he told of it that I had done anything out of my duty and should never have thought of mentioning it, for climbing was always sport for me.

One little incident happened while we were at the wharf in

East Boston. Some boys on the wharf called out that there was a boy overboard. I ran down the side ladder of the ship, followed by the whole gang of riggers all urging me to hurry, though it occurred to me afterwards that they did not get ahead of me. Round the building on the wharf I followed the boys, and there was the little fellow just coming to the surface. I tossed my hat off and made an ineffectual attempt to take off my jacket, but when I noticed him disappearing I jumped in and soon had him, bringing him easily to the wharf, for he was not more than five-or six-years-old. The foreman rigger had thoughtfully grabbed a small coil of rope as he left the ship, so they soon lowered it down to me, and hauled the boy and then me on to the quay. Later in the day, after everybody had gone ashore leaving me, the ship-keeper, alone on board, a labouring man came aboard with the boy's mother and asked if I could drink, as he wanted to treat me. I thanked him and told him I did not drink and that's the last I heard of the affair.

On the voyage out to 'Frisco the weather, trade winds, and everything seemed very like the previous voyage. We had a big row with the crew when we were off the River Plate. Several of the men were put in irons for a spell and afterwards were in court about it in 'Frisco. Somehow in those days we used to have men in irons every voyage. There is a great change in that respect on board ships. I have not put a man in irons for more than fifteen years, and I think I have just as good discipline as ever. Looking back on all those rows they seemed to me to have been nothing but foolishness. In other words, we did not know our business as officers.

After an uneventful passage of one hundred and twenty days we arrived at 'Frisco, discharged our cargo, and took on ballast for Callao. Crews were hard to get and I guess about all of ours were shanghaied, for when our ballast was loaded we anchored in the bay. The men arrived one or two at a time, nearly all of them drunk, and some we had to hoist up with a tackle, but there were no complaints made at the time. Mr. Reed, the Second Mate, left us to go home as Chief Mate of another ship. The man we shipped in his place was a very good sailor but very ignorant.

Quite a fleet of vessels left on the same day, six of us bound to Callao to load guano at the Chincha Islands. As there were no tugboats we had to beat out of the bay. We were the first vessel out and never made a miss-stay, while all the others did. The ship *Ocean Telegraph* could not tack at all, but backed and filled and let the tide take her out. We were a long way outside the Heads with all sail set including a whole side of starboard stunsails, and could easily beat them all, when the *Ocean Telegraph* got out and got sail on her. With the wind on the quarter we were going thirteen knots, but at noon the *Ocean Telegraph* passed us easily, with her skysails and crossjack furled and not a stunsail set. Although we did thirteen knots all the afternoon, by six o'clock I had to go up on the fore yard to see her she had sailed so much faster. As there were six of us bound for Callao, and racing of course, you would have expected the *Ocean Telegraph* to arrive first. In fact the poorest sailor was the first to arrive. By taking a different course she was in port ten days before the next arrival. She had sailed much farther than the rest because her captain knew enough to go away from the land, while all the others made a direct course and were becalmed at the Galapagos Islands. We were nearly three weeks in their vicinity, drifting back every night in a calm what we made in the day, and we might have been there still if we had not taken the whalers' advice and sailed off to the west. There were several whalers cruising in the area. They came on board nearly every day, giving us some of the turtles they catch on the islands.

Arrived at Callao, our crew refused to go further, said they had been shanghaied and demanded to see the Consul. We had to stand watch night and day to keep them from being stolen. We did lose two. The Consul came off and asked each man what he had to complain of. One poor fellow said he had only just gone ashore from the *Andrew Jackson* and before he had been paid off had got drunk (probably been drugged) and was the one we had hoisted aboard unconscious in 'Frisco. All wanted to leave the ship and refused to work until we had two men come off from the shore in place of the two who had got away. These two new men had deserted from another vessel, but had only been ashore a few hours before being taken aboard us, without their clothes and minus a two months' advance of wages. As soon as they had told their story to our crew there was no need for us to watch any more, they were perfectly ready to go to work and to remain in the ship.

Through some mismanagement on the part of the owners at home there was no cargo for us, and as the copper on our bottom was in poor condition we returned to Boston in ballast. It proved to be nothing but a yachting voyage and our ship looked like a yacht when we reached Boston in the summer. The owners and a party came down the Bay in a yacht to meet us. Mr. Bush, the principal owner, said this was just where he wanted her, so I suppose it was his doing that she came home in ballast, though I have heard many say that it was a very singular thing that Captain Freeman could not find a cargo from somewhere. We went directly to the drydock in East Boston.

After the ship was coppered in Boston I joined her again, acting as second Mate going round to New York with a crew of runners. I was thought too young to ship as Second Mate, being only twenty, and looking younger than I was so Mr. Gardner from Cape Cod was shipped in New York. He was a big fellow, but his looks belied him. Mr. Seymour, our live Mate, remained at home and Mr. Reed, our former Second Mate who had left us in 'Frisco joined as Mate. He, by the way, was Captain Freeman's brother-in-law, the two men having married sisters. We loaded a cargo of wheat in New York for Liverpool, and made a fine passage of twenty days to that port, beating the celebrated packet *Dreadnought,* Captain Samuel.

Benny Winsor was still with us and two more boys joined. They were Mr. Seymour's younger brother Frank and an English boy, Ned Deegan. All three of these boys grew up in the ship and I shall mention them again. I will only say now that Benny Winsor eventually died at sea as Second Mate of a ship, while Frank Seymour rose to be master of a ship for some years before carrying on a teaming business at Providence R.I. for a number of years before his death. Ned Deegan was captain of a Chinese steamer for many years before he died.

We had only twenty-one days in Liverpool, discharging and loading back to New York, and made the whole round voyage in fifty-five days. It rained all the time we were in Liverpool, but although it was winter it was not cold. Only once did we see the sun and the Mate told me to loose and dry some of the sails. Before we had them loosed it was raining again, so we gave it up. I met Ned Deegan's sister in Liverpool, a very nice girl of about sixteen. Ned and his only sister had been born in Dublin and when their father died had been left well provided for. Their mother had married again and the stepfather squandered all their money. So his sister was taking care of a baby for a Mrs. O'Neal, whose husband kept the hotel which the American captains patronised. He used to get Kate to tend the bar, for a bar in England without a barmaid would be no good. One of the American captains, in the ship *Gulf Stream*, who had his wife with him, brought her to America and she went to live down east in Maine with the captain's family. Later she came to live with the captain's sister in Charlestown, Mass. She was very smart and capable. I took my father to see her and he thought a lot of her. As long as she lived in Charlestown he used to call on her often and he thought I was blind to her charms. Just to show how things come round, I will tell how Kate later met her husband. A young man from California who came across the plains to join the Northern Army in the Civil War (I think he was one of the so-called California Hundred) was a Lieutenant under Sheridan on the day Sheridan retrieved the victory over Early in the Shenandoah Valley. Lieutenant Roberts was wounded, and lay on the field while both armies passed over him in the retreat of the Northern Army. Later in the day, both armies passed over him again in the retreat of the Southern Army. He was in hospital a long time, and after the close of the war, before going home to California he went to see the Bunker Hill Monument. While at Charlestown he met Kate Deegan in church, and a year later she went to California and married him. He had a position in the U.S. Mint. The last I saw of them they had four boys.

Mr. Gardner left us at Liverpool and I was made Second Mate, Benny Winsor becoming the third. I often think how little a sailor sees of the places he goes to, just through not knowing. I scarcely saw anything of Liverpool, but had I known enough to buy a guide-book I could have seen all the principal places and could have enjoyed and learned so much, instead of wasting my time. It was thirty-five years before I saw Liverpool again, and then it was only to go from the steamer to the station to get a train for Glasgow. It was still raining when I got back, and seemed as natural as though I had not been away a year. Now that I have a Liverpool man for my son-in-law perhaps I shall see it again.

I suppose all my thoughts were on my position as Second Mate, for I remember little that happened on the way home, except that when we made a light the Captain thought it was

D

Fire Island and was steering away to the South until we passed a vessel which told us it was Barnegat, "Hard up the wheel," came the order, and "Call all hands." As quickly as possible we were heading for Sandy Hook, which we soon made as the wind was West South West. We had had no observations of the sun or stars for almost the whole passage so it was not surprising the Captain did not know the lights, which were not so easily distinguished then as now. We were all soon relieved by the sight of a tug, which took us to New York, right up to Twenty-First Street to discharge, for most of the cargo was coal for the gas works. This was my last trip with Captain Freeman, for he left us and Captain Seymour now took command of the *Reynard*. The former only went to sea a short time after this. Then his mind failed, and after a year or more he passed away. This was the second master I had been with who died insane. In those days especially, a shipmaster was not supposed to do anything, and that is the hardest kind of work, particularly at sea where the captain often has no one to talk with, but only worry.

For many years I have made a practice of reading out loud, and that takes the place of talking, or I walk the deck for hours talking to an imaginary audience. How little Capain Seymour thought that he himself would become helpless and go to Snug Harbour to end his days, for I don't believe there was a smarter shipmaster in America and he could read, write, and speak Spanish as well as he could English. But he took to drinking and that made him lose his nerves. It did not seem possible that the lame bowed-down wreck of a man I later used to see at Snug Harbour was the same man who now took command of the *Reynard*. One thing he would never excuse in an officer was being drunk on duty. He would often remark that a man who could not drink without making a fool of himself had better leave it alone. Yet no man ever made a greater fool of himself that way than Seymour . . . Incidentally, the only time I ever got drunk was this time in New York. We were loading at some berth near Fulton Ferry for London. Third Mate Ben Winsor, Ned Deegan, and myself were on board one evening and did not know what to do with ourselves. I do not remember which of us proposed it, but we sent Ned Deegan ashore to get some rum. First we tried a little, then some more, and finished it off. I felt very sick during the night, and in the morning we were such sick-looking objects that Ben and I made an agreement that the first one of us to touch a glass of intoxicating liquor should pay the other ten dollars. I think Captain Seymour must have had a great influence on my life for I have dreamed of him once or twice a year for the last thirty years, and in this dream he is always in command and I am his Mate.

When Captain Seymour took command I noticed a great change in his ideas. For instance, when he was our Mate and there was somebody else to bear all the responsibility (for it is never asked what the Mate did) he used to carry sail till all was blue, but now much to my surprise he would go under easy sail all night, for at first he did not like to trust anybody. His wife told me several years afterwards that he would always go to sleep when it was my watch on deck, but even so he did not begin to carry the sail that Captain Freeman did. I always think of this difference when I hear people tell of what they would do if only they held some other person's place of responsibility. I have always noticed that on a captain's first voyage he is very pleasant. Mr. Reed was Mate, I was Second, Benny Winsor was Third Mate, and as we had all been together several trips we got along first rate.

After loading wheat at Pier 47, East River, for London, we were only just outside of Sandy Hook when it fell flat calm so that we made hardly any headway for four days. Seymour remarked that it was poor weather for a beginner to make a reputation, yet in spite of this calm we made the passage to London in sixteen days. Just east of the Grand Banks we had a terrific gale from the north and it was very cold. When I came down from goose-winging the main topsail the Captain was " splicing the main brace," i.e., giving all hands a glass of grog. You recollect that Ben and I were under a contract, the first to drink was to pay ten dollars. He came to me and asked, " Are you going to have a drink now?" " Yes, I am half frozen." " Well I thought I would ask you, I have had a drink." We had a very poor crew, several of them had never been to sea. Later in the day our main royal got adrift. I sent two men to secure it again, but they did not dare to go out on the yard it was blowing so hard. The Captain asked me if I had a sharp knife, and if so I could cut the sail away. I went up, but instead of cutting the sail away I managed to furl it. Seymour often said later that he had seen me do things that he could not do. I think he thought that was one of them, but I know he would have furled it himself.

This passage I used to take a cold bath every day in my room and I had a jug of Jamaica rum to rub down with. I thought the jug was growing lighter than it ought so I marked the stopple, and found someone was using it. Not until another voyage did I find out it was the Mate and Ben Winsor. I happened to lose a bet to Ben and he said, " We will call it square, for the Mate and I drank your rum, and I owe you ten dollars for being the first one to drink."

By the time we reached London it was spring and we had delightful weather, except when it was foggy. Everybody has heard of a London fog. We lay in the Victoria Dock. The first Sunday I had liberty (One of the officers had to be on board all the time) I went up to London with our Customs officer. We took the train from Barking to Fenchurch Street. I know I lost my ticket and had to pay another fare, something I have been careful not to do again. From the station we walked down to the river, passing the Monument to the Great Fire, which the officer described to me. Then we took a river steamer to the Houses of Parliament, passing under London Bridge. At Westminster we visited the tombs of famous people and went to church in the Abbey. We saw St. James's Park and the Royal Palace, Nelson's monument, the City and St. Paul's Cathedral on this and other Sundays when I could get off. Once Mr. Winsor went with me, but he was not very interested and would never go again. We saw very little of Captain Seymour, for he always stopped ashore in port, coming aboard daily with his gloves on and looking quite a dude.

After discharging we took ballast for New York again, making a very quick passage home. In New York at the U.S. Hotel I met Captain Freeman for the last time. He had made a short voyage somewhere and I think it was his last voyage to sea. He seemed very glad to see me, and asked all about the ship, saying " I suppose you have the *Reynard* in fine order." She was looking pretty well, for coming home in ballast we had nothing to do but clean her up. I took a short run home for a few days, going as usual by the Sound boats, and always enyoying that trip. As I knew I was going out in the *Reynard* again I had no baggage to bring home. In fact it was six years before I took my clothes from the ship.

CHAPTER THREE

Last two voyages in ship Reynard, 1861-1866—American Civil War—Fifth voyage (Second Mate) of forty-four months —London (ship for sale)—Cardiff—Manila—short call at New York, then on to London—Cardiff—Calcutta—Shanghai—Hongkong—Singapore—New York—Sixth voyage (Mate) to San Francisco—Honolulu—McKeen's Island—ship leaking, call at Apia (Samoa)—New London.

My fifth voyage in the *Reynard* was one of the longest I have ever made, lasting forty-four months, though in that time the ship did call at New York once and anchored in the bay for about a week before being sent on to London with the same cargo. If I had thought on that occasion that we should not come straight back from London I would have gone home as the rest did instead of remaining as ship-keeper. We set off with almost the same aftergang as the previous voyage. Seymour was Master, Reed was Mate, I was Second Mate, and Ben Winsor was Third Mate. Ned Deegan and Frank Seymour were Able Seamen now and there was a new boy, Joe Smith from Barrington R.I. The American Civil War had just commenced and when I was at home in Duxbury all my old schoolmates were being drilled for the army. I had no idea there would be a long war. All the talk was of its being over in ninety days and nobody visualised four long years of carnage. Thirteen of my old school mates have their names on the monument in our little graveyard. I little thought I was looking at them for the last time as they were being drilled in front of the Town House by an officer from West Point, and I thought it all sport.

We had a quick passage to London with another cargo of wheat. The *Alabama* was very much in evidence and we crossed her track several times before we got home again, so we kept a sharp lookout for her. When we reached London there was no business for American ships and most of them were being sold. We lay there for thirteen months, while many parties tried to buy our ship but did not come to terms. It was very pleasant to be back in Victoria Dock, for we now had many acquaintances there. All the crew were discharged and no doubt we should all have been had anyone known we would be there so long. As they wanted to sell the ship we kept her in as fine order as possible. In those docks a ship is well taken care of and nothing can be stolen, for the only entrance to the dock area is guarded and after nine o'clock at night no one is admitted, though we were so well acquainted we could get in at any hour and we used to give little tips to the gate-keepers. Our carpenter tried to take out some old copper stowed away in his clothes, but they searched him, found the copper, and investigated further. He was discharged from the ship. Whether he was otherwise punished or not, he was a silly fellow, for he had a year's easy time on board and would probably have been kept on. In those days we were entitled to three months' extra pay if paid off in a foreign port, two months of which went to the seaman and one month to the government.

Of course all the talk was of the War. All the people of England were for the South and sure the South would win out, especially after the battle of Bull Run. Our ship being for sale people came daily to examine her and it was my duty to show them all over the ship. Many asked me if I would remain in the ship if they bought her, but I always said no, if they bought the ship I was going home to war. They laughed at the idea of the North being able to coerce the South, but I said we had to win for I and many others would rather die than see slaves sold at the foot of Bunker Hill Monument. I said, " The War has hardly begun. We will fight to the last man, just as the South is doing now, while we have only got our first men engaged." It is a common belief nowadays that only the English aristocracy were in favour of the South, but actually every man and woman I saw in London (and I was there two years during the War) cheered every Southern victory. Do not imagine that I am down on the English. Queen Victoria never had a more loyal subject, though naturally I put my own country first. Captain Seymour was brought up on a Cuban plantation, of which his father was in charge, and you would have expected him to be in favour of the South. But he was for the North too. The Superintendent of the Victoria Dock used to meet him on the train sometimes and argue about the War, saying, "Well, I will tell you how certain I am the South will win. I have ten thousand pounds in Southern Bonds now, and I am going to invest another thousand this morning." After the war was over Seymour always hoped to go back to London to see how much this man would take for his Southern Bonds.

After remaining in London for thirteen months, and being unable to sell the ship, we started for Cardiff. In the Channel a ship ran us down. It was about two o'clock one morning. We were on the starboard tack standing off shore when we saw a green light on our port bow. As we had the right of way we only kept close to the wind, but the other vessel, instead of keeping away as it was her duty to do, ran into us on the port side, staving a hole in us and smashing in her own bow. We remained by her until morning, as we thought she was sinking and our own hole was above water so we were in no danger. She proved to be a small steamer, with her screw hoisted up and proceeding under sail. Her forward bulkhead had saved her for her bow was all stove in. We both went back to London. Our repairs kept us in London another month, costing eight hundred pounds, which the owners of the other vessel had to pay. We then went to Cardiff and loaded coal for Manila.

I remember one of the sailors that came on board at Cardiff and a description of him may give people ashore some idea of the general run of sailors at that time. He came aboard looking for a job, and was bare-footed, wearing a suit of overalls, no underclothes, and an old hat. The Captain engaged him and he proved a very good man, a good sailmaker, and he could also make clothes. Later, in Manila, the crew bought cloth and he made clothes for them, for he was never idle. When we called at New York he had a chest full of clothes and paid off with one hundred and fifty dollars. We went to London again, then round to Cardiff for the second time, to load for Calcutta, and he appeared on board again in much the same state as when we

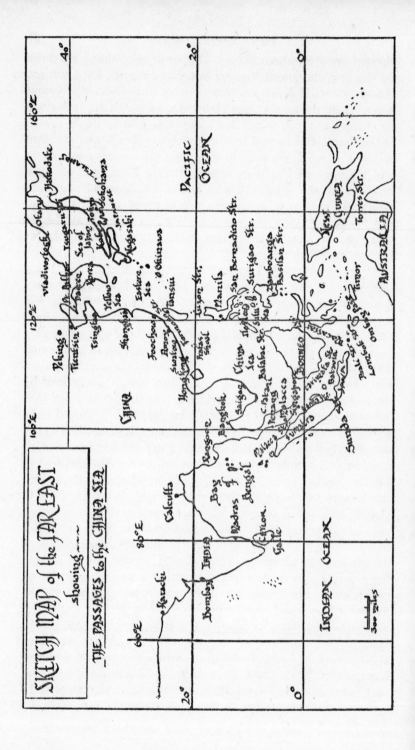

first saw him, and was once more shipped. He told us that he had only been ashore in New York for three days, then shipped for Havre with money gone, clothes gone, and a ninety dollar advance gone. He had just come over from Havre. I mention him as a fair example of the sailors, men that cannot take care of themselves. If such a man could take care of himself he would cease to be a sailor, for any good sailor is a very useful man full of resources.

This time in Cardiff I decided I would learn to smoke. So many had prophesied that I would do so that I fancy I had only put it off so long just to be contrary. Anyhow, I thought it would be pleasant to while away the hours of a long watch by smoking, as nearly everybody that went to sea smoked and said what a comfort it was. So I supplied myself with tobacco and pipes and for a little while was learning, but Mr. Winsor, who shared my room, made so much dirt with his tobacco all over the place that I threw the whole business overboard—tobacco, pipes, and matches, and would not let Ben smoke in the room. From that day to this I have never smoked.

We had a long passage from Cardiff to Manila, as it was the North East monsoon and we had to take the eastern passages through Ombay Strait and Dampier Strait into the Pacific Ocean, then go around the north of Luzon and south to Manila. I enjoyed very much this cruising among the islands, and Captain Seymour, who had been in whalers, always kept two boats on the davits and went ashore to any island where he could easily land. How he dared to leave his ship to the care of the Mate as much as he did is a mystery to me. I have never had officers that I would dare to trust as he trusted us. It must have been the custom in a whaler to go in the boats so much that he got into the habit. They used to call it "gamming," visiting in their boats from one ship to another at sea.

Our coal was for Cavite, about seven or eight miles down the bay from Manila, for the Spanish Government. Little did we think then that one day this country would be governed by the United States. The Captain used to go up to Manila in our boat nearly every day. All our crew refused to work after we arrived in the port. They said they wanted to leave the ship, and when the Captain refused to discharge them they demanded to see the Consul. The Captain said he would see the Consul at Manila, but they must go to work in the meantime. They replied that they would prefer to go into irons, so they were all put in irons except the bare-footed man that came aboard in Cardiff. He told them they were foolish, and as there was no work to be done until we were ready to discharge they certainly were foolish. In about a week the Consul came down from Manila in our boat and told them they could not get paid off there, and then they went to work for we were ready to unload.

"There was another American ship discharging coal, the *Tornado*. One of her sailors fell from aloft and was killed. The only place the bigoted Roman Catholics of Manila would allow him to be buried was on the shore below high water mark, as low down as possible. I should not have thought it so strange if they had not given a decent burial on a point of land to some pirates they shot one morning, these pirates professing to be Catholics. Such things make me think how silly a great many of the observances of all churches are.

In these Spanish ports, unless you give money to the officials you are bound to have trouble, for your cargo must turn out exact or you are liable to a fine. Mr. Reed made his first serious mistake here. He was afraid our coal was going to overrun and kept telling me to give better weight. One evening when we were about two-thirds discharged he asked me how many pounds made a ton of coal. I told him twenty-two hundred and forty. He said it was two thousand, but when he found I was right he was frightened, for he could not make the coal hold out. Though I scrimped all I could, and one man-of-war refused to take any more, we fell short. Due to the fact that Seymour was on good terms with the Lieutenant in command of the Yard, and could speak Spanish so well, we escaped a fine, but no doubt Seymour gave him a present. I recollect bringing off this Superintendent and his family to dinner one Sunday. There were two very pretty senoritas, who walked up our gangway in their bare feet. I brought their slippers up, for which I received a very pretty " Gracias."

After discharging at Cavite we moved up to Manila and loaded a full cargo of hemp in bales for New York, at a very good freight. I was only ashore in Manila once and saw nothing of the place. I used to go boat sailing a great deal though, for Captain Seymour was a great hand for a boat. Hemp is a very light cargo, like tea, and having such a cargo was very like being in ballast.

We went down through the Sulu Sea and Basilan Strait. In that strait we had the most terrific tempest I have ever experienced. The strait is about twenty miles wide and we were becalmed in the centre. Thunderstorms were crashing among the mountains on both sides all afternoon, gradually approaching each other. At midnight they met directly overhead and the two clouds fought like two armies. For four hours it did not cease, but was one continuous flash and roar, with rain coming down in torrents. One bolt struck our main skysail mast, making a complete broom of the pole. It passed down the centre of the royal mast, jumped along the chain topgallant runner filling the bunt of the main royal with splinters, made its way down below and came up the pumps to the deck again. Several of the crew were knocked down and two men were unconscious for an hour or two, but all came round in the morning. I have seen a ship struck by lightning on two other occasions, but nothing like as as bad as this time. All the men were frightened, but our four boys were not, and of course the officers did not show it. The boys had to put the ropes into the hands of the men, for we were under two lower topsails and had to keep bracing round the yards in the changeable wind to keep away from the shore.

During the War we spoke all the vessels we could, to find out the news and where the *Alabama* was last heard of. One vessel told us of the capture of New Orleans. Near the West Indies on the way home we spoke a small schooner loaded with onions from Argentina. The Captain, as usual, boarded her, but she did not know there was any war, and did not dare to sell us one onion!

We arrived in New York and waited a week at anchor in the stream. Captain Seymour, Mr. Reed, and Mr. Winsor went home, while I remained on board with a ship-keeper. Our cargo was wanted in London so we went there and I did not get home at all, did not even get a letter till I arrived in London. I sent one home the day we arrived in New York, but due to a change in the postage rate had not put a big enough stamp on it. The postmaster at Duxbury held it back until my father called to pay the extra postage, so there was no time to get a reply before we sailed. Ben Winsor left us for good at New York. Captain Seymour had always been down on him, even as a boy. I never saw him again as he died at sea on his next voyage, when Second Mate of the *Shooting Star*.

When we had started the voyage the Civil War was just commencing. It was now nearly two years later and the boys I had seen drilling, looking on it all as a kind of joke, had become real soldiers and many of them had been killed. I made a mistake in not joining the Navy, but in the beginning there was so much favouritism shown that I would have chosen the Army, where I knew nothing, rather than the Navy, where I was capable not only of navigating a ship but of rigging her, but thought I would be under boys that knew nothing. However, I was mistaken.

The crew we now shipped for London were a poor lot, but we got there all right. The Captain took his wife over with us this time as we were expecting to come directly back. Of course it was pleasant to be in London again, but after discharging our hemp we went round to Cardiff once more to load coal, this time for Calcutta. I never cared much for Cardiff, perhaps because we lay so far from the city that I saw little of it. Mr. Reed made another mistake here, when we were only in the basin of the dock awaiting a berth and the weather was very bad. The Harbour-master came and told us we must get out another hawser over the stern as it was going to blow hard that night. It was not an easy matter for we were a long way from the pier, so Mr. Reed said, " I don't believe it is going to blow that way," and he put another hawser out over the bow. The Captain came on board late and asked what fasts were out. About midnight we got a squall that parted all our stern-fasts, and we shot ahead on to the dock, cutting our stem to the wood ends, but we damaged several other vessels much more. It was a very expensive job, and all because we did not put the hawser out where the harbour-master told us to. Captain Seymour never knew that the Mate had received orders to get out a hawser. I don't know what he would have said if he had known.

It was at Cardiff that I decided to make an effort to improve my way of life. I had been brought up under strict Puritan ideas and to me as a boy the Sabbath was the most disagreeable day of the week. But I had always intended to be on the Lord's side. A sermon I heard preached in an Episcopal Church at this time made me realise I must make an effort for myself. It was even noticed in the ship that I had left off swearing, for I used to be quite proficient at it, in fact could give lessons in it!

After loading the coal we had to wait a week with the hatches off to let it ventilate. We had a hard time in the Bay of Biscay, but finally reached the Line in forty-seven days, the longest I ever took. In spite of that we reached Calcutta in one hundred and seven days. When the coal was discharged we loaded a cargo of rice for Shanghai. One could write a lot about Calcutta. We had to tow about two hundred miles up the river Hooghli, and parts of it were very dangerous in those days. At one place in particular if the ship touched the bottom she would be rolled over by the tide. As we went up the masts of a vessel were sticking out of the river, the hull having gone down in the quicksands the day before. When we came down the river the masts had entirely disappeared. The pilots lived on board a full rigged brig at the mouth of the Hooghli. This river being so dangerous the pilots have a long training. It takes many years to become a pilot here, but when they are full pilots they get big salaries and are very arbitrary, coming on board with a servant to wait upon them and a leadsman to do all the sounding, this leadsman being in training to be a pilot. A short distance to windward of the brig we hove to, but were still forging ahead with only the crossjack yard aback, so that the boat had quite a pull to reach us. The first salutation we got was, " Why in hell don't you back that main yard?" I thought Captain Seymour would reply, but I guess he thought he had better not. All over the world people think you don't know much if you are not familiar with their local customs. For instance I have several times had the conductor of a trolley car enquire, with impatience, " Don't you know we stop on this side of the street?" More than once I have replied to the same question, " Why no, Conductor, I have a poor memory, but do you know on which side of the street the car stops in Philadelphia, in Boston, in Honolulu, in London, in Paris?"

As we towed up the Ganges to Calcutta I was watching the steering while the rest got their dinner, and I noticed on top of the tug's paddle-box a man who kept getting down on his knees and then standing up. I thought he was talking to someone down below, but the leadsman informed me it was noon and a certain class always pray at that hour no matter where they may be. At sunrise on the bank of the river another crowd was worshipping, and at sunset yet another, praying and shouting. Another class bury their dead in the river and you could not look over the side for five minutes without seeing a dead body floating by, probably with several birds sitting on the corpse and eating it. The birds in Calcutta are scavengers and no one is allowed to kill them.

They were very tame and would grab our food from the steward's hands as he passed from the galley to the cabin if he did not watch out. The dead bodies were so thick in the river then that a gang of men were constantly employed sinking them. I came near to finishing my career here at this time, having an attack of cholera, but recovered after being very sick for several days. Joe Smith, one of our boys, was in hospital and was brought on board in a cot when we sailed, as was another boy from Chatham, Cape Cod, who begged Captain Seymour to take him.

Our passage from Calcutta to Shanghai was very long, ninety-three days. To begin with we lay at the mouth of the Hooghli for ten days, waiting for a slant of wind to take us out to sea. While there we tried to catch a shark but did not succeed, they were so large our shark hook would not hold them. In fact I only managed to get one close enough to see him and he was like a small whale. I have always supposed they have been there for centuries feeding well on the corpses brought down by the river. We called at Singapore for a day, and all the way to Shanghai were on the look out for the *Alabama,* which rumour said was operating in that vicinity. On our arrival at Shanghai we heard she was in Singapore.

Shanghai was full of ships, mostly American with nothing to do, for the *Alabama* had burned a number in the Straits of Malacca so nobody wanted to charter American ships. After we had been in port a week the boy from Chatham asked and received permission to go on board one of the other ships where he said his brother-in-law was the Mate. The next day a boat came alongside and who should be in it but Smith, the old Second Mate of the *Sicilian* who stole the cook's clothes. I recognised him but he did not know me. He asked Captain Seymour to let his brother-in-law join his barque. The Captain said he might go, but as he had been sick all the time (the Captain had nursed him like a child and undoubtedly saved his life by agreeing to take him at Calcutta) he could pay him no wages. On the other hand if he would agree to stay with us he would pay him Ordinary Seaman's wages for the whole of his time on board. The boy said he would remain, but the night before we sailed he got all the money due to him on the pretext that he wanted to buy clothes, then cleared off to join his brother-in-law. Captain Seymour was very mad about it, and it was certainly aggravating to be swindled in this way. I don't think the boy was so much to be blamed as his brother-in-law Smith, and in fact I have been looking for that man ever since.

Our Mate made another mistake in Shanghai. Through not watching the Chinamen discharging we fell short several hundred bags of rice, although I had several casks full that I had swept up. I know it was a good lesson for me. I can tell some very interesting stories about keeping tally of cargoes, some of them almost like sleight-of-hand business. The lesson is, " Do not trust anybody if you are to be held responsible, for if men err they always err in their own favour." I remember what Seymour said when he found the ship had to pay quite a sum for short delivery, " If I was Mate of this ship I would not have waited for the captain to come on board. I would have cleared out."

We sailed down to Hongkong, a very pleasant run in the North East monsoon with only a very little cargo. This port was also full of American ships, laid up on account of the *Alabama*. We only remained a few days and then went on to Singapore. I have often wondered why the Captain sailed directly towards the *Alabama*, for we knew she was in that port, and in fact the day we went into the Eastern entrance of Singapore she went out the other way. Had she come our way she would have burned us up, and it would have been a good job for me if she had, for I would have been amply paid for all my losses from the *Alabama* Claims. Several of my friends who were burned out had quite a windfall after the war from those Claims. But this was as near as we came to her.

We had a fine time in Singapore, where we remained three months, going into the New Harbour, where the dry-dock was, to be coppered. And a more romantic place for a ship to get to cannot be imagined, surrounded by tropical trees. At the time tigers were so thick upon the island (for Singapore is an island and the tigers swim across the Strait from the mainland) that a bounty was given for their heads, in addition to which their skins were said to be worth thirty dollars each. There was an American hunter who made a business of killing them, and it was said that one man a day was killed on the island by the tigers. Seymour was a great hand for shooting. He went ashore one morning at New Harbour, but he soon signalled for the boat to take him off again, there were too many fresh tiger tracks around for his liking.

Our crew were all discharged here and we officers had nothing to do but keep the ship clean. We had several boat races. Our boat always won from the fleet and I always sailed her, but when we sailed against the yachts we came in third, I do not think I went ashore here this time. Finally we loaded for New York, taking with us one passenger. I think he was running away from some financial trouble. After the usual weather on the way home, and speaking one vessel that told us of the capture of Vicksburg, we arrived safely at New York. An hour or two after we had taken our pilot the pilot boat was captured by a rebel man-of-war. Again we anchored in the bay, off the Battery, while Captain Seymour went to Boston to see the owners, leaving the Mate in charge. While the Captain was away the Mate and the passenger went ashore and came off pretty full. We had to hoist the passenger on board with a tackle, but the Mate had been foolish enough to go into the office of our agents, and they telegraphed the owners that they had better send the Captain back to look out for his ship as the Mate was ashore drunk. When the Captain came we hauled into Pier 47 East River to discharge. I was the only one left on board, until later we took a boy from Bristol, Conn. He was a fine boy with snapping black eyes, and crazy to go to sea, but he remained with me only till late in the Fall.

While I was keeping ship this time I went to the Navigation School of Mrs. Captain Thoms and her daughter Isabella, enjoying it very much. Isabella was Mrs. Dr. Brownlow and the first day in school asked me if I was an officer of a vessel. I think I must have looked to her about fifteen. She found she had nothing to teach me for Mate and she put me on to study for Master, but I had only really started when it was Thanksgiving and I went home until just before the ship sailed. I had been away from home for almost four years.

I remember very little of this visit home. One would think that after forty-four months away the home-coming would be exceptional. But it was wartime and we never knew when we would be drafted. My mother told me once that she was glad to have me away, for when they came to enquire for her boys she could truthfully tell them that I was in another part of the world. However, that made no difference to me as my agreements with the owners always stipulated that I was to leave and come home if I was drafted. But most of the boys were away and the war was all the talk.

On the Saturday before I was to return to the ship at New York I took out a boat to have my last sail over to Plymouth. It was blowing hard when I started and while over in Plymouth it increased to a gale, but I set off home for I must take the first train for New York on Monday morning. When I was half-way, and was in what we call the Cow Yard where three tides meet, I could get no further. The boat filled to the thwarts several times and I had to give up and go back to Plymouth. Next morning, Sunday, I set out to walk home, arriving to find the family in tears, for they never knew me to put back in a boat and knew I was coming if possible. The next day I returned to New York and found the ship all loaded.

This was my first voyage as Mate. Deegan, who had been Third Mate latterly, was now Second Mate, and young Seymour was Third. We shipped a Fourth Mate and our black-eyed boy from Bristol was still on board. It was towards the last of the Civil War, men were getting $1800 bounty to join the army, so it was impossible to get sailors. We took anything that came along. I had $90 per month, everybody else $60 and boys $35. I wanted to go to war, but the owner Mr. Bush thought the war was nearly over as Grant was at Petersburg.

We had one boy from Duxbury, Charley Hunt, another from Barrington R.I., and one from New York. It seems that this last one had run away from a rich home. He was a nice boy, but when we arrived at 'Frisco the Captain had several heartbroken letters from his mother and it had killed his poor old grandfather. He was sent home overland and I have never heard of him since, but I think it was a mistake for his mother to call him home. He was in the best school he could have been sent to, and I claim that when we had our big sailing fleet it was worth more for wild boys than all the reform schools in the country. Perhaps he learned his lesson on that passage, he was certainly a smart fellow, and though he had never done any work in his life he was a good Ordinary Seaman when we discharged him.

There was a heavy snow storm just before we were ready to start and the deck was full of snow when we went to anchor off Staten Island. The storm had cleared off bitterly cold. It was an awful job rigging out our jib-boom with everything frozen. The first night out it began to blow, but we got the sail in all

E

right, and though we took a southerly route we still had ice in our channels on the Sunday. All we did for the first week was to drill our boys to take in sail, and we continued the drill every dog-watch till we arrived off Cape Horn, by which time we had the best crew for handling sail I ever saw.

While we were in New York the *Great Republic*, the largest ship in the world, was also loading, and one frequently heard it remarked that she had a fine set of officers. I suppose she had much the same sort of men for a crew as we had, but instead of teaching them they went to abusing them. When she arrived in 'Frisco she did not look neat as we did. They said they had no one to do anything. When the pilot boarded her the Second Mate said to him, " Pilot, I want to show you how I have got my men trained." He clapped his hands and the crew jumped up on the rail and began to crow like roosters. I cannot write all they had been doing to the crew, but it all came out in court, and the Mate and Second Mate got several years in gaol. Her captain said he did not know anything about it and he was not punished, but Captain Henry Otis Winsor, known as " Bully Winsor " and one of the hardest masters that ever sailed, said, " Then he ought to have got ten years for not knowing it." But Bully Winsor was never known to abuse a boy, he always went for a man that he thought lazy.

Of our crew of eighteen only three could steer when we started. Everyone could steer when we had been out two weeks. We had the usual weather and arrived in 'Frisco in 141 days. Our sister ship, the *War Hawk* sailed from Boston about the same time as we left New York. We were both chartered to load a cargo of phosphate at McKeen's Island, the one arriving first to start first. She arrived at 'Frisco the day before we did, and we found the war was now over. After discharging we hauled into the stream and waited forty days for the *War Hawk* to get out of our road, then we started via Honolulu as we did before when we went to Jarvis Island. Reaching Honolulu in fourteen days we found the other vessel had only just sailed. I found Honolulu much the same as it was in 1859 when I was last there, but I did not go ashore. The harbour was full of whalers, and the barque *Ceylon* was there, waiting for a cargo of whale oil. I had met her before in Chinese waters when she was ship-rigged. She now belonged to Charles Brewer & Co., of Boston. I little imagined then that I would sail for those owners for forty years or more. The *Ceylon* lived to be very old and was only lost about 1904.

After waiting a week we started for McKeen's Island, which lies in Latitude 3° South Longitude 175° West. When we arrived the *War Hawk* had not begun to load, so we sailed round for forty days more, during which time we visited all the islands in the vicinity and even went across the Line to Bakers Island. We found it covered with more than a dozen wrecks. As many of them had broken in two and washed around, there seemed to be even more. So many vessels had been wrecked there that it was said the Insurance Companies would no longer insure vessels bound there. But Captain Seymour went ashore there as he did on nearly all these islands, and would spend the day, leaving me to come after him towards nightfall. He had more confidence in me than I ever had in any mate, and not only in me but in any mate he had. Coming home from Singapore on the previous voyage we had passed an island called Pigeon Island. We were becalmed near it and towards sunset we could see flocks of birds going home for the night. So we lowered a boat, took the passenger and two shot-guns and set off. The boat grounded a long way off, but finally we got ashore and found the trees full of pigeons. We did get some, and got back to our ship at eleven o'clock at night, but if a squall had come up we should never have found the ship.

I came very near to losing the ship on McKeen's Island. I had put the Captain ashore in the morning and was coming in for him late in the afternoon, but as I passed to windward of the island the wind died away. I know now that the wind will always die away to windward of a lagoon island, but I did not know it then. We had only the topsails on the ship, and though I made all the sail as fast as I could we only barely scraped past the end of the island. I could see the bottom quite plainly. All the people on the shore ran to see us for they felt sure we could not get clear, Seymour among the rest. It was a good lesson for me, and since then I have had many experiences in trying to pass to windward of these islands in the Trades. I once tried to pass to windward of Pratas Shoals in the China Sea, but had to give it up and go round to leeward though there was a strong breeze blowing. I have never been cautioned against going to windward of these islands in any book of sailing directions. You might think that Captain Seymour would hesitate about going ashore again after seeing his ship so nearly lost, but he went ashore the next day just the same.

McKeen's Island is very much like Jarvis Island, which I visited on my first voyage in the *Reynard*, being the top of a volcano around the crater of which the coral insects have built a circle above the sea, the inside of the circle being full of water. The same kind and abundance of birds and fish are there. A man had been all alone on the island for over a year holding possession of it. One day there had been a hurricane and he had had to ride it out in his whaleboat anchored in the lagoon, for the whole island was submerged. A local vessel was supposed to call and supply him with provisions. She passed the island and he saw her but she did not stop. As he did not have even a dog for company it must have been a frightening experience.

When at last we came in one morning to take the berth of the *War Hawk* to load we very nearly collided with her. As was usual we came close under her stern, but she was all adrift. She had been moored to the reef with one anchor and a hawser to the shore. After slacking out all her chain on that anchor she had dropped the other one under foot. With ninety fathoms of chain out it did not touch the bottom, but was left hanging to prevent her going on the reef in a calm. That morning, when they took the hawser in, the anchor slipped off the reef. So there she was, adrift with both anchors down and all the chain out, and only an old-fashioned windlass to get them in with. In addition to her own crew she had the foreman and twenty-four Kanakas on board. Captain Seymour took our Second Mate and half our crew to help them get the anchors in, which they succeeded in doing by eleven o'clock that night after working all day. In the meantime, of course, I was drifting along with them. By three o'clock in the afternoon the island was out of sight, and it took us four days to beat back to it against the Trade wind and current. The *War Hawk* took her cargo to Mauritius.

When we did get back we let them have one of our bower anchors which they put to a buoy. They also had a mooring chain fast to the anchor and carried up on to the shore, so we lay pretty quietly when the Trade winds were blowing, but had hard work to keep away from the buoy in the calm spells. Loading here was easier than at Jarvis Island, as the cargo was all brought alongside in whaleboats and we had only to take it on board and dump it into the hold. Our chief amusement was catching sharks, playing them with a long line. When we went swimming someone was always posted to look out for sharks. I wonder now how we ever dared to go in at all.

The first night at sea after loading was finished we discovered the ship was leaking. She had been so long out of water in hot climates that she had dried up. We had to keep the pumps going all night, so we put into Apia, in the Navigators Islands, now called Samoa. It was on a Sunday morning with us, but Monday with them as they kept Australian time. We had no chart of the place, only a general chart of the Pacific Ocean, but when we got near the port a pilot came off in a whaleboat. His name was Hamilton, later he became the American Consul there, and he came from New London, Connecticut, where we were bound. We clewed up most of the sails, all hands being aloft furling them, then had a fair wind into the harbour and came to anchor close to the shore in six fathoms of water. It seemed to me the most delightful place I had ever been in, perhaps because we had been so long around those barren sand banks and reefs where we had loaded. I never tired of looking at the mountains, clothed with vegetation to their summits, and at the long valleys in between them with every shade of colour.

The pilot had a boat's crew of five natives, all fine tall fellows, whose only clothing consisted of leaves about their loins, coming down to their knees and sticking out like bundles of hay. The leaves were quite fresh and very fragrant, they seemed to get them fresh every morning. The rest of their bodies were tattooed from head to foot, the finest I ever saw. They told me they were not called men until they were tattooed, that it was a very painful job and sometimes killed the person. The tallest one came to me and said, " Are you my friend?" I said, " I am anybody's friend as long as they behave themselves." " No," he said, " Suppose you my friend you nobody else's friend. Suppose you want pineapple, coral, banana, coconut, me get you plenty." " All right," I said, " I am your friend." " You no got another friend?" " I haven't another friend in the world." Everybody on board had a friend except the Captain, who was supposed to go ashore and get his friend. The Mate's friend was the boss of all the other friends and would tell them when to go ashore, in fact get all the orders from me while the ship was in port.

No sooner were we at anchor than we were surrounded by

the whole population in canoes. Men, women, girls, and boys were in separate canoes, i.e., the men were together, the women together, and so on. None of them wore any clothing except leaves, the children were nude. As each canoe has an outrigger they take up a lot of room and there were canoes for a hundred yards all round the ship. Our decks were soon full of people, but they were so good-natured and honest that we never lost anything, though for the week that we lay there from morning to night there were never less than a hundred sitting around on the rail to keep out of the way of the men at work. If I told my friend at any time to tell them to go ashore they immediately went, and once I found this out I never disturbed them. Soon after we anchored I heard a great commotion at the gangway and found my friend (whose name by the way, was Zulu, tattooed in big letters on his arm, to which fact he had directed my attention) was there in a large canoe loaded with enough tropical fruit of all kinds to last all hands for a week. I asked him what there was to pay. He looked at me in surprise, saying, " Me your friend." There was nothing to pay, and he not only gave me all the fruit I wanted while we were in port but all the coral I would take, twenty different specimens as well as several natural white coral baskets filled with red coral. They said they had to dive in deep water for this red coral. All I could ever get him to accept was one pound of tobacco and two calico bunk curtains which he admired. He made part of one of them into a loin-cloth and turban and gave the other to his sister.

I said the natives would not steal, but they came very near to stealing all our crew, and it was largely by accident that we did not lose them. They had planned to run away with the girls, who were going to hide them in the mountains until we had sailed. We sailed one day sooner than we had calculated owing to the next day being Sunday, so the plan miscarried. It did not leak out till we were at sea, but I have since thought that probably the pilot had kept the Captain informed and he had made his own plans accordingly.

While in port we listed the ship over and caulked the butts on one side, then listed her the other way and caulked the other side, for we could see where many of the leaks were. This stopped a lot of leaking, but we still had to pump all the way home.

There were a number of missionaries here and many of the natives had been converted and taught to read and write. My

friend could write better than I could. Two of the missionaries
were sending their children home to England to be educated.
They left on a German barque that was bound home with a cargo
of coconut oil. When I saw their grief at parting I began to
realise what sacrifices they were making for their religion, and
I often think of those parents when I hear remarks about the
missionaries being an idle worthless lot. The pilot was a missionary man. New London was his native town, and as we were
bound there he sent me a lot of presents for his mother and his
relatives. When we arrived there they told me his history. They
told me that when he was a young man he was an officer in one
of the Havre packets. He married a French girl and brought her
home, leaving her with his folks on his next voyage. They liked
her very much, but while he was away someone with authority
from New York took her away and sent her back to France, in
spite of her begging his people not to let them take her. When
Hamilton returned and found they had let her go he walked out
of the house and they did not hear from him again for eighteen
years. In the meantime he had been in the mines in California
and Australia, and from Australia had drifted up to Apia. Here
he had been converted by the missionaries, had settled down
and married, and then had written to his family. His wife was
the daughter of an English missionary who had married a native
girl and had fourteen children. The U.S. Consul at that time had
married another of these children and another had been adopted
by the wife of a whaling captain while still a child. This whaling
captain was living at Olneyville, near Providence R.I. and at
that time she was a teacher in Michigan. I carried a lot of presents to her from her sisters and corresponded for a while.

After a week in Apia we started for home, pumping all the way.
We passed through the Straits of Le Maire on the passage and
kept close to the coast, for we were leaking so badly we did
not know when we would be obliged to make for a port. After
we crossed the Gulf Stream the leak stopped, and we passed
New York on a beautiful Sunday in late December. It was so fine
that we kept on for New London, although our intention had
been to go into New York. It was so warm that some of the
sailors were going about barefooted, but we had a South East
gale that night and when we got to Montauk Point the wind
came out of the North West and the thermometer fell to four
degrees below zero. The next day we were hove to under a main

lower topsail and began to ice up. We spent all the week off there, twice we sailed round Block Island, and though we saw the Sound boats every day it seems it was so cold all the pilots had gone into Newport.

On Saturday morning it was fine and Seymour decided to beat into New London. We had only an old chart that happened to be in my possession. When we passed Race Rock there was no buoy, the ice had taken it away. We don't know which side of it we went, but we now had a fair wind up the Thames. We did not know the way, black buoys and white buoys were on both sides of us and only twenty-four feet of water, the ship drawing twenty-two. All our flags were flying and when we got to the Fort we anchored. As no one came to us I was busy getting the boat out when a man aloft sang out there was a boat coming. It turned out to be from the U.S. School Ship *Sabine,* which thought we were in distress we were so iced up. Just as the Captain was going ashore in her a tug arrived and a man said he was our agent from Williams & Havens. He wanted to know why we had not come right to town, but when he learned we had no pilot he wondered how we got there at all, for the only vessel in port was a barque drawing thirteen feet of water that had a pilot but got ashore on the way in. It was a case of Good Luck.

As it was Saturday we remained at anchor and Captain Seymour went home. He was a rough-looking man as he climbed over the stern into the tug for he had scarcely slept for a week. He had no time to change his clothes or even to have a wash, only just time to catch a train. In ten minutes or so I saw the train go by. What a change for him, one hour before he had all the anxiety possible, with reefs on both sides of him and the lead going on both sides of the ship, only twenty-four feet of water and his ship drawing twenty-two. Now, all trouble over, his ship safely at anchor, sitting in a warm train, going to meet his wife and family and spend Sunday with them. And what a changed man he was on Monday, when he came on board from the tug, his wife with him, dressed up and with his gloves on.

Now we were all as happy as clams at high water. That night it rained and melted the ice from us. Sunday morning was clear and cold, with a thin scum of ice on the water. We saw a boat coming, and a Mr. Smith introduced himself as the brother-in-law of the Apia pilot, Mr. Hamilton. I gave him all the presents for the family. He brought us bread, fresh meat, and fruit from the market and we had a blow out. He spent an hour with us telling us the news. I forgot to say that while we were at Apia the Consul's flag was at half-mast for the death of Abraham Lincoln. I promised Mr. Smith I would call at his house as soon as I got ashore.

On Monday we moved up to the town, as near to the wharf as we could get, stuck her in the mud and unbent the sails. The crew were paid off, only two stopping with me on board. Mr. Smith sent me word that he could not come off, but to come up to the house. After tea I went ashore and made my way to his house, where the door was opened by one of the loveliest visions I ever saw. It was Annie Smith, just eighteen and the belle of New London. I had not seen a white woman for a year and I hardly knew what to say, but she and her mother and her sister Nellie, another beauty of sixteen, made me very welcome. They were all good singers and I spent a most pleasant evening. I remained by the ship for about a month until she was discharged, alone but for the two sailors. Then Captain Seymour, Mr. Deegan, and Mr. Seymour came to relieve me, and that was the end of my service in the *Reynard*. I had been in her about eight years. Ned Deegan fell in love with Nellie Smith and they were engaged some years afterwards, but as he was in China they finally gave it up. For several years I used to call at New London to see this family, but it is a long time now since I have heard from them.

CHAPTER FOUR

Negotiating for Command—Subsequent history of Reynard—
One voyage as Mate of ship Nevada *1866-1867—San Francisco
—Altata for Logwood—Crew troubles—Sickness—New York—
Interlude of two years ashore—The Bitt business—Marriage—
Wrecked schooner—Back to sea.*

When I said good-bye to the Captain and officers of the
Reynard at New London I left all my clothes in my room as
usual. I knew she was going to load for 'Frisco again and expected
to be sent for to join her in a few weeks. After a voyage lasting
a year I was very pleased to get away from the ship and was
soon in my old haunts in Duxbury and Plymouth Bays, having
a large boat called the *Liberty* in which I spent every day except
Sundays for a month.

There was some talk of my taking command of the *War Hawk,*
but Captain Williams, a man with more influence than I had,
took her. Then Captain Calahan bought into the *Reynard,* as
Captain Seymour had decided to take a piece of a new barque
called the *Pekin,* which was building in Bristol, I believe. Captain
Seymour advised the owners, Bush & Comstock to give the
Reynard to me as I had been in her so long and knew all her
points. They said they would like to, but did not feel rich enough
as they had a chance to sell a master's interest.

One day when I came in from sailing I found a letter from
the owners. They wanted to see me immediately about taking
command of the *War Hawk,* so I went at once to the Boston

office. When I arrived they said I was too late, they had given the ship to Captain Williams. Then I learned my first lesson in business. They had known I could not get their letter in time and had no idea of giving me the ship, but wanted to make it appear as though it was my fault, so they could keep me in the *Reynard* as Mate. They asked me if I would go again in the *Reynard*, but I said "Perhaps Captain Calahan will not want me." They said, "We are sure he will," to which I replied, "I will write to Captain Calahan, and if he wants me I will go." So I wrote to him saying I thought I could suit him, but I was a religious man and some captains did not like them, so I wished him to know it before we sailed. When he received my letter he went to Mr. Deegan, who was acting Second Mate, and asked him if it was true that I was a religious man. Deegan told him that he knew I had a great deal of respect for religion. In a few days I received a letter from him saying he would not require my services, which was all I wanted to show the owners. Then I went on board and got my clothes. Captain Calahan was very pleasant and wanted to know if I found all my things all right, in fact he seemed sorry I was leaving. When Deegan found I was not going in the ship he left her too, and I heard that Calahan had considerable to say about religious mates. He was a big man but very ignorant, in fact had to leave his last ship when she was put under the English flag because he could not pass the Board and get a Certificate. Yet Bush & Comstock placed him in command of the *Reynard* just because his friends had a little money, when I had served them faithfully for eight years. Well, they got all they deserved and more than they wanted of Calahan.

He boasted that he would make the quickest passage the ship ever made, and restored her skysail yards which Seymour had taken off as being quite useless. I guess I was lucky I did not go with him for I should have had trouble, he had three different mates before he left New York. A few days out the crew took charge, refusing to do anything but sail the ship. He made the longest passage she ever did, and going into 'Frisco without a pilot ran the ship ashore, necessitating expensive repairs for which the insurance refused to pay because he had no pilot. Bush told Captain Seymour they might as well have given him $25,000 to stay out of the ship, and Seymour told them, "You should have put in Josselyn, he would have been all right." Mr. Bush told me, " If you had gone in the ship we would have given her to you now," for I was still home when she arrived in 'Frisco. I said nothing, but probably had I gone there would have been no trouble and I might have been Mate of her for years. Calahan had all his crew arrested in 'Frisco but got no redress, I did not hear the details. On the voyage back he came in partially dismasted and leaking badly. Had I remained at home I would have got her then, but by that time I was away Mate of the ship *Nevada*. Captain Calahan then took command of the ship *Dreadnought* and lost her somewhere on the coast of Patagonia. Later he was mate of a ship again and a few years afterwards was a wharfinger in San Francisco.

After spending the most delightful summer of my life up to that time I joined the ship *Nevada,* belonging to William F. Weld & Co. She was originally the *Fear Not*, of 1100 tons, and had been in the government employ during the Civil War. She was the fastest ship on the wind I ever saw, making 264 miles in a day's sailing sharp on the wind, and that is all she could do anyway. Captain Nichols was in command, a very competent man when he was sober, but he was full most of the time. It was a very disagreeable voyage. The carpenter was a very fine man, making his first trip to sea. He only wanted to get to 'Frisco. I had any amount of trouble with the crew and carried my revolver almost constantly for the last month of the passage.

Having made a reasonable passage of 126 days we discharged, then went to anchor in the Bay for a month, during which time I do not remember seeing the Captain once. I understood that he was up in Monterey visiting his brother-in-law, but from what Mr. Frederick Weld said to me when we reached home, I think he was having a spree. Only the cook and one man were with me on board. The carpenter wanted me to join him and go into business in 'Frisco. When I met him again two years later he had done very well and was then up in Portland, Oregon.

Eventually we sailed for Mazatlan, in the Gulf of California, and loaded a cargo of log wood for home in a place called Altata. All I could see of it was the beach off which we were anchored. We had a very able crew of sailors, and if the Captain could have kept sober it would have been a pleasant voyage. Three of the men were over six feet tall, but the Captain used to give them rum till they got to fighting among themselves. When I discovered the cause of the trouble I used to just let them fight it out. The steward told me what was happening, and I have seen men come from the wheel who could scarcely stand from the liquor the Captain had given them.

Approaching Mazatlan we had a violent tempest and were struck by lightning. It did not do much damage, but after the storm was over we had three fireballs, called corposants or compisants, one at the top of each mast. I could hear them buzzing like bumble bees, but no one else could hear it and I began to think I imagined it. While we lay at Altata we had one of these tempests or electrical storms about once a week. When they do not get one of them the local people look for a gale of wind. The only week we did not get one we had a bad storm which made us buoy and slip our anchor and go to sea for several days. After each tempest it would be calm and we would be covered with corposants up aloft, buzzing so that everybody could hear them. I went aloft to examine them after one such tempest, but the Captain came out and called me down, said I was a fool and would be killed. However, I had my hand on some small ones. They felt cold, but that was all, they were quite transparent.

There was a gang of men from shore to help load the wood. One Saturday night they did not get ashore on account of a tempest so I took them in our boat on Sunday morning, landing them on the beach. Two of my four men walked ashore with them, and one never returned, the other, who could not speak Spanish, came back in about a week almost dead from starvation.

During the voyage home we had a great deal of sickness, in fact when we passed Cape Horn there were only five sailors fit for work in both watches. It commenced while we were loading, the men complaining of intestinal pains. The Captain, cook, and steward said they were only loafing, but I considered them sick, and later when these three were laid up themselves they did not call it loafing. I think Providence must have favoured us with fine weather, only once during the whole passage home did we have all hands on deck at once and that was in the South East Trades. On the day we arrived in New York half were sick. Of course we could not do much work about the ship. Captain Nichols wanted to know what I should tell the owners. When we passed Pernambuco I was all ready to paint ship, but the Captain was half full and said first we must sandpaper. We spent four days sandpapering the paintwork. It made it all fine and smooth, but then it began to rain and in eighteen days we were in New York and anchored in the Bay. Captain Nichols went ashore and I have never seen him since. When the boarding-house runners came off the crew drove them off the ship, something I never saw before or since. They remained with me four days and we painted the ship, but the paint had been mixed so long it was slow in drying. Then a tug took us to a wharf in Brooklyn and all the crew went ashore. The Shipping Master paid them off, and since the Captain was not there I had to identify the men. After two days all alone at the wharf I went and found Mr. Frederick Baker, of the owners, who sent me a ship-keeper.

They asked me about Captain Nichols's drinking, so I told them. They said, " Why did you not write us that the Captain was away on a spree in San Francisco?" I told them I did not know where he was, he had told me he was going to Monterey. They said, " Had you written us we would have given you charge of the ship, but you people will never tell of each other." Asked if I would go another voyage in the *Nevada* I replied, " Not with Captain Nichols." " Well, we have plenty of other ships," they said. It would have been better for me to have remained in her, for when she was ready for sea again Captain Nichols could not be found. After waiting for a week Captain " Bully " Lunt, about the worst man that ever commanded a ship, took her.

Again they had a lot of sickness and could not make it out. Doctors called in to examine things condemned a molasses tank that had a lead pipe to it, but still the sickness continued. In my opinion the trouble was caused by our having scraped and painted the tops of our houses. Before the paint was properly dry we had caught rainwater and filled the main tanks. That water was still in the ship. Captain Nichols did not live long afterwards, and " Bully " Lunt to whom I shall refer again, died and was buried at sea a few years later. This was the most disagreeable voyage I ever made, and I made up my mind to try and get a living ashore.

One of my friends from Providence who used to go gunning with me in the Bay had gone into the bitt business at Forestville, Connecticut. I happened to go over there to see him one day without the slightest intention of going into the business. The weather was very cold just then, and I went into the factory with my friend. They were engaged in trying to hoist a turbine wheel out of its socket to repair it. It was a very simple job for a sailor, not more than getting the anchor on the bow, but they had been at work a week and could not manage it, although they had purchases enough to lift a ship's mainmast. I saw at a glance, as any sailor would, that they could not lift it the way their gear was rigged, and involuntarily said, " They will never get it out that way." Now these men were working for love, not money, and in their own time. It was at their suggestion that Andrews had consented to have it repaired, and they had spent a week in the ice-cold water. To have a young fellow dressed up like a dude make such a remark in their hearing at such a time was enough to make anyone swear. Darwin Reed, an old soldier under Banks at New Orleans and lame from a wound in the foot, who was the leader of the gang and head machinist in the factory, looked up and swore that he thought he could get the wheel out as well as I could. Andrews said, " This man is a sailor, he's been round Cape Horn." " Well, I wish some — would take this — thing out." His tone implied that he would like to see me try. I was only twenty-five then and immediately accepted the challenge, saying, " If someone will lend me their overalls and rubber boots I will show you how." They quickly supplied me with the old clothes, and soon as I commenced work they never said a word but watched me. The only trouble was that they had very little room and did not know how to lash their blocks. In about fifteen minutes I was ready for them to pull on the fall, and out she came. To them it seemed like a miracle, and as long as I was around, for nearly two years, whenever there was any weight to be lifted they sent for the sailor.

During this period ashore I had some experience of another kind of knot-tying. A man came around exhibiting another fellow who claimed that no one could tie him up so that he could not escape. The Exhibition took place in the Methodist Church Vestry, about one half of the audience being Spiritualists who maintained that the man had help from the other world in getting clear. I was invited to try my hand at tying him up and was given three or four pieces of rope far too large for such work. When I told the audience he could not be securely tied with such rope, they insisted I try, so I secured his wrists as snugly as possible without hurting the flesh. As I was doing this the man who was exhibiting him tried to frighten me by saying he might turn ugly if I hurt him. After he was tied the audience asked me if I thought him secure. I said, " No, but it is the best I can do with these big ropes. If he was a burglar in my house I should not be satisfied with the way he is fast." However, he was placed in a cabinet, instruments began to play, ghostly hands appeared at the opening at the top of the cabinet, which rocked and twisted for some minutes. When the door was opened he was free from his ropes. I was not satisfied, so the next night, at Bristol, I was on hand to tie him again, and this time I came prepared with a new clothes-line and a mackerel line to tie him to my satisfaction. But there was no performance, for after much argument there was such a disturbance that the police were called in to keep order. Some ten years later, at Surabaya in Java, I met by chance again the man who had been exhibiting. He was now on the other side, going around the world exposing fake spiritualists and mediums. When we talked together he assured me that had I tied the man with my ropes he could never have escaped, the explanation of the trick being that this man's wrists were very large and his hands were very small.

Since then I have met Houdini, in fact am quite well acquainted with him. He is a man nobody has succeeded in tying, nor can he be kept in handcuffs, but he does not claim any ghostly help. He comes out before his audience and says it is all a trick, which he could explain to them, only he does not intend to, as he would lose his easy job and reputed income of $80,000 a year. I hope some day to have the chance to try and tie him. He was once arrested in Germany for dealing with Spirits, but proved to his captors that it was all square by telling several men whom he could trust how it was done.

I finally decided to go into the Bitt business and spent one of the most interesting years of my life there. After learning to do all parts of the work with my own hands, which was not too hard as we had water power, I was able to take the place of anybody who was absent. It was very annoying to have a man go off on a spree and stop the work. However, I had just got fairly going when I found we were infringing on the Jennings Bitt Patent, so I swapped places with one of the Andrews brothers in Plymouth, spending six months in the newspaper business. During this time in Plymouth I met my wife and was married. It was my intention after the honeymoon to go back to sea, and I engaged to go as Mate of one of William F. Weld's ships again.

Poster advertising sailing of "Matchless"

Barque "John D. Brewer"

"Matchless", from a painting

When the time came to part we concluded it would be better to live ashore, so I wrote to Forestville, receiving a reply that they would give me $3.00 a day to take charge of the machine-room. So I backed out from my ship and remained at Forestville about a year. My eldest daughter was born there and I have many pleasant rcollections of the place. While I was there I had a visit from the black-eyed boy who had been on my last voyage in the *Reynard*. I don't know how he found out I was there, but he called to see me. The poor fellow was all broken up. He had been in the Navy, had fallen from aloft, and was now a cripple. There were a few men in the factory who had been to sea and two of them had been whaling. A great many tramps used to call at the place, and the Boss would send all that claimed to be sailors to me. About half of them said they had been wrecked at Hatteras. Actually most of them had never been afloat, but up in the country they thought no one would know.

I had begun to hanker for the sea, in fact all the time I was ashore I had a longing for it. As we had been obliged to stop making that kind of bitt, business was slack, so I again went to William F. Weld & Co. for a job. They did not receive me very warmly, calling my attention to the previous time I had agreed to go but changed my mind, and saying they wanted a man to go if he had agreed to. I did not find out until later that they had at that time sent me a letter to join a ship and that my people at home did not send it on to Forestville, which was very wrong of them. I was about to leave the office, when they said " Hold on till Mr. Baker comes to see you, he will be free in a moment." So I sat down and waited what seemed an hour, then thinking they were only fooling I got up and left. I discovered about two months later that as soon as they missed me they sent a boy after me, for they wanted me all the time. He did not find me, however, and in the meantime, as I went up the wharf, I met my old Captain Dawes, of the *Sicilian*. He was just building a new ship, the *Matchless,* and gave me a chance to go Mate of her, but as she was not ready I went down to Duxbury to wait.

Meanwhile I had nothing to do, and my youngest sister was at home teaching. She suggested that I apply for the Island Creek School, which had been having a lot of trouble, the boys making life unbearable for the teachers, causing several of them to resign. I was prepared to do it for a month, and was sure I could handle the boys and win them to my side, for I have always

F

had a way with them. I never met enough sailors to frighten me, and the first essential in all kinds of command is to have no fear. But it was not to be, the Committee decided to close the school until the next term, and a month later I was called to join the *Matchless* building in East Boston. Four years later I was asked to take the school on, but I was Master of a ship then and not looking for a country school at $40.00 a month.

One night during this month there was a storm and in the morning I found a schooner piled up on the beach. I went out to her in a dory with some others. The Captain had gone to Plymouth to telegraph his owners, and the Mate was having hard work to keep the crowd from stealing. There were two barrels of fish oil which they tried again and again to steal, and they also stole canned goods, of which there were two hundred cases. I would not have believed it possible if I had not seen it with my own eyes, men who owned a house and had money in the bank stealing from a poor wrecked schooner. It seemed as though they had gone crazy, and they said in excuse, " What's the odds, it all comes out of the insurance." For all they knew it might be the private property of the captain, and no insurance. Later in the day, however, an insurance agent came down and looked after her.

In those days there were no Life-Saving Stations on the coast, only a house for the shipwrecked seamen should they get ashore alive. In helping the Mate move some sails in the cabin and make room to sleep, for the schooner was lying over on her side, I came across a half jug of whisky. The Mate gave me all particulars of the wreck. On reaching home that afternoon I took a horse and sleigh and drove over to Plymouth to give an account of the wreck to the paper in which I had an interest. Telling the story I happened to mention the whisky jug. The editor in his account in the paper next day wondered if the whisky jug might have something to do with the wreck. When they read the account the Captain and the Mate were awful mad about it, but never suspected I was the guilty one, as they could not imagine who could have given such an exact account and known about the whisky. Two months later, when the *Matchless* was loading at Lewis Wharf, in Boston, I met them again. They had another schooner then, but were still trying to find out who had given that report to the paper. They could have found out by asking at the newspaper office, but perhaps they felt a little guilty and did not care to have the matter probed.

I helped to strip the wrecked schooner and carried her cargo across the beach all alone. It was lonesome work. I used to spend the night at the Gurnet Lighthouse. The keeper was an old captain and we used to play checkers after supper in the long winter evenings.

CHAPTER FIVE

Mate of the new ship Matchless, *1870—Boston to San Francisco—Queenstown for orders—Antwerp—North Shields—San Francisco—Manila—Iloilo—London—North Shields, the great gale—First Command—Hongkong—Iloilo—Boston, February 1874.*

Some time in March 1870 I joined the *Matchless* on the stocks, as she was building at East Boston. I was employed by the builders and made myself generally useful, in salting and around the ship, until she was launched. I think I earned my month's salary on launching day. She slid off the ways much sooner than expected, overturning forty blocks that had not yet been split out. For some reason or other there was no anchor to check her and the tugs could not catch up with her, unprepared as they were. There was no steering gear on the rudder and the tiller was securely chocked to prevent its turning, in case the pintles might be twisted off by the speed of the vessel's sternway. We were going straight for the Navy Yard wall at Charlestown. Up to now I had been nothing but a boy among the ship carpenters, giving no orders and always asking their advice. They all said, " She will go into the Navy Yard wall." But once the ship was afloat it came natural for me to take command of the situation. " Clear away the tiller," I yelled, and I soon had some of the carpenters with their top-mauls to stand by. As soon as the ship had lost a little of her sternway we knocked away the shores from the tiller, and using watch tackles were able to put

84

it over and steer the ship broadside to the shipyard. Then the tugs came alongside, taking us to the sheers to have our lower masts put in.

I was now the ship-keeper and it was a cold job, for the cabin was not finished and the only fire was in the galley. My dog, a fine pointer I had brought up from a pup in Forestville, was with me and about midnight I tried to get some water for him. The barque *Jennie* was lying near us, and seeing a light on board I thought her ship-keeper would give me some. But he took me for a thief and would not allow me on board, so I had to get some snow off the wharf and melt it down for drinking water. It was at least a month before the *Matchless* was rigged and ready for the owners to take her. Then we hauled to Lewis Wharf and started to load for San Francisco.

She was a costly ship, of 1198 tons Register, old Carpenters' Measurement. Ready for sea, with 300 tons of coal on board, her cost was $111,000. She had thirty-six owners, for almost all who had worked on her had a piece, but Captain Dawes was the biggest single owner. While we were loading at Lewis Wharf a young clerk of my acquaintance in the office of William F. Weld & Co. came on board. He asked where I had gone on leaving their office, said he had been sent to look for me as soon as they had noticed I had gone. It was some satisfaction to know they had wanted me, but I was no longer available.

We shipped a Mr. Bartlett, from Sandwich, as Second Mate. I asked Captain Dawes if he wanted a Third Mate, but he said he did not care for one. I knew a young Duxbury fellow, John Alden, who wanted the chance. The next day a fine-looking lady came on board and enquired for Captain Dawes. I showed her into the cabin, and after remaining a while she went ashore. Shortly afterwards the Captain came to me and said, " Did you see that lady who came on board?" "Yes, Sir." "Well, I am going to take her son as Third Mate." Which just shows what influence a woman has over a sailor. The day before a Third Mate was useless! However, she was an exceptional woman. Her son had been at Annapolis, and each time he was turned out his mother had gone to Washington and got him reinstated. When Grant was elected President a Commodore Porter took command at Annapolis. It was no use for his mother to go to Washington then, he told us, and he and some other young men who had broken their parole left. He knew very little about a ship but he learned quickly. Twelve years later I met him again at Singapore, where he was Mate of the ship *Henrietta*.

We had rather a poor crew going out, but made a fair passage beating the *Herald of the Morning,* a celebrated ship. The day before we arrived at 'Frisco the previous captain of that ship called on Mrs. Dawes and told her not to worry, the *Herald* had not arrived yet. Much to his surprise we arrived the day before the *Herald.* In my opinion she would have beaten us by a good many days if he had still been in her for he, Captain Otis Baker, was a driver. A few hours after leaving Boston we had a very hard tempest and several places in the city were struck by lightning, but it did not worry us although we were only at Boston Light. There was one passenger, a doctor from Boston, who spent all the latter part of his life taking voyages to sea until finally a ship he was in failed to arrive in port.

Off Cape Horn we fell in with the ship *Japan,* both ship and captain belonging to Bath, Maine. She was on fire so we took off her crew of twenty-two, heaving to in fine weather while they came over in their own boats. Her captain, officers, cook, carpenter, and steward went to 'Frisco with us, but we transferred the rest of her crew during the next week or so to two English barques which were bound for Valparaiso and some other South American port. They had saved all their clothes and tools. I was very pleased to get the carpenter, for our own was useless and had refused to do some work I had given him. Next day this new man came to me and offered to do this job, doing it so well that I kept him at work until we reached 'Frisco, and never gave any more work to the one that had refused. Very seldom does an officer get a chance like that, you have to put up with what you have got till the end of the passage or even the voyage. It did me lots of good to see this fellow with nothing to do for two months. I don't know if Captain Dawes paid him his wages or not, for a man that refuses duty is not entitled to them, but in 'Frisco we signed on the carpenter from the *Japan* and he remained in the *Matchless* for many years, saving all his money until he had several thousand dollars. He finally got married in Liverpool and left the ship the voyage before she was lost. I hope he got a thrifty English wife. His only fault was that he would keep drunk in port all the time, but he never made any trouble and kept in his room. Strange to say, during the time I was in command of the *Matchless* he was sober in port. I guess he was afraid I would not put up with it. But to really tell the truth, I think most of the men that drink in port are the best men, otherwise they would rise to better positions.

Mr. Bartlett left in 'Frisco to make way for the Captain's son, who had been away in the barque, *Emma C. Beal* when we sailed from Boston, and now came overland to join us. I met Bartlett again thirty years afterwards in a Boston street, just by chance. He had then left the sea for many years and was a travelling salesman, married with a family. We recognised each other at once, and I think we both regretted we could not spend a longer time together talking.

As we came to the wharf there was a big crowd to see the new ship, and we had her in fine order. Our quarterdeck was as white as snow and I gave Bartlett special orders about making her fast to the wharf, so as not to soil the deck. As our mooring chains were new and black with coal tar I put them on the wharf from forward and told him to just haul the end on board. Who should happen to be the wharfinger on the wharf but Captain Calahan, who had not wanted me in the *Reynard* two years before. As soon as I had made the ship fast forward I went aft to see how Bartlett had done his work. It made me very mad to find he had taken all the spare chain from the wharf and pulled it across the deck, making an awful mess that never would come off till the deck was holystoned again. When he told me the wharfinger had made him do it I deliberately took it all ashore again. Captain Calahan then appeared from forward and yelled at me, for he wanted to show his importance to the crowd on the quay. Remembering old times, and thinking I would let him know how a religious man did his work, I gave him such a talking to, calling him anything but a sailor and telling him the wharf was for our convenience not his, and that Captain Dawes would give him fits when he returned and saw his quarterdeck. The crowd were all laughing at him and I thought he would pitch into me, but he could not get a word in edgeways. I suppose the poor fellow only did his duty from his point of view, and afterwards he was as good as pie to me.

When we left Boston there had not even been a rumour of war between France and Germany. But it was now all over and Louis Napoleon was a prisoner. Such things can only happen in a sailor's life. We loaded wheat in 'Frisco for Queenstown for Orders and made an uneventful passage. Our crew, who like most sailors on long voyages became very economical, would scarcely buy clothes enough for comfort. They would not buy any boots from the Captain, preferring to go bare-footed although it was cold weather. Arrived at Cork *Little Buttercup* came on board. A first they refused to buy anything, as prices for clothes and boots were higher than the Captain charged. But as soon as they'd had a drink from the flask they bought all they were allowed to have, up to $50.00 per man, which shows that "when rum is in wit is out." I always remember one voyage in the *Nuuanu* to Honolulu and back to Philadelphia in '97 or '98, when owing to plague in Honolulu the crew did not leave and hardly went ashore. On the way home there was one young Scotsman who came round the Horn wearing oilskins that were useless to protect him. A new suit was only $2.50, yet to save this money he went wet and cold for two months of the Cape weather. All the crew were paid off on a Tuesday with an average of $150 each. They had made their plans, it was spring-time, some were going up on the Lakes, and to hear them talk they could give points to the Kaiser, King Edward, or Roosevelt. By Saturday one of them came on board and asked the Mate if he might sleep in the forecastle till Monday. His money was gone, and his clothes. I asked about the others, especially the Scots lad who was so very economical. He had already gone to sea, money gone as well as a month's advance (allotment). All the others were gone too, except one Russian who had gone home to Russia taking his money with him. The unusual thing about this story is not that their money went so quickly, but that one man got away from the Land Sharks. Yet you continually hear "how terribly sailors are abused at sea."

From Queenstown we were ordered to Antwerp. As the Franco-German War was just ended there were so many vessels in the port that we could not get up the river. After waiting a week or more we received orders to come up, but we had only gone part of the way when down came the Harbourmaster ordering us back again. Here was a fix. The pilot said we could not go back, there was no room to turn and the river was full of shipping. A couple of brokers from the shore were on board and they told the Captain to go ahead as he'd had orders. However, I took the liberty of advising Captain Dawes not to proceed, since he now had direct orders to stop and as long as he obeyed the latest orders those giving them could be held responsible for any

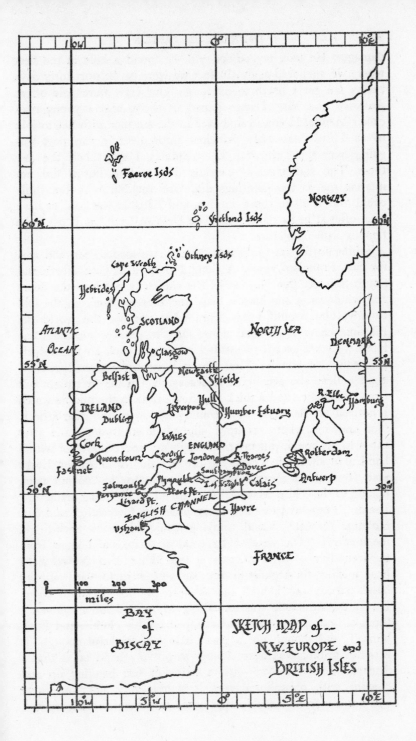

damages. He took my advice and we found a hole in the fleet where we anchored again. In fact we were in the port forty days before we got a berth to discharge. Our crew were paid off at Antwerp and Mrs. Dawes joined us there, also a young man called Mendal Holmes came over in the steamer with her to join us as Third Mate. My principal amusement in this port was going over the Cathedral. Each Sunday I spent half the day there. The statuary was considered very fine, but it did not interest me as the paintings did. One familiar with the Bible could find it all in the paintings, and £30,000 was said to have been offered in England for " The Descent from the Cross," the famous Rubens picture.

Sailing in ballast for North Shields, we loaded iron and coal for San Francisco again. A thing I noticed at both North and South Shields, also Newcastle, the similarity between the doors and windows of the houses there and those at home in the Old Colony. One would know from what part of the world the Pilgrims came from that alone. On the passage around Cape Horn we were loaded too stiff. I never saw such an uncomfortable ship. No wonder Mrs. Dawes went home from 'Frisco, I don't believe she ever went to sea again. On the first night out from Shields we had a thick fog. Some time in the middle watch I noticed all the crew were coming aft on to the quarterdeck. Not knowing what was up I slipped down through the after cabin to my room, put my revolver in my pocket together with a handful of shells, then came out through the forward door. Every man from the forecastle was there, even to the lookout man, talking to the Third Mate. " What are all hands doing aft here?" I said. " They say there is a ghost under the forecastle," said Mr. Holmes. " Ghost?" I said, thinking it might be some trick to get me forward. " Oh, yes," said several of them, and I knew from the trembling of their voices that they thought so. Now I have been looking for a ghost all my life, so I went forward with all hands strung out behind me as near as they dared to come. Under the forecastle was something white, and for a moment I thought one of the crew had stripped off his clothes and hung himself, and though not a ghost it looked frightful enough. It was not until I was near enough to put my hand on it that I discovered what it was—just a string of fish hanging up and glowing with phosphorescence. It sounds silly now, but there was not a man in the ship that dared to go and investigate it. I imagine most ghost stories have just as simple an explanation.

When we arrived at Frisco this time a Scottish boy called Sam Clark, who had joined us there on the previous visit, was made Third Mate in place of Holmes. The latter had cowboy ideas, seldom went ashore without being "heeled," as he called it, i.e. with his revolver in his hip pocket. He was a smart fellow, but he had money and that spoiled him for work. I never met him again but I believe he got in tow with an actress or something and died some years ago. One day I was down in the hold and heard a familiar voice calling me from the deck. It was my old carpenter from the *Nevada* three years ago. He was now living in Portland, Ore, and doing well, had made one trip to China as a passenger to see that country, and had gone into politics.

We loaded a full cargo of flour for Hongkong. Before we sailed from 'Frisco, Captain Dawes chartered to go to Manila and/or Iloilo to load sugar for the U.K. for Orders, and made a great mistake in doing so. Had the freight rate been high it would not have been so bad, but to charter at a low rate was the height of foolishness. It is something like this. In chartering a ship ahead the broker bets that freights will go higher, and as a rule he is in a better position to know than is the master of the ship, who is at sea most of the time. I will say here that during the four years I was in her the *Matchless* lost over $50,000 by being chartered ahead. When we arrived at Hongkong the broker came on board almost before the anchor was down to get the ship to go directly back to 'Frisco at a big rate. But we were already chartered and had to make a long voyage, so a Captain Bowden took it.

Some time later, after I had left the ship and Captain Dawes took her again, he loaded for 'Frisco and before he sailed he chartered to load wheat from 'Frisco to the U.K. for Orders at a high rate of freight. I said to him, "Are you going to charter ahead again?" "Yes, I will charter her for as long as she floats at that rate." Well, when she arrived at 'Frisco that time the tables were turned. Freights were away down, and as Captain Dawes went up the wharf who should he meet but Captain Bowden, who was not chartered. Dawes, with head up, said "It's a long lane that has no turning, Bowden." But, alas, in a few days the brokers failed, and not only did Captain Dawes lose his fine charter but he had to pay a thousand dollars to get clear from them or else wait for a long time, and then take the lower rates. Of course that was an exceptional case.

From Hongkong we went to Manila to load 1,000 bales of hemp, then filled up with green sugar in Iloilo for London. The sugar drained about fifteen per cent, and we could not pump it out as our new ship did not make enough water to work the pumps. Back in London the first news we heard was of Boston's big fire. It seemed a long time since I had been in London before and there were many changes visible, apart from my old shipmates being scattered all over the world.

After discharging in London we started down the river looking for the tug *Liverpool* which was to tow us to North Shields. We anchored somewhere in the river. During the night a steamer was sighted passing rather a long way off which our pilot thought might be the *Liverpool*. It was a quiet night with a full moon and I thought I could make them hear, but the pilot laughed at the idea. Anyway, I let out a yell *Liverpool* and they heard me and came to us, but I could not speak out loud for a week. At daylight we started in tow for North Shields and the next night were caught in one of the worst gales ever known in the North Sea. Our tug had to leave us and we lay off the Humber under a main lower topsail, and that blew away. Next morning it moderated, so we bent another topsail and, the wind being about East South East, started north. It was mid-winter and not daylight till eight o'clock. We had a Coast pilot and he was steering to the north, till I went and told him and the Captain that by my reckoning we were already past Shields, advising them to keep away until we made the land as we could always haul away to the north again. I probably should not have had the nerve to advise the Captain and Pilot, only I was to take command of the ship at Shields. Our crew, who were runners, were aloft bending a new main topsail, and before daylight reported a light right ahead. The pilot thought it was Shields Light, but just then one of the crew aloft (who happened to be a Shields pilot) sang out, " That's not Shields Light, it's Farne Island." We were thirty miles beyond Shields and had to turn round and come back in the face of this gale if we could.

It was still blowing a hard gale with a tremendous sea, and we could see vessels ashore all along the coast as we came down just along the beach. All that saved us was a new ship and a brand new suit of sails just bent on in London, also a good set of ballast of moulding sand that would not shift. I never saw such carrying on of sail, we could not keep our feet she jumped so, but down the coast she came, carrying whole topsails, courses, jibs, and spanker (the crossjack was furled) while even steamers could not keep off and went ashore. About 2 p.m. we were down to the entrance to Shields, where two piers are built out to sea at the mouth of the River Tyne and a ship must enter between them. There was one wreck on the right-hand side and several on the left. Some of them had just gone on shore and all the lifeboats were out trying to pick off their crews. Several tugs were pulling on one they evidently hoped to get off, they were side-wheel boats and in some cases the seas had washed their paddle boxes completely off. Some of the lifeboats had capsized. The shores were lined with people, friends of the lifeboatmen and thousands who had come down from Newcastle to see the wrecks. They were crying so that we could hear their voices above the gale.

As we kept away to enter the river the pilot set our main topgallant sail, for the other vessels that had gone ashore had done so because they could not steer in the high following sea, and I did not know that we should. The sailor who was a Shields pilot went aft and took the wheel. We almost turned around once or twice, and the jibs would draw on both sides as we yawed about. I wanted to take the wheel myself, but I had plenty to do and could only take a glance now and then at the wrecks. I thought we should be dashed into the shipping inside for we were going about ten knots and I had only fifteen fathoms of chain overhauled clear for running. All the rest was in a tangled heap, we had jumped about so, and it took me days in port to clear it. Both chains had been thrown over the fore hatch back and forth several times. But as we rushed into the crowd of shipping a number of tugs grabbed us, catching hold anywhere they could. We let go topsail halyards and let everything fly. In a few minutes we were safely at anchor, all our troubles over. I believe there is a very fine marine painting of the ship *Matchless* coming in from sea that dark day, her new cotton sails as white as snow, as some watching artist saw us.

Captain Dawes went ashore, but immediately returned to say he had a telegram from Liverpool asking if we were safe. It seems that the night we were off the Humber a brig called the *Matchless* had tried to run in there and was lost with all hands. This report had been telegraphed to Liverpool, and had gone on to Boston U.S. "*Matchless* and all hands lost." As soon as he knew of this Captain Dawes telegraphed home that we were all well, but the other report had been published in the papers with our obituaries, and caused distress to some of our families before his good news could arrive.

After the ship had loaded coal for Hongkong, Captain Dawes went home, leaving me in command, with his son John C. Dawes as Mate. However long a man sails as Mate he will find a great responsibility when he assumes command. Everything has to be referred to him and he is responsible for all mistakes, no matter who makes them. The first thing I discovered wrong was the ship's chronometer. Due to foggy weather on the English coast we had no chance of the observation which all commanders take as soon as possible. Our pilot left at the Isle of Wight on the fourth day out and with fair winds we were soon in the latitude of Madeira which much to my surprise we sighted, our longitude being ninety miles out. But when I worked the sights using the old correction the position was right. The chronometer man had given me the wrong correction. This is always given in figures and also in writing. When I looked at the correction before sailing I had noticed they were different, and when I asked him about it he said, "Oh, how could I have made that mistake?" and changed one of them—the wrong one!

The next mistake occurred through Captain Dawes. I had no new chart to go up the China Sea and he said I would not need one as I would be taking the eastern passages. Well, a Mate never likes to argue with his Captain, so I accepted his word for it; but when I got well out to sea and had more time to go into things I found that the season would make it necessary to go up the China Sea and I had no suitable chart. Luckily I found an old one somewhere on board, which I made do, I had a fair passage to Hongkong, similar to other trips up the China Sea, of which I had made several.

The owners made the next mistake, which I got over by accident. My orders from them were to proceed to Manila from Hongkong. Shortly before I was ready to sail I wrote to Manila telling them when I would be likely to leave. A reply came by the next mail saying the voyage had been changed and I was to proceed direct to Iloilo. The owners had never notified me, though it saved them a good deal of money when I found out, for I got a ballast of salt at $1.00 per ton, saving the buying of ballast, to say nothing of two weeks' time and the expenses of an extra port.

Our Consul at Hongkong at that time was nothing but a sailor thief. He kept a sailors' boarding house and his man came on board persuading all my men to leave. There was another American ship in and he just swapped the two crews, they were only ashore two days. I tried to keep my men, but they were determined to go, and rather than have any trouble I let them go. The next day when I went to pay them off they wanted to come back, but the Consul would not allow it. I should like to see an American Consul play me such a trick now. My new crew got a big advance and the Consul got nearly all of it. We certainly did have a race of scamps in our Consular service in those days.

At Iloilo we loaded a full cargo of sugar for Boston. I always got along first rate with the Spanish and they were certainly very cheap ports. I would like to visit the Philippine Islands now to see what changes have been introduced since the Americans took possession of them. It must have made a great change for the Manila men. For instance, our pilotage was $14.00 in and out, but the pilot told me he only got $2.00 in and the same out, the government taking the other $24.00.

When loading was finished the South West monsoon was still blowing and the owners of the cargo wanted me to wait until the monsoon changed. I waited a few days, but very impatiently, for I had not been home for nearly four years. A fine English ship, the *Golden Spur* was also loading and as soon as he finished he did not wait for the monsoon, but hove up his anchors and went out the other way. This was too much for me. I went and got my papers and, though the shippers told me the charts of the eastern passage were not good, I started at noon the next day just twenty-four hours after the *Golden Spur*. I had not gone far before I wished myself back again. We had only two feet of water to spare under us, and at four o'clock we found the *Golden Spur* ashore in the mud, heaving sugar overboard out of all hatches. I can tell you I really wished myself back then, but we kept on and the next day passed out into the Pacific Ocean through the San Bernardino Straits. I had worried myself into a fever and was quite sick for days. We had a fair passage home round the Cape of Good Hope, reported at St. Helena and then had a fine run as far as Cape Hatteras. We then hoped and expected to be in Boston in a short time, but it took us another twenty-one days. It was the month of February and we certainly had a hard time back of Nantucket with North West gales, but I would not have so hard a time now. I have learned a lot since then and see where I made mistakes.

I had been away from home for forty-four months and was now within one hundred miles of my wife and child. And there we remained, covered with ice and snow and with many of our men sick with scurvy, the only time I ever saw it. One morning the wind had gone down to a calm. A schooner was near, so I took our boat and went on board. "Why," said her captain, "You will be in tomorrow. I only left Long Wharf at five o'clock last evening and saw Cape Cod Light this morning." It was encouraging, but we had been where we were two weeks already. He was very kind, supplying me with fresh meat and vegetables for which he would take nothing. He had twenty passengers, bound to the Argentine Republic. I returned on board, and when the wind sprang up from the East went through the South Channel and would have reached Boston, but kept away for a pilot boat, and then we only reached Marshfield, for the wind had backed again to the North West. But it was good to have a pilot on board, in fact it always is, but this time especially so. Under reefed topsails and foresail we stretched away for the north shore, wore ship in the morning, and then just fetched back to Marshfield. The fact is that we ought to have carried sail all night and been up to Boston Light in the morning, but like a great many mistakes I made that voyage, I trusted to the pilot. Fearing that we might be blown out to sea again I got the pilot to run us into Provincetown Harbour. I don't believe the Pilgrims were more glad to get there than we were. We only had the three lower topsails on her and when we let go the anchor at four o'clock in the afternoon it was blowing a howling gale, but before we had those sails furled it was a flat calm. Shortly afterwards a tug came alongside, but he wanted so much that I went ashore and telegraphed the owners. Having received an answer the next morning we took the tug and started, the bay as smooth as glass but the ship well covered with ice and snow. Half-way across the bay another tug met us with Captain Dawes on board and before night we had the third tug. By eleven o'clock that night we stuck in the mud off the East Boston wharf, and as Captain Dawes was on board, I jumped into one of the tugs and was soon landed in the city, making my way

Captain Walter Lyman Josselyn

Barque "Nuuanu" leaving Honolulu about 1906

Barque "Nuuanu" at Honolulu

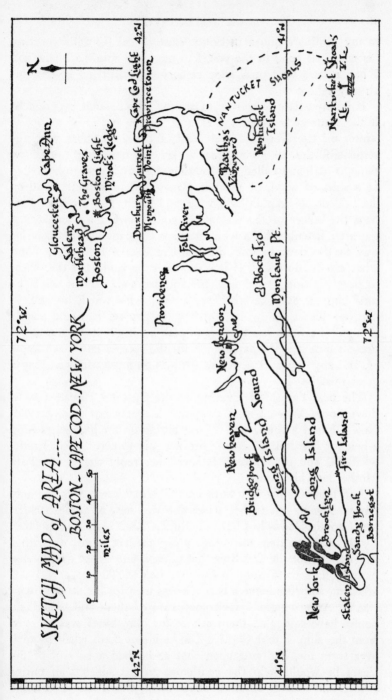

SKETCH MAP of AREA....
BOSTON-CAPE COD..NEW YORK

miles
0   10   20   30   40   50

N

Gloucester   Cape Ann
Salem
Marblehead   The Graves
Boston   Boston Light
          Minot's Ledge

Duxbury   Cape Cod Light
Plymouth   Provincetown
           Point

Fall River

Providence

New London

New Haven

Bridgeport
Long Island Sound

New York   Long Island   Fire Island
Staten Island   Brooklyn
Sandy Hook
Barnegat

Block Isd
Montauk Pt.

Martha's   NANTUCKET SHOALS
Vineyard
        Nantucket
        Island

Nantucket Shoals
Lt. V'l.

72°W   42°N
72°W   41°N

G

to my brother's house in South Boston. All the family except his wife had gone to the wharf to meet the ship, so Nellie and I had a long wait until they came back, surprised to find me already ashore.

It is impossible to convey to anyone who has not experienced it the contrast between the care of a ship and crew at sea in winter off the New England coast, and being ashore with the responsibilities all gone, able to lay down at night with no thought of being called, no listening for sounds on deck telling of a shift of wind, or what is worse still, no sounds at all on deck. Then the captain will wake and listen. Not a sound. Perhaps the officer of the watch has gone forward for something, but after listening for a while perhaps the captain will make his way to the deck to find the mate in charge fast asleep. And what can he do then? If it was ashore he could tell the officer to pack his things, and look for another man. But at sea if he puts him off duty he will have to stand his watch himself. If he gives him a hiding he will have to pay for it. Some people think all a captain has to do is to pick his finger-nails, but at the present time it is the hardest job for the poorest pay that I know of, and any boy in America who starts on a sea life is making a great mistake.

The next day, after entering at the Customs House, I went down home. When I went away my daughter was one year old. Now I found a young lady of five sitting on the lounge, making a belt for her doll. When my brother said to her, " Well, Bessie, what did you say to your father?" her reply was, " Oh, I let Mother love him first."

And that was my last work on the *Matchless*. I was the only one who went out in her when she was new to come back in her. Captain Dawes lost her near Sunda Strait several years later. By the way, another annoyance a captain has to put up with I experienced for the first time that voyage. Our agent who loaded us in Iloilo sent to Captain Dawes a box of 500 cigars, and also asked me to bring home a box of chess men for his brother, who was an Army officer. I took good care of them and would, no doubt, have smuggled them ashore for him, but I was relieved from the ship. I told Captain Dawes about them when he took over from me, and presumed that as he had a present of the cigars he would help the gentleman to get his box of curios ashore. Not hearing anything about them, after I had been home about a week I wrote to ask him if he had received them safely. I got a very saucy answer, " Yes, he had them, but no thanks to me, he'd had to pay duty on them at the Customs House, etc." He seemed to think it was my duty to smuggle them ashore for him. Well, I am wiser now.

CHAPTER SIX

Building of the ship Charger *and run to New York—Master of ship* Coringa, *1874—Cargoes of ice from Boston to Calcutta and Bombay—Renewal of Class—Tuticorin—Calcutta—Boston —Honolulu in 1877—Tidal wave—Pacific Hurricane—Hongkong —Nagasaki—Shanghai—Amoy—Java 1878—Boston with sugar —New York—Case oil to Bombay—Akyab to Kangasanthra with rice—Singapore—New York—Case oil to Batavia—Singapore— Surabaya—Uncharted reef in Carimata Strait—Singapore— Bangkok—Rice for Samarang—Typhoon—*Coringa *wrecked near Cape Patani—Rescue—Steamer* Kongsee *to Bangkok and Singapore—Steamer* Benalder *to the U.S.A.*

About four weeks after I arrived home in the *Matchless,* Mr. Henry Hastings asked me to go Mate of his new ship *Charger,* which was building in East Boston. When I told him I did not want to go away again as Mate he asked me to join her in that capacity until she was finished, and for the short run around to New York. This I agreed to do, and I spent the next few months on her seeing that she was properly fitted out. She was a fine ship of 1400 tons and it seemed like the *Matchless* over again, for she was from the same builders.

When she was ready for sea one of Hastings' old masters, Captain Henry, took her to New York with a crew of runners, men who did not sign any articles but are paid so much for the trip or run, be it long or short. We usually expect to go round in three days, but I have known vessels take three weeks and come in dismasted! Mr. Hastings and four more of the owners went round with us on what proved a regular yachting trip. A New York pilot joined us in Boston, we had a first-class cook and steward, and lived high, with plenty of liquor for all those who drank—except Captain Henry. He was all of a shake for the want of it, but told me he would not ask for it if he died. We had a calm for one day, just where I had been a few weeks before in the *Matchless,* covered with snow and ice. Now all was fine and beautiful.

In coming down Boston harbour I had a little controversy with Ned Hastings, the old man's son and himself a part-owner. The wind was fresh from the South West and we had all the jibs set. Someone of the crowd who were returning to Boston in the tug told Ned that we should carry away the jib-boom. I was all over the ship stowing away stores, clearing decks, and seeing to everything else, for I was the only mate, when I happened to look forward to see them hauling down the Flying Jib. I went along and made them hoist it up again, the runners saying that young Mr. Hastings had ordered it down. When Ned had his attention called to the fact that we were hoisting it again he wanted to know what we were doing and told us to haul it down once more, but I would not allow anyone to touch the halyards. " You will carry away the jib-boom," he said. " Mr. Hastings, there is a Captain on board, and a Pilot in charge, and I am Mate, and that jib don't come down without their orders while I am here." He went aft without a word. There was not the least danger to the jib-boom, and even if there had been the jib would have had to stay there for orders.

After the calm in the South Channel a fine breeze sprang up from the East and we increased our speed until we were doing fourteen knots. I marked the line myself and Mr. Hastings had it hove every half hour, being much pleased to find she would sail so fast. Schooners were double-reefed, but we flew along with three Royals set. The only cargo we had was two hundred tons of iron, and a ship without copper, sails a knot faster when she is new and clean. At eight o'clock the Captain asked me to give him a sight, and again at ten. I told him where I put her, but he said, " Oh, she can't be there, you are forty miles out." I knew my reckoning was correct, but it is not etiquette on board a ship to contradict the Captain. The four passengers were round the chart with him. At noon I went to my room and worked her up again. Finally Mr. Hastings said, " Where do you make her?" I told him, then the Captain said " How much have you been giving her since morning?" " Fourteen knots since eight o'clock." " Oh, she hasn't gone twelve." I did not reply, and we all went up on deck. Just then one of the owner's boys said he could see a lighthouse. For a time nobody else could see it, but finally I saw it and said, " I see it. It's Fire Island Lighthouse, on our beam. My observations were correct." Then the Pilot spoke up, " That ain't Fire Island, 'tis Shinnecock." When I insisted it was Fire Island he said, " Don't you think I know the land? Besides, if it was Fire Island we should be in sight of the Highlands now." " I don't know if you know the land or not, but I know how to work a sight and our chronometers are only three days from Boston." Just then, " Land Ho," sang out the men forward, and there was Highlands in plain sight ahead. " Oh," said the Pilot, " the Mate is right, that is Fire Island Lighthouse abeam." Then old man Hastings, with his gruff voice, said " There don't seem to be a — one of you knows where she is except the Mate." She had been going fourteen knots and he was pleased to know I had not been fooling him.

We soon had a tug and towed to an anchorage in New York Bay. All the owner's party went ashore in the tug and later in the day Captain Henry went ashore. I never saw him again. He was quite an old man, probably had he had a glass to steady his hand he would not have made a mistake in his longitude. Then he was bothered by all the crowd around him, while I had gone into my room and closed the door until I had worked out our position. The next day we went into dry-dock to be coppered, and as soon as the water was out of the dock I went down into it. The first man I saw was the boss carpenter, Sampson, a towney of mine, and I believe one of the owners of the *Matchless*. " How does she sail?" " Fine." " She runs away from folks, I hear." " No, I guess not, but she is good for fourteen knots." " Well, old man Hastings said she ran away from everybody but the Mate." I remained on board in New York until the ship was loaded and her captain, a Cape Cod man, arrived home from Liverpool to take over. Then I returned to Boston.

Very shortly after this I took command of the old ship *Coringa*, belonging to Charles Brewer & Co., of Boston. That was in the spring of 1874 and I am still with the firm thirty-six

years later. Their trade was mostly with the Hawaiian Islands,
to which they have run a line of packets from Boston for a great
many years. During that time there have been tremendous
changes in our cargoes and the development of the Islands can
be seen in them. And what changes have taken place there since
my first visit in 1859. Now there are more Europeans and people
of all races than there are natives.

The *Coringa* was twenty-four years old, 777 tons, and small
for a ship. My first job was to rig her as a barque, by sending
down all the yards on the mizzen. We then loaded her with a
cargo of natural ice in Charlestown for Calcutta. This is another
trade which has long passed away, since the commercial manu-
facture of ice. My wife and daughter went with me this time
and we had a fair passage out. I found the *Coringa* the easiest
vessel I was ever at sea in. She had been built as a copper ore
trader, but only made one trip with it, and for years now had
been in the Calcutta trade. As copper ore is one of the hardest
cargoes to carry she had to be the best sea-boat possible. You
might ask, " Are not all vessels built to be the best kind of sea-
boat?" The answer is " No, they are built to make money, and
the one that carries the most cargo makes the most money, but a
cargo of copper ore will only half-fill the ship so she can be
built with less regard for such factors as economy of space and
more concentration on her sea-keeping qualities. Probably the
dimensions of Noah's Ark are those of the finest sea-boat possible,
but of course any ship is a compromise." The first gale of wind
we encountered in *Coringa* we hove her to, and she lay so quietly
I could hardly believe there was any gale at all—and I had just
come from the most costly built ship in the U.S.

I had a Mate by the name of Top, a German I think, a very
quiet man. One night in the North East Trades it was very dark,
and sometime in the night my wife spoke to me, " I believe there
is a mouse in my bunk." As I struck a match to light the lamp
she said, " It's a rat, I've got him." " Hang on to him," I said,
and then I took hold of him in the sheet and carried the whole
lot on deck. Mr. Top was walking back and forth on the quarterdeck, and when I met him with this sheet in my hand he thought
it must certainly be a ghost. I had hard work to get him to take
hold of the other end of the sheet while I threw the rat overboard.

When we arrived at the pilot brig outside Calcutta I remembered the last time, twenty years before, with Captain Seymour in the *Reynard*. I steered straight for the brig till I was so close her captain shouted, " Haul your main yards aback," then " Haul your fore yards aback." I was not going to touch him, but I was determined he should be satisfied I was near enough. When the pilot boarded he said, " What made you come so close, we thought you would run into us." I told him of the salutation I heard on my last visit and that I did not want to get another like it.

We had a very pleasant time in Calcutta. There were several American vessels in the port so we had quite a company of our own, and I think all my crew remained by the vessel. After discharging our ice we loaded a full cargo of jute butts for Boston and had a very fine run home, beating the whole crowd of six vessels. They were earlier than I was and were a long time north of Hatteras, as I had been the year before in the *Matchless*, while we came along in fine weather. One day in the Gulf Stream it was dead calm, so I took a boat and went on board a schooner. When I left the side of the *Coringa* it was as quiet as alongside a wharf, but the schooner rolled so much that we had to put the boat astern of her and I thought the sea was getting up. Back alongside our barque she was as quiet as ever, which goes to show the difference in the models and the loading of the two vessels.

After coppering the barque in Boston we loaded ice again, this time for Bombay. Here old Captain Brewer, the head of the house, made a mistake. Our Class had run out and before we could renew it the surveyors wanted to open the ship (cut holes in the side to see if the wood was rotten). A Class is a Certificate from the Insurance Company stating that the ship is a good one to carry cargoes and that they are willing to take a risk on her. We could have got a Class, but as we were loading ice we could not stop for it, since the ice must be covered with sawdust as soon as possible to keep it from melting. Without one we should have difficulty getting a cargo home. Captain Brewer said I must do the best I could.

This voyage my family remained at home, but a lot of friends came down the harbour with me. I bid them goodbye at Boston Light, and with a fair wind was half-way to Cape Cod before I went below. When I walked into my cabin all was quiet—no wife, no little girl. It seemed like entering my tomb and I did not get over it on the outward passage. We had a fair passage to Bombay, and being loaded with ice were anchored close to the Apollo Bund, the landing place built of stone. Ice ships have a special privilege, they not only have the best berth but they work Sundays and holidays. Once the holds are opened the ice must get into the ice vaults ashore as soon as possible, it melts so fast in these hot climates. One Sunday our ice carts were stopped from passing the Scottish Church as their noise interrupted the service. However the police quickly started them again, for the ice people of Boston were under heavy bonds to keep a supply of ice in Bombay, and if the carts were stopped for long the bond would be forfeited.

Soon after we commenced discharging the Prince of Wales arrived, making a tour of India. All the ships in the harbour were moved to make room for his fleet of warships, but the *Coringa* remained, the only merchant vessel near the fleet, consequently we had a fine view of all that went on. I shall never forget one night when the Prince returned from visiting some tomb inland. He arrived in his yacht or tender after dark and all the vessels of the Fleet were illuminated. Not only was every ship illuminated by countless rows of Chinese lanterns, but on every yardarm was a man with a bundle of rockets. The yards of all the men-of-war were manned and every man had some kind of lantern with different colours, which all changed at once. The effect was wonderful, but greatest of all were the bouquets of rockets. Never before or since have I seen such fireworks.

One day I visited the Towers of Silence, where the Parsees exposed their dead to be eaten by the vultures that hover in clouds in the vicinity.

From Bombay I took a cargo of rice to Tuticorin, a quiet little place with only about a dozen white residents in the Gulf of Manaar, just across from Colombo. At first I went to the hotel, but my agent invited me to stay in his house, where I had a very pleasant month. The *Coringa* was anchored some distance from the shore and I could only go off to her in the morning when the wind was from the land. I engaged stevedores to discharge and load, thinking to make life easier for my sailors. They complained later that the captain would not let them work cargo, and had I known they were going to do this they could have worked till their fingers bled on the bags of salt. Since that time I have given my crews all the cargo they wanted to handle.

A young lady at the house, Miss Castiers, had been to school with American missionaries on the Madras Coast and could sing all the American War songs. As I was acquainted with them we used to sing together a good deal. An orphan, she married a Mr. Underwood, the head of an English house, while I was there. The Bishop came down from the Coast for the occasion and stayed a week. It seemed strange to me to see a minister of the Gospel and his wife take their regular liquor, not only at the table but twice a day, and they would not believe me at home when I told them such a man was a Bishop of the Church of England. We had a fine time at the wedding and at the dinner that night at our house, where not only all the Europeans were present, but also the Natives of quality. The only one that did not drink was a Native. He sat beside me at the table and wanted me to drink his share, it was against his religion. It seemed odd that the ones who had come out to convert them should be so far behind them on the alcohol question—and that is not the only lesson they can teach us.

We loaded salt at Tuticorin for Calcutta. Before leaving Bombay I had written to the Calcutta agents that I was coming there with a cargo of salt and that the barque had no Class, explaining to them the reason why. So on my arrival I was fortunate enough to get a freight home, the only one in the port and a very good one for the times. There was one other vessel in the port, a new ship, and her captain thought he would get it, for the *Coringa* was old. In Calcutta at that time every captain had two horses, one for day and the other for evening, and a " Syce " to take care of them. The first one they gave me wanted to go so fast that I could hardly hold him, but had to pass the reins behind my back and lay my whole weight on them. Of course I asked for a different horse and the next day had a nice quiet one. As I passed by the other ship I saw my horse of the day before alongside her. Her captain had taken him, said he wanted a horse that could go and that he was used to them. Well, he let him go, and before noon had killed him, and had to pay for him. I felt glad I was not used to horses.

We had a fine passage home, and this time had the barque surveyed and got a Class, old Captain Brewer complimenting me on my success without one. The other ship, although new, had waited several months and then come home at a less freight than I had.

The *Coringa* was now loaded for Honolulu and we sailed on the 28th November 1876. Mr. Dawes, who had been Second Mate the previous voyage became the Chief Mate. He was a nephew of Captain Dawes of the *Matchless*. We had several Duxbury boys among the crew, Charley Gifford the carpenter and George Freeman, Loud from Plymouth, one from Watertown and one from Charlestown. The passage out was long, 157 days, the longest I was ever at sea. We were a long time off Cape Horn with head winds, but the *Coringa* was such a comfortable vessel we were not worn out. When we reached Honolulu in May 1877 there were still a good many whalers there. Brewers' vessels had been bringing home oil, but there was none for me. We were ordered to Hongkong, and kept on board for ballast 180 tons of coal we had, and also took 150 tons of sand.

During our stay at Honolulu there was an earthquake in South America, giving us a high and a low water every hour in the twenty-four. We first noticed it on the morning we commenced discharging—our port hole would come up above the wharf, then go down again every half hour, so that it bothered us a good deal in discharging from it. That forenoon I went riding up the Nuuanu Valley with my wife and on the way back we had a view far out to sea. We saw a tremendous spouting far out, like the explosion of a mine, and later fishermen reported the top of the water covered with pumicestone and dead fish. On the same day at Hilo the ships were aground, and one whaler whose oil was ashore had to send his men away up country to collect the oil from where the tidal wave had carried it. I believe he only lost one cask.

The Missionary brig was in Honolulu with us. Her Captain Colcord was an Adventist and was convinced the world was coming to an end before the present Pope died. Alas, the Pope has died and many other Popes since, but still the world goes on. I also knew at this time a Captain Fuller, who was in a barque trading between Honolulu and San Francisco. His eldest daughter used to play with mine, but she is now a widow and her eldest son is in Brewer and Co.'s office. Old Father Damon was the sailor missionary and we all looked for him. His little sons are now prominent men of the place and his grandchildren grown up. *Tempus fugit!*

The passage from Honolulu to Hongkong made this my first voyage round the world. We took thirty Chinese passengers, among them a little girl called Ah Kow, who was about the same age as my little girl. We had her in the cabin a good deal, and all the time during the hurricane, or typhoon, we experienced. As this is the only bona fide Hurricane I ever passed through I will attempt to describe it.

Where there is plenty of sea room a hurricane can usually be dodged, for they move according to the Laws of Storms, and in many cases we can make a fair wind of them. Sometimes they recurve unexpectedly and then the mariner, if his ship is hove to, can do nothing but wait and let the storm pass over him. It is impossible to describe properly how hard it blows, it is like the blast from the muzzle of a gun. We were sailing along before the North East Trades from Honolulu towards China in about latitude 18° N., with day after day about the same. When about a thousand miles from Guam I noticed a swell from the South East, remarking to my wife, "How can we have a swell from the S.E. in these Trades?" The next day it was higher, a regular long rolling sea such as you would expect off Cape Horn, and I realised that in the distance there must be a hurricane. We were in ballast and travelling about 250 miles a day, but it was apparently gaining on us. The day before we passed Guam there was an immense sea, but no other indications of a hurricane approaching and the barometer steady at 30.00 inches. As we passed through the line of islands at Guam the sea went down, but the next day we had it again, and there was an arc of clouds in the South East, and the barometer began to fall. Had we been loaded I should have kept away to the South West and let the gale go by us, but I thought we could stand it, being in ballast (I have not fooled with hurricanes since), so kept directly on our course of due West. It followed us a week before it reached us, during which time we had travelled more than 1500 miles. On the last day we made 250 miles under two lower topsails and a reefed foresail. It was noon and we were at dinner when the Second Mate reported, "It's a dead calm, Sir." We had run directly into the centre. Such a sea and no wind, but being in ballast we did not mind the sea much. We furled the foresail and fore topsail and waited all the afternoon, tumbling about in the sea. About four o'clock we saw it coming from the North East and there was just time to get the hands on deck and furl the main topsail before it struck us. Such a roar is indescribable, one could only make signs and if the men had been aloft I don't think they could ever have got down again. One half of our mainsail blew away, though furled as snug as we could make it. It was the 20th June and a full moon. From 8.0 p.m. till 11.00 p.m. the barque lay on her side, with rain and salt water blowing over us so that one could not see the mizzen mast only thirty feet away. There was a continuous flash of lightning, but no thunder could be heard. At 11.00 p.m. my wife came to the cabin door and made signs that the barometer was rising, and by daylight the storm was over. In the course of it the wind backed round the compass from North to West, South, East, and finally North East, the regular Trades again. In the morning we had quite a list to port, but the only damage was loss of half a mainsail. The passengers were unhurt but their baggage, which had been laid out around their sleeping place, was all in a heap on the lee side.

Ten days later we arrived in Hongkong after a passage of forty-five days, to find a lot of American vessels laid up, among them the *Matchless*, Captain John C. Dawes, Sam Clark as Mate, and the same old carpenter I had picked up off Cape Horn. All the crowd came outside to meet me in a launch and one of them had served a long apprenticeship in the *Coringa* when she was new. He and one or two others remained on board with us until we got in, the rest going on to meet another arrival. They all asked me what I was going to do with that old tub out there, since there was nothing for them with their newer vessels. " Oh, the best I can," was my reply.

As it was the hurricane season and I had had all the hurricane I wanted, I sent down royal and topgallant yards after unbending sails, but the very next day I was offered a fine business to load for Saigon and back with a cargo for $5,000. We had the charter all made out, but the vessel being twenty-five years old they could not insure her and I lost that. The next day I was offered $2.00 per ton on coal from Nagasaki to Shanghai. I accepted it, sent up my yards again, and began bending the sails. Meeting one of the old traders ashore he said, " Why are you bending sails?" I told him. " Do you suppose I could get it?" And he did get it, only he had to pay three cents a ton for trimming. Finally the whole fleet followed me to Nagasaki, though I got the highest freight of the crowd. The *Matchless* loaded for home in Hongkong and I never saw her again.

I was first to arrive in Nagasaki, for nothing could beat the *Coringa* on the wind. No sooner was my anchor down than a boat from an English man-of-war came to enquire if I had seen any wreckage. It seems that two vessels had left Nagasaki on the same afternoon and neither of them had been heard of since. It was supposed that they had collided and both sank. When the other vessels of our crowd arrived we again made a society of our own, meeting on board some ship every evening, for we all belonged around New England. I found a very interesting hotelkeeper in Nagasaki, Captain Smith, and his wife and daughter. His vessel had been condemned, so he became a pilot there, and they had set up a hotel, which was very pleasant for us all. It was like home as most of our crowd had their families with them.

From Nagasaki I made three voyages to Shanghai with coal, and in fact became quite a pilot in the vicinity. One day we visited the old walled city in Shanghai. I have since visited those in Amoy and Canton. In these old Chinese cities the streets are too narrow and crooked for anything but pedestrian traffic while one would soon get lost without a guide. The stench is terrible, and I believe it is only the immense amount of firecrackers consumed that purifies the air enough to support Chinese life.

The freights went down to $1.50 per ton, which did not pay, so I chartered to go with a cargo to Amoy for a lump sum. My wife and little girl went home by steamer to New York and I was alone again. It was only two days' run down to Amoy with a fair wind, and there I found an American barquentine. Her captain and I had a pleasant time there, going gunning a good deal in our sampan. It was winter and I had nothing to do with the cargo, the Chinese loading it and discharging it. The young men in the place used to go gunning on Sundays and wanted me to go with them in their house-boat, but I did not care to go on Sundays when I was free to go all the week. I used to go out early on Monday in my sampan and get more birds and ducks than the whole crowd did, but I expected they were more for the good time than the birds, and anyway it was the kind of gunning I had been brought up to as a boy. Monday afternoon I would make them all a present of birds. The other captain and I made one trip up in the country in the house-boat and had a fine time. The Chinese boys would gather around us in crowds and frequently stone us, but our guns kept them from coming too near. When I fell into the mud on one occasion they laughed and cheered, just as our boys do when they get a chance to torment a poor Chinese. Human nature is about the same the world over. My four boys from home were now Able Seamen and the balance of the crew were Chinese. They make excellent sailors, but in a bad time they require someone to lead them.

One gruesome sight I shall always remember. The captain of the barquentine and I used to keep together a good deal as ours were the only vessels in port. One morning we had scarcely sat down at the ship-chandler's when our pilot came in, saying he would not want anything to eat for a week as he had just seen three Chinese have their heads cut off. I always want to see a thing once for myself, so we made our way quickly to the execution place on a small hill just outside the city walls, although everyone advised us not to go. There we found a big crowd of spectators on the hill-top, while a little way below lay the three bodies, a soldier with a drawn sword marching back and forth to see that no one disturbed them. I was told that they were left exposed for several days for all to look at and take warning. I had always supposed that decapitation was one clean cut with a sharp sword or axe, but these poor creatures had been hacked and hacked. Their crime was stealing. They were said to belong to a junk that had hooked up a telegraph wire from the sea bottom, hauling on board all they could get. The whole crew were served the same way, being sent around to different cities and executed as examples. Well, I was not sorry I went, but it was several days before I cared for my food and I should have to be paid high to see it again. I might mention here that the Chinese are the greatest fishermen in the world. Immense fleets of junks work off all the ports and they have to keep together, for if a Chinese vessel gets ashore in a province where she does not belong they will kill all the crew and take the ship and contents.

Our ship-chandler was a very pleasant man of about thirty-five. With his hat on he was a nice-looking fellow, but a very low forehead spoiled his beauty. Most of the Europeans on the China Coast at this time used to take tickets in a lottery drawn in Manila every month. This ship-chandler had won a first prize and thought he would get married to a young lady he corresponded with in England. They exchanged photographs, but in

his picture he had his hat on. She agreed to marry him and he
sent her the passage money to come out to Hongkong. He went
on board the steamer to meet her and spotted her at once, but
she did not seem to recognise him, although he waited till everybody else had gone ashore. When he finally introduced himself
she saw him without his hat, then said she could never marry
him. I knew another man who won a first prize in the Manila
lottery. He was trading down to Borneo and bought a ticket just
before sailing. When he returned months later he had forgotten
all about it, but something reminded him just in time and he
found he had won $60,000. He gave a big supper, invited all
his friends, bid them goodbye, and went home to Denmark.

I chartered to carry a cargo of tea from Amoy to Samarang
and Surabaya, with passengers on deck and bricks for ballast.
The tea was supposed to be worth over one million dollars. With
200 seasick passengers on deck there was hardly room to get
about, but it was a fair monsoon down the China Sea. There was
a Chinese doctor to take care of them, but about all he did for
them was to pinch them. He was a big man with very strong
hands. They thought one poor fellow would die, he was black
and blue from head to foot where the doctor had pinched him.
I took him in hand, and after an examination gave him some
medicine which brought him round all right. Then all the sick
wanted to come to me.

We were only fifteen days getting down to Samarang, where
our passengers discharged themselves and the cargo in quick
time, all but the bricks which we were to take to Surabaya. I was
glad to get clear of the passengers, for when we came to anchor
and lay head to wind the stench from two hundred coolies was
something awful. This was my first voyage to Java and after I
had chartered the other captains enquired if I had any Blue
Flag days in the Charter Party. No, I had not. Then they told
me such awful stories about Samarang that I went there in
fear and trembling but one thing I knew, the *Coringa* was old
and well-insured and the owners would be pleased to have her
go. The first day I was ashore in Samarang I asked the ship-
chandler how many ships had been lost there (for I thought
from what I'd heard it was as bad as the back of Cape Cod in
winter). He replied that there were never any lost there. His
partner said, " Oh, yes, don't you remember the so-and-so?"
" That old thing! " he replied. " Why she was so old her chains

were rusted through. If she'd had proper anchors and chains she would never have gone ashore." I find one half of the stories about places are about the same, but I was greatly relieved, and had a very pleasant time there. My only annoyance was caused by a young man called Gilmore whom I had taken on as an unpaid Third Mate to please our Consul in Amoy. He had been put ashore there by some vessel in which he was a passenger, but we thought he had been a Second Mate and I was trying to be helpful. However, he knew nothing and could not even get along with our crew. In Samarang he asked if he could go ashore to see a dentist as he had a bad tooth. In Java no one is allowed ashore and the ship is held responsible for all bills incurred by anyone permitted to go. Once ashore this man ran up accounts at the ship's expense, giving me a lot of trouble with the Consul and ship-chandler, so that I had to seek him out and take him back to the ship in my Tambanga, a type of local boat.

From Samarang it was only a short run around to Surabaya, and being in ballast we could use the northern entrance. The first boatman that came alongside said "I am your Tambanga man," and I found he was. I had to take the first that came. I found quite a fleet of American vessels in port, and few of them with anything to do. They were all new ships, and as usual wanted to know what I was going to do with that old vessel when there was nothing for the new ones. There were Captain Frost of the ship *Hoogley,* Captain Higgins of the *Southern Chief,* Captain Bowden of the ship *Regent,* and several others. I have mentioned Captain Bowden before in my *Matchless* days. Two of them were loading for home. Since the Chinese were in no hurry for their bricks I kept them in for ballast. Incidentally, I always liked to sail for the Chinese, they were the fairest men to sail for that I ever met.

I put my vessel in the hands of a Dutch house, the name of which I forget. It was very pleasant to let the owners do the worrying after one had done all one could, and all we captains used to go ashore in the morning and remain until after tiffin. To amuse themselves several of the others put up a job on me. Before a ship loads in Java she must be surveyed, no matter how new she is, and this cost forty guilders at 40 cents U.S. to the guilder. They asked me if I had been surveyed, saying I had better get it done before I chartered or the surveyors would certainly make me copper, which would cost like fury there. This

H

would have been excellent advice if there had been the least prospect of my loading, but under the prevailing conditions a waste of money. Perhaps I had talked too much in telling them what I was going to do, for I had made a plan. I was only going to wait one week more, and was willing to spend the forty guilders. Next morning I had the surveyor come off, and he duly said I would have to copper before he would give me a survey. I knew better than he did the condition of my copper, as I had rolled her down with her yards almost in the water to patch her as I took in the bricks at Amoy. In fact the people ashore thought she was capsized, but you can't capsize a ship by putting cargo in the bottom on one side. So I told him, " That is what I thought you would say. Now the *Regent* has two hundred tons of coal to sell, and the *Anauhack* has two hundred more. I can buy it cheap and it will just make me a set of ballast for Nagasaki, where I can sell it for three times what I pay for it to the U.S. Government. Then I will load a cargo of coal for Hongkong, and have enough money to copper the vessel and have some left." I meant it too, and the surveyor, who only wanted the forty guilders and never imagined I could get a charter in Java, said, " I suppose I can give you a certificate, but if you should charter you will have to patch your copper."

" Of course," I said.

I was always the first ashore in the morning from the fleet. Next morning, when I went into my broker's office with the intention of telling him I was going to buy this coal, he said to me, " Captain, would you take part of a freight for Boston?" My heart fairly jumped, but I said, " I guess so, who has it?" " Martin Dyce." " What is the freight?" " Forty-two and six. If you take it I will not charge you any commission." I went to see Martin Dyce, who said there was about eight hundred tons and that I could take my time to consider it. There was one captain who had sold his ship and was living ashore while he collected payment, so I went to him and he said, " I would not let the grass grow under my feet till I got it. No one has got more than forty shillings this year." I scooted back to Martin Dyce and accepted the freight, but in the interval I thought perhaps I could get enough cargo from another house to fill the ship, so I asked Martin Dyce, " Can I have the privilege of filling the barque from another house if I can find it?" He thought for a moment, then said, " Yes, but we will claim the first privilege of filling you if we can." So the charter was made out and signed. In half an hour I was back with the captain who was living ashore and showed him the signed Charter Party. "Well, that beats the Dutch! Your vessel is twenty-seven years old and gets the best freight out of Java this year."

I had supposed I would have to go to one or two out-ports to load, but no, the cargo was here and I could have it at once. I was late to tiffin at the hotel, for I had been notifying the Chinese to take out their bricks, engaging a stevedore, and so on. The great joke was that only two days before, Bowden and Frost had been advising me to get surveyed, just for fun because my vessel was so old, and here I was chartered and surveyed. When they came ashore they always called on the captain who was living ashore, as his place was on the way to the hotel. It was a standing joke with all of us to ask, "What's the news?" for there was no news. But this morning he replied, "The *Coringa* is chartered." Thinking it was all part of their fun Bowden said, "Yes? What is she getting?" "Forty-two and six." "That all? A ship like her should get three pounds!" "But she really is chartered, I have seen the Charter Party." It was not until we were all together in the hotel and they had seen the Charter Party themselves that they believed him. I said, "I want to thank you fellows for putting me up to getting my vessel surveyed." I never saw a more astonished set of men, but no more so than I was myself, for I would have been happy to get a ballasting of sugar for Boston instead of the full cargo they gave me. Frost remained there fourteen months before he got a freight for home, and he had already been to Batavia twice to see if he could do better there. Bowden remained five months, then went in ballast to Bangkok. I loaded as rapidly as possible and was all ready to sail on Saturday, but my cook, a man from Chatham, Cape Cod, was taken with cholera and I had to leave him. He got better, but died at Singapore on his way home.

On Saturday I was clearing out and had only to remit 2,200 Guilders home, the balance of my China freight, and I came near losing it all. I went to the bank opposite Dandells', my bankers, accompanied by a young clerk from the office. Telling the banker I wanted a draft on Boston I waited with the money in my hands while a clerk made the bills out, for sometimes they liked to count the money first to make sure there is no mistake. While I was waiting in came a German captain, "Have you got my draft made out?" They brought it to him and he paid them 30,000 Guilders. When they handed me my draft I handed them my money, took the bills, and crossed the road to my brokers. Before I got to their door the clerk who had made out my drafts came running to me, " Captain, Captain, you did not pay for your drafts." " Why yes I did." " No, there is no money there," so I went back with him, saying to myself, " Possession is nine points of the law and I have the drafts." The banker said, " Captain, you forgot to pay for your drafts." " I beg your pardon, Sir, I paid for them when I took them from your clerk. I held the money in my hand all the time he was making them out." " But my dear Sir," said the banker. " You don't pay for them here, you pay the cashier." " That is what I thought, but I saw the German captain pay thirty thousand guilders here, in fact he pushed himself in ahead of me and I had to wait until he had finished. I did as he did, passed the money with one hand while I received the drafts with the other." The banker said, " There is no money here, I am afraid you have lost it. You must return those drafts." " No, Sir, I paid for them and I will keep them," but I did not know what the end would be. I went to see the Consul, who said, " You hang on to those Bills. The banker has been here and wants me to stop your ship. I told him I could not, but I guessed you would stop till Monday. Let them hunt for the money." It was a relief to have him on my side. I did stop till Monday, but it was on account of my cook, for in those sickly places no one wants to stay longer than necessary. On Sunday forenoon I went on board the German ship. At first her captain did not know me, then he said, " Ah, I know what you are after, those twenty-two hundred guilders I found in my wallet. I could not think where it came from, thought my Chinaman had paid me too much, until the clerk from the bank came off." So it was all right. When I told the Consul (who, by the way, was a German himself) on Monday he said, " Oh yes, I know that captain of old. He knew he had it all the time, but was afraid someone saw him take it."

Gilmore, the man who had given me trouble at Samarang, persuaded Captain Higgins of the *Southern Chief* to take him to Boston, before we knew we were going there too. I was glad to be rid of him, and Higgins told me afterwards that the police at Boston had instructions to send him home to Brooklyn as

soon as the ship arrived. About a year later he came to see me
in New York, with an invitation from his mother who wanted
to thank me for my care of him. She was a widow and a writer
for the papers. I believe he was only a spoiled darling, and perhaps in later years became a man. I have never heard from him
since.

We came near running the barque ashore on Nantucket Shoals.
The young fellow from Watertown that I had made Second
Mate was in charge of the deck from eight to twelve, the wind
was South West, and I was steering to just clear the South
Shoal Lightship. I went below at nine, telling him to call me
if he saw a light, and knowing we could not run ashore without
seeing it. As I lay down I thought to myself there were two
lights on the lightship and that I had said to call me if he saw
a light, and I was on the point of speaking to him again. Then
I thought, " He will surely call me if he sees two lights." I
knew about where we were by soundings, we generally keep in
about eighteen fathoms of water. Just before twelve I came on
deck and hove the lead. Nine fathoms only. I turned away to the
East till in eighteen fathoms, then South to get around the shoals.
I said, " I can't imagine how we could get into such shoal water
without seeing the South Shoal Lightship," and turning to the
Second Mate I said, " Didn't you see any lights?" " I saw two
lights, Sir, but you said to call you if I saw a light." " Well, what
did you think it was?" " I thought it was two fishermen, Sir."
It was true that we had seen several fishermen the day before,
and they had seemed to be in pairs. We had passed directly by
the lightship for the shoal and in another half hour we should
have been ashore if I had not taken that sounding. I can remember half a dozen just as narrow escapes in my experience, and have
got so that I scarcely trust anybody when I am near the land.

When we arrived in Boston on July 18th, 1878, the pilot said,
" Those people you are consigned to have failed." Going later
with Mr. Brewer to see the man I was greeted with, " I was in
hopes that the *Coringa* would never arrive." I said nothing, didn't
know enough then, but I would not accept such a greeting today
without giving it full publicity. But it made me think why they
had chosen the oldest vessel in port, when so many new ones
were available. Probably this man had bought this sugar, and
as the price had gone down, had told them to ship it on something that would never reach port with it. In that case, why did

they pay such a big freight? I don't know, unless to make the Commission larger.

After being coppered the *Coringa* was towed to New York and loaded case oil for Bombay. Mr. Dawes, from Duxbury, was still the Mate and we had two more green boys from Duxbury, the four from the last voyage having left the sea. We had a long passage of 140 days to Bombay, but got there all right without having to jettison any cargo. The barque was very crank, so I had to send down the fore topgallant mast and the main royal yard. It was hard work to get round the decks, she lay over so much you could not get to windward without a rope and we rove life-lines for the purpose. Going through the Trades in the Atlantic I lashed eight water casks out in the channels and filled them with water, which made a great difference though we still could not carry much sail.

At Bombay we chartered to load a cargo of rice at Akyab for a small place in the north-east of Ceylon called Kangasanthra. They had a fire in Akyab while we were there and a good deal of the place was burned. Several other vessels were loading for the same port, among them the ship *Carondelet,* Captain Stetson. On the passage to Ceylon we passed close to Point de Galle, where several boats came off from the shore and we spent a day trading for jewellery, but we got awfully cheated.

One of the Duxbury boys had been sent to sea to remove him from the influence of a young lady who was much older than he was. At Akyab he received a long letter from her, but as he was coming up the ship's side it fell out of his pocket before he had even read it and the strong current carried it away. I have often thought that that was the most aggravating thing that ever happened to anyone. Poor boy, he was always in trouble and once fell down a hatch, nearly killing himself. I know when we got back to New York and he had gone home I felt quite relieved, but next day I received a telegram saying he had sent his trunk home by the wrong boat and I had to hunt it up. Anyway the match was broken off.

We arrived at Kangasanthra just after the South West Monsoon had set in, in fact it caught us about ninety miles to the East of the island. The off-shore wind brought a wonderful spicey fragrance which the missionaries told me when I arrived was from the tobacco plant just then in bloom. Here we remained about a month, and at the end of it I was glad to get away. All my freight money was paid to me in cash and about once a fortnight we had to go across country to Jaffna, where there was a bank. I think this was the first year the merchants had tried shipping by big ships, because so many of the junks and praus had run away to Sumatra and other places and sold their cargoes, and were never heard of again. I suppose steamers do the trade now.

The missionaries here were a very interesting crowd and they were very kind to us, inviting us to their homes. Most of them had been driven out of India shortly before, and on their way home had stopped at Colombo, but were not allowed to land. The authorities had decided that the missionaries only made trouble, but told them they might land north of the river Jaffna in the northern part of the island. Jaffnapatam was good for nothing and the people so wild that no white man could live there. The missionaries went there and under their care the northern part of Ceylon has become the finest part of the island. Everyone can read and write, there are schools and a college, and the population has increased. They have their own language. Jaffna was an old Dutch place, very clean, though there did not seem to be much business except for a pearl fishery. The drive there across the island was very pleasant.

After discharging we went in ballast to Singapore to load a cargo of cutch, pepper, and rattans for New York. Singapore is the finest place I know in the tropics, and the healthiest for a place so near the Equator. There were six of us loading for New York.

When we arrived home we found the largest fleet of vessels that had ever been in New York. According to the papers there were 600 barques, 400 ships, and 84 tramp steamers in the port. Five of us were at Pier 47 from Singapore and had only one Customs officer between us. I had a bit of trouble with the searchers who sealed up my cabin while I was ashore so that I could not get to bed, but we finally got friendly and I gave each of them a malacca cane. While at home this time I also sent a malacca cane to each of the men in the factory at Forestville, Conn., where I used to work.

The *Coringa* now loaded case oil for Batavia, Java, on what was to prove her last voyage, my wife and daughter sailing with me. About a week out we had some bad weather and leaked so badly we had to throw overboard a considerable amount of oil before we finally weathered the gale. The last cargo of pepper had dried up the caulking about the stanchions. In good time we arrived at Batavia, finding several other American vessels in the port. In these tropical places it is better for the master to live ashore on the high ground up above the fever, though it is also healthy on board the ship at anchor a mile or more from the low shore. At this time most Batavia people lived twenty miles away in the mountains at Buitenzorg, where one required a blanket over one at nights. The steam cars run you up, and we spent a few days there.

Mr. Dawes, the Mate, was sick and under doctor's care, so when we went to Singapore to load rice for Surabaya he went home on a tea steamer, while I promoted the Second Mate to Mate and took the carpenter, Gibbons, as Second Mate. On the way from Singapore to Surabaya we struck a reef which was wrongly charted in Carimata Strait. It was not enough to make the vessel leak, and I backed her off with her own sails, but as we had been aground I could not charter for home. So I went back to Singapore from Surabaya in ballast, went into dry-dock and had her caulked and coppered. As the new Mate could not keep sober I discharged him and shipped Mr. Philip W. Weeks of Winsor, Nova Scotia, as Mate. When we came out of dock I chartered to load rice at Bangkok for Samarang. We went up in about a week, anchoring off the Bar so far from the shore that you could only just see it. It was the quietest place I ever remember, we were all alone except for the occasional steamer which would anchor for a day or so near us.

Leaving Bangkok bar with our ship deeply laden with rice on November 12th, 1880, we ran into a hurricane which was to prove too much for the old *Coringa*. This typhoon was in a latitude and at a time of year when they are not generally encountered, in fact there is no record of one being met so far south before. Later that day strong gales from the North East and an ugly sea obliged us to reduce sail and caused the ship to leak more than usual. We manned the pumps every two hours and steered to the South East. By mid-day on the 13th, we were close to Pulo Panjang and getting out of the sheltered waters of the Gulf of Siam. A heavy cross sea was flooding the decks with water and causing the ship to leak badly. Sail was reduced still

further and the ship kept away to S.S.E., while we were standing
to the pumps all day. At midnight it was blowing so hard and
there was such a sea abeam that I kept away before it to the
South West. In spite of all hands at the pumps the water was
gaining in the hold. All our starboard bulwarks were washed
away and we commenced to throw overboard cargo from the
main hatch and fore scuttle, but it was slow work as we had to
keep closing the hatch on account of the seas. The galley was
washed out so that we could not light a fire. We reckoned there
was thirty inches of water in the hold and a good deal more between decks.

Daylight on the 14th, found water going through the cabin
where the bulwarks had been smashed and we were obliged to
heave to on the starboard tack with the ship's head North. The
first roll washed away the best boat from the davits. We pumped
and threw cargo overboard all day and at 3.0 p.m. let go one
anchor and slipped it, as the ship was settling by the head. The
fore topmast and mizzen staysails blew to pieces. The barque
would not lay to the wind, and away went the fore topmast and
the jib-boom, taking the main topgallant mast with them. With
the vessel apparently sinking we launched two boats, but could
not keep them away from the ship's side and both were stove
in. All hands were at the pumps all night, all water casks and
spars were adrift and the casks washed overboard.

By the next morning the wind and sea had moderated slightly,
but hard squalls blew away the foresail and fore topsail as we
could not leave the pumps to furl them. Land was visible to leeward so I got a sight and found our position was 15 miles South
East of Cape Patani, on the Malay peninsula. We left the pumps
then and bent another fore sail, but it was old and soon blew
away. We spent all forenoon trying to get enough sail to weather
the cape, but at 3.0 p.m. with six to eight feet of water in the
hold and our deck almost level with the water, I kept away for the
shore. An hour later we struck the sandy bottom about three
quarters of a mile away from the beach and ran up into the
sand for a quarter of a mile before we stopped. Mr. Gibbon and
a cabin boy tried to get ashore on a raft, but a current set them
seawards and only Mr. Gibbon reached the beach three miles
to the northward, Henry Echelman being washed from the raft
and drowned. Seas were breaking over the vessel and she was
working closer to the shore. We spent a dreadful night, with my

wife and daughter lashed in chairs to the top of the deck house to keep them from being washed overboard.

Tuesday morning, the 16th, saw the ship within 500 yards of the shore, which was lined with natives. Mr. Gibbon, whom we had supposed drowned, was among them and we were much encouraged. Our only remaining boat was a very old one. Covering it with canvas nailed on with tacks I took wife and child and four men and backed ashore with a line. We got there safely, but stove in the boat, then hauled the others ashore with a rope secured to a raft. The Raja of Tuluba (or Tabulan), in whose territory we had landed, took us to his place and they treated us as kindly as possble, guarding our few possessions on the shore from theft. The Chinese were very kind and fed the men but wanted pay.

During the next few days we recovered our spirits as the gale moderated and we had some rest. It rained continuously and the mud in the village and in the camp we set up was knee deep, while the current was very strong in the local river. As the weather improved Mr. Weeks and Victor Wisell swam off to the ship where they made a raft and succeeded in getting some things ashore to add to our comfort. The Raja was most anxious to help us and I wrote letters to send to Singapore and Bangkok, consulting with him as to how to get them away. On the 22nd Arthur Courtney, when trying to cross a rapid, was swept out to sea and drowned. Carl Sudbury, who could not swim, let go of a raft some of them were bringing ashore and was drowned in spite of efforts by Mr. Weeks to reach him.

Tuesday, the 23rd, was our first fine day since we got ashore. Mr. Weeks had secured a piece of the general chart of the area and suggested he might try to walk to Penang, which is only 110 miles across country. After a consultation the Raja gave him two guides and we agreed to pay them $60.00 if they conducted the Mate safely via Singorah to Penang. Two days later they started off, the river having fallen four feet or more indicating that the heavy rains up country must be over. The Raja had a house made on the beach for the men to live in, where they were much more comfortable than camping under the old boat. As the days went by the natives were busy gathering their harvest from the paddy fields exposed by the receding flood waters. Some of us visited the ship occasionally at some risk to get clothes, bedding, and tools. A few canned meats supplemented our diet of rice and salt fish, which was causing us all to suffer stomach pains and to feel sick and faint, though after Carl Sudbury was drowned few of the men cared to venture off to the wreck. Two men became sick with fever, and others who had set off to explore the surrounding area reported back that they could get no help and hardly enough to eat. From time to time parties of natives, some of them armed with guns and one accompanied by a large elephant, visited the camp, and this disturbed our Raja so much that he sent his guard to watch the camp and ship at nights. He and his people were as kind to us as ever, though the Chinese appeared to get tired of us when they realised there was nothing to gain. My family and I slept on the veranda of a hut raised a few feet from the ground, with all kinds of filth and garbage thrown underneath. We found the dirt the hardest thing of all to put up with, but managed to keep free of lice.

On Thursday, December 2nd, I found the sea had washed the spare topmast and the top of the cabin table ashore, and this I gave to the Raja. He was very much interested in learning English and spent two or three hours every day at it. One day I drew him a chart of the world, and when I explained to him that it was round and showed him the motions of the heavenly bodies he readily understood, but was quite struck with his ignorance. They are all very anxious to learn.

On the 5th, a party of Chinese arrived from Kelantan and one of them who could talk quite good English said there had been a report of our vessel and he had come to see it. He said that the gale which had wrecked us was the worse ever known on the coast and that more than 200 people had lost their lives in Kelantan, houses being unroofed and coconut trees blown down. These Chinese talked about buying the ship, provided the Raja would protect them, but made no offers.

Wednesday the 8th, was a fine day and I had just returned from a morning visit to the camp when we heard two cannon fired. A native came in, and after sitting down for five minutes, said there was a steamer coming. Going down to the camp again I found they had seen her, but she had gone past and was now out of sight behind the Cape. About 8.0 p.m. another native came to tell us that the steamer had returned and had anchored near the wreck. Going down to the beach we found that it was so. She was the *Kongsee* and her Mate had come ashore in the vessel's gig. He handed me a note from Captain Uldall, her Master, saying that Major Studor, the U.S. Consul at Singapore, had received a telegram from Mr. Weeks at Penang and had requested him to stop for us on his passage north and to take us to Bangkok and thence to Singapore. He asked us to hurry up and come off at once. I immediately made arrangements to send off the crew in a canoe, then went back to the village for my family. Saying good-bye to the Raja at 10.0 p.m. I gave him about 175 yards of canvas we had saved from the wreck, and at 11.30 p.m. the last of us left the beach in the steamer's boat. We arrived on board about half an hour after midnight and were very kindly treated by her Captain, officers, and steward. She at once got under way for Bangkok.

By morning it was blowing hard, so it was fortunate we had got on board during the night. We were all very seasick, and for some days suffered from nausea and diarrhoea, probably due to the unusual food we had eaten for the last three weeks. We anchored at Bangkok Bar at 4 p.m. on the 10th, and next forenoon proceeded up the river to the wharf at Bangkok. There a doctor prescribed for us and our Consul, General J. H. Holderman, said that as all preliminary steps had been taken by the Consul at Singapore he would waive his right to the settlement of the crew and vessel, particularly as the vessel was insured in America and the cargo at Singapore and as there was no telegraphic communication at Bangkok. I was too sick to attend to business, but advanced a small sum of money to each of my crew. One of them, Victor Wisell, came to the cabin and said his money was bad, though I had received it from the Consul and had no means of changing it. He became very abusive and used a lot of profane language. Fortunately for us both I was too sick to say much and my wife sent him from the cabin. Had he resisted her I would have shot him.

Early on Monday morning the *Kongsee* steamed down to the Bar to load the remainder of her cargo and at midnight a harbour launch brought the ship's papers down, whereupon she got under way and proceeded to Singapore. She had arrived in Bangkok on Saturday after the Customs House had closed and left on Monday before it was opened. We reached Singapore on Friday, 17th December, by which time I was feeling more like myself again.

At Singapore I made a full report of all that had happened, of course, and after some months the State Department in

Washington ordered a Gold Medal and a magazine rifle with suitable ammunition to be prepared as testimonials of the occasion and presented to the Raja of Tuluba in consideration of his very humane attentions to me and my family and crew when we were thrown within his care. These articles were accompanied by suitable mementoes of manufactured goods as suggested by the Consul at Bangkok to be distributed to the natives who had distinguished themselves in contributing to the necessities of the destitute crew."

Our agents in Singapore were Boustead & Co., but I was well acquainted there and had several times discharged men before the Consul, Major Studor, always having to pay one month's pay to the U.S. Government and two months' to the seaman. This time I had my crew but no money or ship. These men had about forty dollars each due to them and I was advised by my friends to give them orders on the owners at home for the amounts due. The next morning when I went to call on the Consul I found he was giving the men two suits of clothes apiece. Now they did not require any clothes for they had saved all their clothing from the wreck and had washed and mended them while waiting for the steamer, and they also had all my slop clothes which they had taken from the wreck. Some of them had as many as a dozen shirts and twenty pairs of stockings. They thought they were going to get these clothes from the Consul for nothing, but he knew they had wages coming to them and intended to deduct the cost from their pay, getting his commission from the tailor. However, it was none of my business. A few days later he asked me when I was going to pay the crew off. I told him I had no money but intended to give them orders on the owners at home. He was very put out and told me I must wire for the money. But I thought to myself, " You have had your way with me for several years when I had a ship you could bother, now I am free and I will have my way." The Mate and three men shipped aboard a vessel for New York and I would have given them orders on owners but the Consul said that all must be served alike and all their accounts would go through Washington. The Mate came to Charles Brewer & Co., in due course and got his money, but the three sailors never came. I have their accounts to this day, ready to be paid with interest if they would call for it.

As soon as possible I put up the hull and cargo of the *Coringa*

to auction, as she might be found, and received for the hull
$100 and for the cargo $800. Then the Consul said, "I suppose
now you will pay off the crew?" "How can I? If you had let
me give an order on owners to the men who sailed the other day
I could do so, but you said all must be served alike." Really I
intended to pay them off all the time, and when I had shown
the Consul and the men that they could not force me to do so,
I paid them off.

When my wife had gone home from Shanghai two years previously she wrote me a letter from Singapore, describing what
a nice place it was, only there had been no rain for some time
and the drains smelt dreadfully. On our arrival this time she
said, "Why, the drains smell just as bad as they did two years
ago." I had to laugh, "Don't you know what it is that smells so
bad?" "No, it smells as bad as a skunk." "That is the celebrated
fruit, the durian, remember the Raja sent us a piece of one while
we were wrecked and it drove us out of the hut till we gave it
away?" It is said to be the finest fruit in the world when you
have learned to eat it, but I never learned, the smell is too much
for me.

So ended my seven years experience in the *Coringa*. My wife
and daughter and I returned to New York in the steamer,
Benalder and enjoyed the trip very much. The Captain gave us
his stateroom, for we were the only passengers and all the other
rooms were full of tea. He was eighty years old, but a smart man.
He told me it would be a good chance to study steam, so I stood
watch with the Chief Engineer from eight to twelve all the way
home, and could handle the engines as well as any of them when
we arrived. Of course my two years in the machine-room of the
business in Forestville had given me a knowledge they did not
all possess about machinery. I spent two days in Malta plugging
tubes and two more in Gibraltar overhauling circulating pumps,
and every evening recited my lesson to the Chief Engineer, for I
studied the Engineering Manual through, and he thought I could
pass a pretty good examination when we arrived. There were
thirty-six men on board, all Scots, and I took so much interest
in it they seemed to like to teach me.

CHAPTER SEVEN

Fourteen voyages in the barque John D. Brewer, 1882-1896 *—New ships and the Hawaiian flag—Building the* John D. Brewer*—New York to Shanghai with case oil—Daughter born —Poles from Foochow—Rice to Whampoa—Hongkong, New York—2nd Voyage case oil to Shanghai—Krakatau explosion— Iloilo—Boston—3rd Voyage New York—Shanghai—Nagasaki— Iloilo—Boston—4th Voyage Shanghai, Iloilo, Boston—5th voyage Shanghai, Nagasaki, Hongkong, Cebu, Boston—6th Voyage Honolulu, Hongkong, Iloilo, New York—7th Voyage Hongkong, Cebu, Boston—8th Voyage New York, Honolulu, Manila, Iloilo, New York, 9th Voyage Boston, New York, Honolulu, Manila, Iloilo, New York—10th Voyage Shanghai, Cebu, Philadelphia— 11th Voyage Shanghai, Colombo, wife's death, Cochin, New York—12th Voyage Batavia, Lossum, Cebu, Boston—13th Voyage Port Elizabeth, Colombo, Cochin, Alleppey, New York— 14th Voyage, Buenos Aires, Anjer for orders, Surabaya, New York, hospital with pneumonia.*

After coming home in the *Benalder* I was ashore for nearly a year. Mr. Brewer bought the ship *Victoria* on the way from Europe to San Francisco and I was all ready to take her as soon as she arrived. I took an eighth of her, and had she arrived we would have made a good bargain, but her captain lost her on the coast of Terra del Fuego and I lost $500, for she was not fully insured. We then tried to buy the ship eventually called *Luzon* which had been on the stocks for nearly a year awaiting a purchaser, then tried to buy the barque *Rambler*. Failing in these attempts we finally decided to build a new vessel. We thought of building an iron barque, but could only get one offer in the United States, to build her for $100,000. At the time we could have built her in England for $60,000, and that is what we should have done, placing her under the Hawaiian flag as Brewers' later did with four vessels. In fact Mr. Brewer ought to have built two steamers and placed them under the Hawaiian flag. He would have made a fortune. But we were too patriotic and must sail under the American flag. I never could see why we were not allowed to build ships, or buy them, where we could get them cheapest, to sail in foreign waters and compete with foreign vessels. All my life I have had to support my family and pay for goods that were protected. It has cost me twice as much to support a family as it costs a foreign sailor. It certainly did not protect American carpenters, for most of those building the *John D. Brewer* came from Novia Scotia and returned there to spend their money. Had it not been for that foolish law our merchant marine would have retained its place as second only to that of Britain.

Eventually it was decided to build the *John D. Brewer,* a barque of about 1,000 tons, at the yard of Smith & Townsend in East Boston. They were the builders of *Matchless* and *Charger* so I was right at home. With the laying of the first keel piece I went into the yard and it seemed almost as though I had built her myself. I took my family and lived at the Maverick House, East Boston. In that hotel was a table known as The Captain's Table, for an old Navy captain had lived there for years and had the same place in the dining-room. All the captains went to that table. During our stay a young couple also sat with him, the lady being a sister to Lieutenant Danenhower, who was one of a party missing in the Arctic Ocean at that time. We were talking about them at dinner one day and the old captain, who did not know that she was Danenhower's sister, said, " Well, I suppose they are all in the bellies of the white bears now." His gruff old voice made it sound all the worse and the poor lady left the table in tears. I was always up early in the morning and the first thing I heard next day was the news-boys shouting the rescue of Lieutenant Danenhower. He was somewhere in Siberia coming home overland. Of course I lost no time in sending a paper to his sister, and she had a smiling face from that day. He arrived home and she met him, but he did not live many years afterwards.

It was during this time that I got a lesson in playing checkers, at which I thought I was pretty good. Of course I knew everybody staying in the hotel. One evening there was a young fellow in the Smoking Room who wanted to play a game of checkers with a man from Bath for $100, but the man from Bath would not play for money. So I took on the Bath man and beat him three games out of four. Next evening the young fellow asked if he might come to my room and play me a game. He told me to take my time, and I did so, but he won every game. I said, " Aren't you the greatest checker player in the world?" " Oh no," he replied, " I am only third rate." He mentioned two famous players as the greatest, said there were many second rate players, and called himself third rate. What was my rate? Since then I have never played checkers except to please someone, but it was a good lesson.

As soon as the barque was finished in April 1882 she was towed to New York, where we loaded case oil for Shanghai at 31st Street, East River. We had a very quick trip, making Anjer in 80 days and Shanghai in 107, in spite of being loaded very crank with one thousand cases of oil in the poop. Although the ship was not built for speed she was beaten only three times during the fourteen years I was in her, and I think she was about as nearly perfect as a wooden ship could be. I planned the cabin to suit myself and family, who came with me on this voyage. It so happened that we sailed on the same day as the *Luzon* which the builders reckoned would sail a knot faster, and beat her to Shanghai by forty days. We spoke one vessel in Formosa Channel, the *Pendleton* of Searsport, Captain Laffin. She was 157 days out then, in fact she had sailed from New York before the *John D. Brewer* had been launched in Boston. I could see she had been in bad weather as her bulwarks had been partially washed away.

I was half-way up the river to Woosung before I got a pilot. He was an immense man called Knott, and I can see him stepping over the rail now. He gave me a whistle which has been in my pocket ever since. I don't know what I should do without it as it exactly balances the jack-knife in my other pocket. The K inscribed on the whistle is almost worn off after twenty-seven years. We arrived in August and my youngest daughter Elizabeth was born at the Astor House Hotel in American Town on

I

September 14th. Shortly after this event I made a quick trip down the coast to Foochow, and back with a cargo of poles, leaving my family at the hotel in Shanghai.

According to the Sailing Directions a vessel beating up the China Coast against the North East Monsoon should go out into the Black Stream or Japan Current, which is very similar to the Gulf Stream on the Atlantic Coast of the U.S.A. I found it much easier and quicker to hug the coast. That is the secret of beating the monsoon on the China Coast, the wind will always haul towards the land at some time during the night. You have to wait around on short tacks till the time comes, in some places till nearly morning. Then when the wind comes from the land up you go, making more in a couple of hours than you could by beating all day farther off shore. This time I was only seven days from Foochow to Shanghai. On the day I went to my agents a fine Nova Scotia barque with a fore and aft mainsail came in to the same agents. I asked her captain how long he had been. " One hundred and thirty days from New York, thirty days from Formosa, and I have a vessel that can go to windward with anything." I did not tell him I was only four days from Formosa, where he had been thirty, but he had gone by the book and kept out in the Black Stream.

Whenever I see a cargo of Foochow poles I think of the barque *Fruiterer*, Captain James H. Dawes, my old captain in the *Sicilian* and *Matchless*. The *Fruiterer* was making the same voyage with poles when a steamer ran into her and cut her stern off. She saved all the crew except the young man at the wheel, Trescott Tupper, of Kingston, who hung on to a piece of the taffrail for four days and nights with nothing to eat or drink but a snake he caught on the second day. Then a German barque picked him up, and took good care of him, and landed him at her next port. There are plenty of snakes in the China Sea, but I don't know that they are good eating, and he was lucky to escape the sharks too. In those days we were not obliged to carry side-lights and Captain Dawes always said they were useless, until he was run down that time. Afterwards they had to be lit at sunset and remain till sunrise, no matter how long the twilight.

After discharging my poles and picking up my family again we loaded a cargo of rice for Whampoa, the nearest point a sailing vessel can get to Canton, eleven miles up river. We had a nice run down to Hongkong, and as the tugboat wanted so much money I sailed up to Whampoa, about the last square-rigged vessel that ever did so. This is where the vessel used to load tea in old times, and there is quite an extensive graveyard which is rapidly decaying owing to time and Chinese vandalism, every stone worth taking having been stolen. I often think the Chinese are the greatest and the cleverest thieves in the world, in spite of the severity of their laws against theft. In any Chinese port I had to hire men to watch the copper on the outside of the ship. To the Chinese all Europeans are barbarians and it is no crime to steal from them, but in my view the Chinese themselves are most barbaric in the way they rob and murder one another. My sampan man did not dare to go down to the ship from Canton after 3.0 p.m. for fear of pirates. Money would not hire him, and once when I could not come at that hour he would not wait, but I had to hire a steam launch. As everyone knows, many thousands of people live in boats at Canton. These sampan people are a distinct class, being born in the boats, living in them, and only marrying among themselves. The Chinese trust each other so little that it seems to me the so called " Yellow Peril " is a long way off. Only a united people can succeed—witness the Japanese in the late war against Russia, and France after the Revolution. There was no European society at Whampoa, though the Harbourmaster was from New Bedford, Mass. He was a Quaker and married to a Chinese, and had several children. Such marriages between a European and a native woman of no education seem to me a mistake, as the children are neither one thing nor the other.

One day in Canton we visited a Chinese Court Room. Eleven men and one woman were being tried for breaking into a house. The men were on their knees, their thumbs tied to their big toes, the thumbs over their shoulders and the toes pulled up behind to meet. To prevent them from falling over there was a frame of wood behind each man, and his queue or pigtail was drawn through a hole in the frame. Each wore only a loincloth and their backs had been beaten with bamboos until they were bloody and raw. This was only a preliminary, for they had not yet been tried, only found in the vicinity. The woman was standing and she had not been beaten. The two judges were reclining on lounges and seemed to enjoy their easy position the more for seeing these poor creatures in agony. I suppose they were proven guilty and decapitated, or worse, as I had seen done in Amoy a few years previously.

I had to travel down to Hongkong to charter the barque for New York. The river steamers are much like our Long Island Sound boats, only smaller. No Chinese were allowed in the saloon, apart from an occasional well-known official, and there were racks of loaded rifles and revolvers, swords and pikes, also a hot steam hose ready to turn on. No one knew who the hundreds of Chinese deck passengers were or if they included a gang of pirates. While I was away in Hongkong there was a bad row on board the barque. The men got some liquor and became wild, and would have killed the Mate if my wife had not come with my revolver and driven them away from him. She then hoisted the ensign with the Union down and the Harbourmaster came off and stopped the row. The subsequent trial took eleven days and cost the U.S. Government a lot of money, and then it was only a farce, for the men admitted what they had done. Our Consul was new and did not know what to do, but like all people ashore he thought that Jack was abused.

We towed down to Hongkong and loaded for New York. Our Consul at Hongkong at that time was Colonel Mosby, of the Southern Army. He asked me all about the row at Whampoa, then said, "I think I could have settled that in about ten minutes." Here we had to leave the Chinese woman who had taken care of the baby since her birth. How she cried! When we reached New York my family stayed at home and I was alone in the *John D. Brewer* for the next thirteen years.

Again we took case oil to Shanghai, loading it this time at Fly Island, up the Newtown Creek. The place was well-named Fly Island, I never saw so many flies in my life. I shipped the Second Mate from the *Martha Davis* as Mate, and again we had a fine run of eighty days to Anjer.

About a week before we reached Java Head the sun looked very peculiar, you could look directly at it like the moon till its altitude was over fifty degrees. When we came to Java Head I was still more surprised, for the trees seemed to be leafless and instead of the most luxuriant vegetation in the world everything was barren. The sixty feet high perpendicular cliffs of the shore were black as though painted, and there was a very disagreeable odour as from dead fish. As it was very rainy I put it all down to that.

It was dark when we approached Anjer and as I could see no light I anchored till morning. It was still raining in the morning, so I sailed on without knowing of the terrible eruption of Krakatau, or that I was the first vessel to go through after it excepting the American warship *Enterprise,* Captain Barker of Pembroke, Mass.

I had a description of the catastrophe from the captain and mate of the barque *Western Bell,* the only vessel known to be in the vicinity at the time. She was anchored behind St. Nicholas Point, on the western end of Java, so the sixty-foot tidal waves did not reach her, but the current ran by them so fast they had to put down both anchors and all their chain to hold her. They estimated the strength of the tide as twenty knots at times. They thought the end of the world had surely come as for forty-eight hours it was so dark they could hardly see one another.

Krakatau is a small island about 2,000 feet high midway between Java and Sumatra and about twenty miles from each. It used to be a perfect sugar-loaf in shape, but now the west side is blown away. I have forgotten how frequent the eruptions were, but their roar could be heard many hundreds of miles away, the noise being worse at Batavia than at Anjer, where it passed over their heads. It raised tidal waves sixty feet high on the Java side and over on Sumatra, where there was a bay, they came up one hundred and thirty-three feet to the door of the British Consul's house. A great many people were killed including all the white people living at Anjer, where the lighthouse was also destroyed. All vegetation was stripped of leaves, and branches were broken off up to the mountain tops by the mud. This mud and dust was what had made the sun look so peculiar as we approached five hundred miles away. When I passed again on my way home four months later I sailed for a whole day through pumice stone, only seeing the water at intervals, and I found patches of it as far as Mauritius. A year later I met patches of it as far away as St. Helena in the Atlantic.

On reaching Shanghai I went on board the U.S.S. *Enterprise* by the starboard gangway and asked to see Captain Barker. When I was ushered into his cabin he greeted me by name, which surprised me until I found he had been born at Hanover, Mass., my father's native place. I have always wondered why there is not more intercourse between the Navy and the Merchant Marine. Many shipmasters think the Navy officers stuck-up, but from my experience they are perfect gentlemen. I left my chart of Sunda Strait with the Navigating officer, who corrected it for me. Captain Barker had come to the Straits the day after the eruption, and when he wired home about it the U.S. Government gave him instructions to survey the Straits as he had a deep sea sounding apparatus on board. He told me they counted forty dead bodies the first day, to say nothing of dead animals, houses, and other wreckage.

I was soon discharged, then took mud ballast from Shanghai to Iloilo, to load sugar at that port for Boston. We found fourteen vessels at Iloilo, and several of the captains had their families on board. I had been to the Philippine Islands a good many times and had always been fortunate enough to get along pleasantly with the officials, though many of the captains had been fined and were in trouble with them daily. I had always given them about $10.00 when we arrived and the same when we left, and it was money well spent, for the port charges were not heavy. Most others did the same, but I was always very courteous to them, and I consider that the secret of success. On my arrival this time I was boarded, as usual, by a large boat pulling twelve oars. A file of soldiers mustered by the gangway, while the searchers looked over the ship to see that nothing was being smuggled. The officer in charge of them was very young, just out from Spain I should say. Taking him down to the cabin, as usual, I tried to entertain him with my broken Spanish, for he knew not a word of English. Then I handed him fourteen dollars, at which he became very excited and indignant. As he would not take the money I told the Mate to give it to the searching officer. He did so, and it was accepted, but the Lieutenant would not talk any more, and when the searching officer came to the cabin to make his report the Lieutenant asked him if he had been offered any money. At first he denied it, but finally he confessed he had received fourteen dollars. " Give it to me," the Lieutenant said, and seizing his hat he ran up on deck, called everyone's attention, and threw the money into the sea. His own searching officer, who stood beside me, whispered, " Damn fool, damn fool," then getting into the boat they went ashore to make their report. I have no doubt his superiors ashore said " Damn fool," too, for I heard no more about it. The other captains all said I would have trouble, but the Consul agreed with me it was the custom and no crime to make a man a present. However, ever since then I have made them ask for what they expect, and they never fail to do so.

I had a number of sheep on board, as they are very cheap in Shanghai, and I used to kill one every Saturday and distribute it among my friends in the other ships. Being invited to dine at the Consul's one Sunday I took along a quarter of mutton for him. As we were pulling away from the ship's side the carbinero, or native soldier, on board called us back. Thinking he wanted to go ashore with us I returned, but all he did was to point at the piece of mutton and take it from me. I told the Consul about it and he sent a man for it, but by that time the Customs officer had sent a letter ashore about it, so could not let it go. Eventually it was returned to me on Monday with apologies, but by then it had gone bad and I could only throw it away. It seemed a wicked waste as there was no good meat in the islands.

Carrying a full cargo of sugar to Boston, we made the passage in 105 days. Of the fourteen vessels bound home from Iloilo the nearest to me was 115 days to New York, while an English tea clipper specially chartered because of her speed took 156 days, passing St. Helena on the day I arrived in Boston. Coming up the harbour the pilot ran us aground twice, scraping over the bottom off Point Allerton and again when we were coming to an anchor inside. The tide was extremely low, but he ought to have known there was not enough water for us and waited until it had risen a little. He was the oldest pilot in the Company. Our shoe was all gone and the keel split for twenty feet.

Fortunately we had to dock to copper, so repairs to the keel were completed at the same time and only cost two hundred dollars. Then we towed to Bayonne, in the port of New York, and loaded oil for Shanghai again. I shipped Walter Pendleton as Mate, and he continued with me for the next four years. As soon as we were alongside at Bayonne who should come on board to see me but Captain William F. Seymour, with whom I had sailed for many years in the *Reynard*. We had both left her at the same time and he had built and commanded the barque *Pekin* afterwards. In those days he was one of the smartest shipmasters sailing out of the U.S., now he was a wreck and dragged his feet like an old man, all through drink. He came to see me every day while we were there, and each voyage afterwards until he passed away, for the Sailors' Snug Harbour is only across the water from Bayonne.

We had another quick passage out to Shanghai, but on the way I was beaten by Henry Hastings' new ship *South American*. She passed me in the South Indian Ocean near St. Paul's Rocks, though we both arrived at Anjer on the same day. About a dozen of us were held up in the Sunda Strait together, all bound up the China Sea. One of these vessels, a Novia Scotia ship, bound for Japan myseriously disappeared on her way north. One morning, after we had been at anchor all night, we finally got through, all hurrying to get under way and make sail. I was the first to get away and led the crowd, the *South American* was the last. I noticed her captain took infinite pains in setting his sails, every sail was set like a board. Then she passed us all, going up the Sumatra coast without making a tack. I was leading the rest, but had to tack twice. It was a good lesson for me, and I have been more particular about setting my sails since that day than I was ever brought up to be. I am convinced now that had my sails been properly set she would not have beaten me in smooth water. A small vessel on the wind has the advantage, she answers her helm so much more quickly in varying flaws. The *South American* arrived at Hongkong in 95 days from Cardiff. I went away up to Shanghai, discharged, took 5,000 cases of oil as ballast to Nagasaki reaching there in 52 hours, discharged the oil ballast, loaded a full cargo of coal, came down to Hongkong, and had my coal out before the *South American* finished discharging.

It was this time in Shanghai that I had a big row with the pilots. They were a notoriously drunken crowd, one reason being that the many lines of steamers that ply there all keep their regular pilots, and as it is an easier life to go back and forth to Hongkong and get good pay without the trouble of keeping a pilot boat, the steamers get the pick of the men. As I owned a piece of the *John D. Brewer* I would not take one of the drunkards and had an arrangement with the pilot Knott. I was anchored outside the Bar and saw two boats coming for me, one of which was Knott's boat. The other boat boarded me first, but I refused them and took Knott as I thought they allowed a captain his preference. They went to the Harbourmaster, who decided in their favour. I went to the American Minister, who said I should pay the pilotage to Knott. There was a good deal of talk and I said I would not have a drunken pilot on my ship if I could get a sober one, and it passed for the time. However, on my last voyage to Shanghai several years later there was a sequel.

At Nagasaki it was a pleasure to renew acquaintance with the Smith family. The old captain from Maine was still acting as pilot and insurance surveyor for Lloyds, while his wife and family of two girls and two boys formed the nucleus of our little society of captains and their families who used his hotel. The Japanese workers are the smartest I have ever seen. All our coal was passed on board from boats in baskets of 20 or 30 pounds each, and all weighed on board. We were loaded in one day, and all done by girls, several hundreds of them.

After unloading the coal at Hongkong we waited there until we received orders for Iloilo, where we again loaded a cargo of sugar for Boston, and made a fair passage home.

Looking back over this period of my life I find it difficult to separate the incidents of one voyage from those of another. Mr. Pendleton was again Mate on this, my fourth voyage in the *John D. Brewer,* and it is by remembering who the Mate was that I can best bring my memory into focus. It has been said of the sea life that, " Sometimes you see a ship, and sometimes you ship a sea." These voyages of a year each do seem monotonous in retrospect, but no more than does life ashore in the country. There are so many pleasant things about the sea life that one can put up with some discomforts. Pure air to breathe, time to read and think, these more than pay for the absence of world news and seeing only the same faces for months, and even those are repaid when you reach port by a zest that only abstinence can give.

Again we towed to New York, again old Captain Seymour came daily to see us at Bayonne, again we sailed for Shanghai and, with almost the same winds and weather, passed into the China Sea through Sunda Strait, finding the same boatmen with yams, fowl, and eggs to sell. Many of them had their limbs twisted out of shape, having barely escaped with their lives at the time of the eruption. No doctor to help them, nature had to do it all. The shores of the Strait were covered with vegetation again now, three years after the eruption. All the dust and mud in the air had settled, covering what had in places been barren rocks.

Someone asked me the other day, "Where is your home?"
That set me thinking, for I am at home among all nations and
this little earth doesn't seem as large as my native town did
once. Arriving in Shanghai it seemed like home, I had been there
so many times. Just before we reached there, outside the Saddle
Islands, we had a terrific gale of wind. We spent all night under
two lower topsails, with continuous lightning but no thunder.
My old pilot Knott was in an English mail-boat, and he called
it a typhoon, said they were hove to all night and he was on the
bridge with the captain, a young man, till it moderated in the
morning. I was within fifty miles of the steamer so she could not
have had it much harder than we did, but it was nothing compared to the one we had in the Pacific in the *Coringa*.

We took mud ballast for Iloilo and loaded a full cargo of sugar
there for Boston, which we reached in good season. As an illustra-
tion of the difference between the Japanese and the Filipinos—in
Nagasaki I could dischage my 300 tons of ballast easily in one
day, while in Iloilo I never got it out in less than a week.

The ship's fifth voyage was again very similar—case oil from
Bayonne to Shanghai, mud ballast to Nagasaki, and coal to Hongkong. Then I took a cargo for the Chinese to Cebu in the Philippines and sugar from there to Boston.

While in Nagasaki this time Mrs. Smith gave me a kitten, one
of thirty in their backyard, all descended from the cat that was
on their ship when she was condemned there. This kitten became
very attached to me and was in the ship three years or more. He
was very clever and was the only cat I ever saw who could catch
Cape Pigeons as they swirled down to him off the Horn. I think
he attracted them, for he was mottled like a pigeon. Perhaps they
wanted to know what species he belonged to. Anyway, if they
came within four feet of him they were gone. Eventually he was
lost overboard.

Cebu is a nice place and I always enjoyed being there. Like
all parts of the Philippines everything was going to decay
under Spanish rule, the officials making all the money they could
during their limited time in office. There are four large churches
or cathedrals and each has a chime of bells. It seemed as though
one of them was ringing all the time. Many millions of people
must have travelled up their steps for the stones are worn down
several inches by the constant tread of the bare-footed worship-

pers. I remember once seeing a thousand mothers with their babies being baptised, or sprinkled. They had waited until a certain bishop could perform the act. It was here that Magellan, the first man to bring his fleet round South America, and so round the world, was killed. He lost his life in some trivial affair on the island of Mactan, which makes the harbour of Cebu, in much the same way as Captain Cook lost his in the Sandwich Islands. I would like to go there once more, to note the changes since the United States took over the islands, where at that time we were only just allowed to breathe. In those days a Spaniard hardly dared to go out of town the natives were so hostile. A friend of mine was in the only vessel in port at Cebu when the islands were captured. He went ashore and hauled down the Spanish flag, hoisting the Amercian flag in its place. I wonder someone did not shoot him.

Our sixth voyage was probably the last time I loaded a full cargo in Boston for Honolulu, and even so we took a part of the cargo, 10,000 cases of oil, on to Hongkong. It was an uneventful voyage out. From Honolulu to Hongkong we carried about a hundred Chinese passengers, the vessel furnishing only water and firewood while they brought their own food and did their own cooking. I never had one die, but heard of one vessel which lost several. The others paid the Mate to put the bodies in empty beef barrels, which were then put down the hold with the firewood. One of the barrels exploded from the gas generated inside it, and after that none of the Chinese would go down below for firewood, but had to hire the sailors to get it for them.

We had a hard time to get a crew in Hongkong owing to a strike of seamen, and I was fool enough, being the first ship ready to leave, to take anything I could scrape up, even sick men. The other captains said that if the first vessel took them it would break the strike and the rest would get a crew at the regular wages. The consequence was that I had two men sick with cholera and had to go into quarantine at Iloilo, where I loaded sugar for New York. But for the fact that I bribed the doctor with $100 I would have had to sail up to Mariveles, near Manila, which would have meant at least a month's detention. In beating into Iloilo we carried away our main topgallant yard, but had plenty of time while in quarantine to repair all damage. There were quite a number of vessels in the port with us and we used to go across the bay to Negros Island for picnics.

We arrived in New York on a Friday. My officers lived in Boston and naturally wanted to go home to their families, having been away a year. Our crews have to be paid off before the Commissioner and I asked him if I might give them their money and let them go, explaining how hard it was for them either to wait until next week or go to a good deal of expense travelling back and forth. He said very crossly that he would pay them off next week in a tone which made me reply angrily, " You do not pay my crew off." " That is the law of the United States," he said. " I beg your pardon, Sir, the law says they shall be paid off in your presence." " Well you shall pay them off." " When?" " This afternoon at one o'clock." He thought he had me, for it was already ten o'clock, but when he found me ready at the specified time he changed completely, paid them off himself in about fifteen minutes, and my officers got home after all. Sometimes one gains by getting mad a little. I notice that nowadays the captains all pay their own crews in New York, and in my opinion the crews would be better off if that were the case in all United States ports.

This was Mr. Pendleton's last voyage as Mate with me. He later commanded the barques *Martha Davis* and *Amy Turner* and is now an Insurance Broker in New York.

Mr. Haskil was the Mate on the ship's seventh voyage. We loaded at Fly Island for Hongkong direct and experienced the usual weather until, down in the South Indian Ocean, we met a terrific Easterly gale and were hove to with our starboard side completely under water all one night. Towards morning we kept away to the eastward as the wind had veered from North East to North West and moderated. It was not quite a hurricane with us, though no doubt we were on the edge of one, and we carried the main lower topsail all night. Another time I would furl it though, for it only made the ship dive into the head sea, washing away our jibs through plunging the jib-boom under as we luffed up when the wind hauled.

On sounding the pumps we found four feet of water in the hold, so got up steam on the donkey-engine and pumped her out by steam while the crew were bending new jibs. We found the water had gone down the air strake under the topgallant forecastle. It was a common practice, in ships built about that time, to leave an air strake for ventilation, no one supposing water could get up there. I had mine all closed up tight after that experience. Had the gale lasted a few hours more the *John D. Brewer* would have been among the missing vessels and no one would have known the cause. Both the *Annie W. Weston* and the *Foohng Suey* took a lot of water on different occasions in the same way, which makes me think that many of our missing vessels have gone down from similar causes which were not discovered in time.

From this time to Sunda Strait we had normal weather. I usually passed between St. Paul and Amsterdam Islands. On the former, they say, are hot springs of boiling water, so close to the shore that you can catch a fish in the sea and, without taking it from the hook, turn round with your rod and hold it in the boiling water until cooked! I suppose there are submarine volcanoes in the South Indian Ocean, for the sea water will often change its temperature many degrees in a few hours.

We loaded in Hongkong for Cebu and on approaching through the northern entrance we got aground. It was night time, but fortunately there was no damage, only one sheet of copper torn from the bottom of the shoe. It was low water, so we hove her off with a kedge as the tide rose. We loaded sugar for home.

Back in Boston, Mr. Charles Macdonald of Novia Scotia joined us as Mate for the ship's eighth voyage. We part loaded there, then towed to New York to finish, being bound around the Horn to Honolulu and from there going on across the Pacific to Manila with 10,000 cases of the oil loaded at Boston.

A young man named John Measury joined us as an Ordinary Seaman at Boston, but his grandfather, who was a very rich man in New York, made some arrangement with the owners for him to live in the cabin. He proved a very capable fellow. Later, in Manila, he wanted to leave the ship, but his grandfather would not agree to it so he continued the voyage, being made an Able Seaman on the way home. I don't think he ever went to sea again until after he had studied and become a doctor. Then he made several cruises in his own vessel with Mr. Charles Macdonald as his sailing master.

In Honolulu a Mr. Goodale joined us as a passenger for the rest of the voyage, and I found him a very pleasant companion.

He had suffered poor health and after leaving Yale College had come out to Honolulu round the Horn in one of Brewers' ships. There he had a very varied experience, having been a tutor to the Royal Family of Hawaii, a Collector of Customs, and manager of a plantation. During the American Civil War he had served as a private in the Northern Army. Later he had married and brought his bride out to Honolulu round the Horn. Now he wished to complete his circuit of the globe so came with us, bringing several trunks and boxes filled with his life's correspondence. After reviewing this he threw it overboard, keeping only a few of the most valuable letters including one from Abraham Lincoln. He taught me to play chess, of which he was very fond, and I proved an apt scholar.

From Manila we went to Iloilo and loaded sugar for Sandy Hook for orders. On the way home the Second Mate, a young Scotsman from Glasgow, fell from the fore topgallant yard to the deck, landing on his head and being killed instantly. Among his effects were several letters, all without an address, one to his mother, one to his sister, etc. Possibly the British Consul was able to trace his folks. About $300 was due to him, which was paid to the Government. Every man that ships on the articles has to give the address of his relatives, but there are always one or two men and sometimes an officer, who have no one, and in the event of their being lost their pay goes to the Government. After the Second Mate's death some of the men were afraid to keep a lookout on the forecastle, said they saw his ghost.

We arrived off the Delaware Capes in November. Having had a South East gale, and the wind having come round the right way, with a mild-looking sunset, I felt sure of a fine day. There were a lot of schooners around and we were all steering for New York, but next morning the wind backed to the South East and about ten o'clock it came out of the North East, beginning to blow hard without any warning. So suddenly did it come on that we clewed up all the sails down to lower topsails before we furled even the royals, and none too soon. Later in the day we furled the forelower topsail and were hove to. I never remember so severe a gale coming on without warning, with the barometer steady at 30.00 inches indicating the finest weather. Next morning we had not only several schooners in sight but two steamers were hove to near us. After sunrise it moderated and we all commenced to make sail. In the course of the day we saw four schooners which had lost their jib-booms. A day later we arrived off New York and towed up to Staten Island, only to be ordered to Philadelphia. Mr. Goodale went around with us. He bought me a book of Hoyle's Games as a parting present. I never saw him again for he died a short time later in Honolulu.

We took a Philadelphia pilot in New York, and with a Baltimore tug-boat started for our destination. On the day following we were towing up the Delaware, a fine day with the wind South East. We had set our sails to dry them and as we were well into the river, with the pilot in charge, I lay down to take a nap. I had had little rest for several days. Coming out on deck an hour later I saw a very nasty-looking squall coming down from the North West. I called all hands, and with the pilot at the wheel began to clew up our sails. There were twenty schooners in sight, with all sail set. It seemed to me they must be crazy, for they not only had to let everything go with a run but they had to let go both anchors, and even that hardly held them against this terrific squall. To make it worse the hailstones cut so that one could not face it and the men's hands were cut badly. For two hours our tug could only just hold us against the wind. Then it moderated, but cleared up freezing cold. As we towed up the river we passed schooner after schooner with their gaffs aloft and the sails blown away, only the rope remaining, and one barque with both his anchors down. He told me afterwards how he was below and the pilot in charge or he would not have been caught. I had to stand watch most of the night for the pilot had to go on board the tug. Her captain was a Baltimore man and a stranger in the Delaware. We were the only sailing vessel to reach Philadelphia that night. I found my family in the port awaiting my arrival.

After discharging our sugar we loaded a cargo of coal and proceeded in tow for Boston. I shipped a full crew by the run, and my wife and daughter and her cousin went around with us. We had hardly got out of the Delaware when a heavy Easterly gale came on and the tug had to take us into New York. I spent a most anxious night, keeping reefed topsails on the barque till we were up to Sandy Hook, and was relieved to get into the smooth waters of New York harbour. It was a Sunday, and as we towed through the Narrows the Customs boat tried to stop us, but we did not want him for anything so paid no attention to his signals. Proceeding on through the East River we anchored near Hart Island while the tug went back for more coal as the gale was ahead. We remained at anchor all day Monday, the revenue cutter anchoring near us. Next day, the wind having moderated, we towed as far as Vineyard Haven, where we anchored for another day as there was still a big sea on the shoals. We had no sooner dropped our anchor this time than the revenue cutter which had followed us from New York came near and lowered a boat, which came alongside. As we were not expecting visitors we had no ladder handy and they had to wait some time for us to get it out. Eventually a young officer came on board, demanding in a very short manner to see our papers. I invited him into the cabin, but he would not sit down. When he saw we were from Philadelphia he was greatly surprised. They had been chasing us thinking our intention was to get rid of some smuggled goods in Vineyard Haven. They were so sure that we were from China, with our bright yards and masts, that they did not even hail us and ask where we were from, which would have saved them a lot of trouble. A day or so later we towed to Boston and discharged our coal at the Cunard Wharf.

Voyage nine saw a new Mate in the ship. He was Mr. Turner, who came from the *South American,* one of the finest and fastest American sailing ships of the day, which had just been a total loss on the South African coast near Cape Agulhas. It seems she sailed ashore with a South East wind, going about as fast as she could, and though they saw Cape Agulhas light the captain took it to be the light of a steamer they had seen during the day. According to the Mate's account he told the Second Mate when he went on deck at 8.0 p.m. that the ship would be ashore before midnight on the course she was steering. "Why didn't you tell the captain so?" I asked him. "Oh, no one could talk to that captain." I thought to myself that it would be a curious captain that I would not tell if I thought the ship was going ashore. A cast of the lead would have told them at once. I would have thought the captain had run her ashore on purpose if she had not been a fine new ship, and if he had not also had his wife on board. Several of her crew were drowned in trying to reach the shore. Her captain told me later there must have been a big current which set them to the northward. My own idea is this. At the Cape of Good Hope the compass variation is about two points. On my charts of this area one has a magnetic compass rose and the other a true compass rose. I think that perhaps when he changed from the Indian Ocean chart to the South Atlantic chart he forgot to allow for the variation and so was steering two points more north than he intended. I have made the same mistake more than once, but always found it out in time.

Mr. Turner was a good sailor, but coming from a big ship thought he had nothing to learn from a small barque. I soon showed him that he was very deficient, not only about sailor-ising but especially in navigation, and he soon learned his lessons. He was always so cocksure he was correct, no matter how many mistakes he made.

After loading part of our cargo in Boston we towed to New York and finished loading for Honolulu. Going again around Cape Horn to Honolulu, we discharged all but 10,000 cases of oil, which we took to Manila. Here Mr. Turner made a mistake in tallying out the oil, but I discovered it in time and a few dollars to the Customs officials made it all right. Proceeding to Iloilo we again loaded a full cargo of sugar for New York. According to Mr. Turner's accounting I had signed Bills of Lading for more than we had on board, but going over his figures we found his mistake and rectified it. However, his most serious mistakes were made on the passage home. Off the Brazilian coast we were running before the South East trades with square yards and studding sails set and a bright full moon in the sky. He called me in great trepidation with " There is a ship running us down." Of course I flew on deck. " She's on the lee bow, sir," said the man at the wheel. Seeing her red light I said " Put your wheel down." " Helm is hard down, Sir," and there we were already, all aback, lying helpless. Instead of getting out of the way of a ship on the wind the Mate had deliberately hove to under her bows. Any Cape Cod boy brought up in a boat would have known better what to do. The other ship passed so close to us that you could have thrown your hat on board. Not a word was said by either ship and I would have been ashamed to let her know what vessel we were.

Again, near Nantucket Shoals a steamer was reported right ahead. It was four o'clock in the morning, all hands were aloft furling the mainsail, and the Mate was forward watching the steamer's light. She came straight for us, and as she began to get close Mr. Turner yelled to me " Hard down, hard down," and

K

almost went crazy because I kept the ship on her course, Full and By, just a little closer to reduce our headway. She did come very close and almost ran us down, and I did give them a tongue-lashing, but here was our Mate, who had been mate of a fine ship for several years, did not know the Rule of the Road. No wonder the *South American* was lost.

On the passage home I changed the swinging bed in my cabin into a stationary one, which left a space that could only be reached by taking out the bed, springs, and boards—an ideal place for hiding anything one wished to smuggle. We arrived in New York on a Saturday and I had to go to Boston that night, leaving Mr. Turner in charge. Just before starting on my journey I went on board the barque at Brooklyn to make sure all was well. Mr. Turner met me on the wharf, much excited, saying, " There are three Customs officers on board. They are in the cabin. I don't know if I have done right, but there was a bottle of gin in the locker and I let them have it." That was all right, and I found them having a delightful time with the gin, and they greeted me warmly. I asked them if they wanted to look in my room, for I was going home. " Oh, no we don't want to look at all when we are treated as well as we are here." So I went to Boston, returning on Tuesday. Going to my room I noticed the bed was tumbled, and not smooth as I had left it. I called the Mate, " Who has been in my room?" " No one, Sir." " Then how come my bed tumbled up?" " Oh, that was done by the Customs officers last Saturday. When they first came on board they went straight to your room, took the bed off, took out the springs, and looked in that hole the carpenter made." Had I known this on Saturday I would have probably talked differently to them. Someone had taken pains to inform the Customs House that I had built a place for smuggling.

There used to be a well-known ship-keeper in Boston called Mike Donahue, sometimes known as Clothes Pin Mike and sometimes as Stove Pipe Mike on account of two occasions when he had been very quick-witted over helping two captains of newly arrived ships to smuggle ashore a box of cigars and a roll of silk respectively.

For our tenth voyage Mr. Macdonald was back in the ship as Mate, and this was his last trip with me. He has been a captain for many years now. We loaded case oil at Bayonne for Shanghai, then mud ballast to Cebu, and finally a full cargo of sugar to Philadelphia. I can think of no incident on the voyage worth mentioning, though we must have grown a year older.

While we lay discharging in Philadelphia there arrived in New York two new vessels just off the stocks, built in Scotland. One of them was owned in Novia Scotia and a Captain Macdonald had her this first voyage. He made a very quick passage to Shanghai. I think he only made one more trip in her and then was lost overboard in the Shanghai river. The other was a barque of 2,100 tons, the largest three-masted barque I ever saw. Her mizzen mast, a single stick, was too tall to go under the bridge at Brooklyn. Both ships came over from Scotland in sixteen days and one heard every day what wonderful sailors these two vessels were but on my way to Shanghai the following voyage I passed the barque in the China Sea.

The *Helen Brewer* was also built in England at this time, and sailing a few days later than the other two was forty days coming across. She was a most unfortunate vessel, though very costly for her size. To begin with, just as she was finished and while in the hands of both builders and owners, for she was paid for, but the owners had not yet received any Bill of Sale, both parties had her insured. The owners had their Captain Newell and the Mate on board and the builder had their ship-keeper there too. During a gale she parted her stern fasts and she swung off the quay, her keel touched the bottom, and she turned completely over, filled, and sank. It cost half what she was worth to get her up and rig her again, for all her rigging was condemned except the lower masts. After her slow passage across the Atlantic I saw her lying at Staten Island as I went to sea and she was certainly a beauty. Her first voyage was with oil to Hongkong. When they got outside Sandy Hook she was so crank they threw over part of the cargo, and when they got down south they jettisoned some more. Then they got among the ice and lost a man overboard. She passed through Bali Strait, then off the east coast of Luzon in a typhoon she lost sails and had to cut away her topgallant masts. Going by way of San Bernardino Strait to Cebu she lay there a month, then towed to Manila, but had to stop on the way and get another tug. From Manila, where her cargo was sold, she towed to Hongkong, and there was another big insurance job. She had a long passage home.

On her second voyage Captain Mahaney took her, and in the

Shanghai river she took the bottom and had to dock, but was undamaged. On her third voyage Captain Mahaney got her ashore in Formosa Channel, but by good luck and skill and throwing cargo overboard got her off and to Shanghai and then home. On her fourth voyage a French man-of-war ran into her off Woosung and cut her bows off. She was at anchor, but just getting under way, with two tugs alongside. Here was not only another insurance job but a long lawsuit to decide who was at fault, the French warship claiming she was not exhibiting the proper lights. She lost a fine charter and had to go to Java and take a poor one. I only remember one voyage that she did not have trouble, the Mate had her that voyage. On her return Captain Mahaney took her again, went to Java and loaded for home in Surabaya, but she was never heard of again after she sailed. The captain had his wife with him.

The Mate on our eleventh voyage was a very uneducated man whose name I forget. Had anything happened to me I am sure he could not have navigated the vessel to port. We loaded with oil at Bayonne for Shanghai and this was the last time I ever loaded at Bayonne and the last time I saw my old Captain Seymour, for he only lived about a year longer. It was also my last visit to Shanghai. Down in the South Atlantic we had the misfortune to carry away our main lower topsail yard while running before a heavy gale, but four days later we had another one up. Then I had a terribly sore right hand, so swollen that all my fingers seemed as one. For four days and nights I could not sleep for the pain, the steward changing the poultices every four hours. Then at last it broke and I nearly fainted. It was a month before I could hold a pen and a year before it was back to normal.

In the lower part of the China Sea, sailing straight up that sea before the South West monsoon, near the Anamba Islands we overtook the large English barque that was supposed to sail so fast. We were then 85 days out and towards dark saw what we took to be a brig ahead, but next morning we could see it was a large barque. We kept gaining, although the winds were very light. She looked like an old vessel she was so rusty, but when we got within hailing distance I found it was the same barque they had talked about so much in New York, which had come from Glasgow in 16 days. At noon we were close to her, and I hailed,

"Where are you from?" "New York." "Where are you bound?" "Shanghai." "How many days are you out?" "One hundred and twenty." Then he hailed me, "Where are you from?" "New York." "Where are you bound?" "Shanghai." "How many days are you out?" "Eighty-six." "You will beat all the fleet." "No, the *Mary L. Stone* has beaten me already by four days to Anjer." "What kind of weather did you have running down your easting?" "I had too much wind." "I didn't get enough. This vessel wants plenty of wind." As the wind was very light I sheered off and we wished each other a pleasant voyage. Two hours later the monsoon became strong and by nightfall I could just see his topgallant sails astern, so the breeze did not help him. I reached Shanghai about a week ahead of him. Many vessels have the name of being fast sailers when they only happened to have a good chance once.

We took a pilot outside the Saddles, and immediately it began to blow from the North West, lasting several days. The pilot boat sought a harbour to leeward somewhere, and as we had taken the last pilot only her Chinese crew were left on board. At the harbour where she took shelter the natives took the boat, and after robbing her they destroyed her. I believe the Chinese Government had to pay for her as she was owned by Americans, and I presumed there was some more decapitating.

I had quite a lot of trouble with pilots at Shanghai this time, having five of them before I got to sea. When the barque was ordered up to Tungkadou to discharge I went into the billiard-room of the Astor House Hotel to tell my pilot, who was a partner of the one who had brought me in from sea. He was half full, and when I asked him to order the tugboat he said he was not going to do any damned coolie work. "Well I will get a pilot who will do coolie work," and I went to another party who, after some demurring, consented to pilot the vessel. However, when the tugs came alongside the man that had refused to order the boats was with them and was coming on board to take charge, but I would not allow him to board the vessel. Then he sent in his bill, which I refused to pay. The Harbour-master wanted to know the reason, so I told him about the pilot refusing to do "coolie work" and added that he was probably drunk at the time. Then he said, "You captains are always talking about drunken pilots, but you don't dare put it in writing." He went on to tell me of the time the American Minister had decided against him, and when I told him I was the captain concerned he was determined I should pay this time. I told him, " If this pilot wants his reputation in the papers he shall have it." He found I didn't scare worth a cent, and as he was an American himself from New Bedford, Mass., I have thought since that he was only talking for effect. He said I would have to pay it, but I did not. Now people said I must not go near the Astor House as I would be attacked. There was not the least danger of this, for I had as many friends as enemies and was quite fearless myself. Had I not been I think something might have happened to me. I have always noticed that no one cares to attack man or boy if they are fearless, but if they run they will chase them.

We were ordered to take ballast and proceed to Colombo. As this was a new route to me I went on board the steamer *Bokharah* to discuss the best way to get there, via Malacca Strait or out through Sunda Strait. She was a regular trader. Her Chief Officer very kindly gave me all the information in his power. We got to talking about crews and he told me they only carried Indian crews, mostly Hindus. He said the European crews were always drunk in port but there was never any trouble with the native, or Calashee crews, as they called them. Just then the Third Officer came to the door and said, " I wish you would come and see if you can get these men out of the forecastle. They have been in there half an hour now and won't come out for me." " All right, all right, I'll attend to them in a minute." I did not think much of their good discipline and wondered what they would call poor!

On the way down the China Sea I ran through Formosa Channel before a heavy gale of wind from the North, part of a typhoon. We kept reefed topsails and a reefed foresail on the *John D. Brewer* and ran out of it, finding it flat calm with a heavy northerly swell by the time we were down to Pratas Shoals. I think we must have escaped the worst of it, for the same steamer *Bokharah* was lost in Formosa Channel. She became unmanageable and ran ashore on Sand Island. The Captain and a great many of the crew and passengers were lost, including a number of Army officers from Hongkong who had been up to Shanghai for a cricket match. The Mate was saved and I have often wished I could see him again to get particulars. It seems to me that a magnificent steamer of many thousands of tons like the *Bokharah* ought to come safely where a small sailing vessel does, and I have thought perhaps he might have done so had he had some of those drunken English sailors instead of his Calashee crew.

I had one passenger for Colombo, a Shanghai pilot. After a forty day passage we arrived on a Saturday evening and next morning our cabin boy, who had been begging to go in swimming, was given permission. It was his first voyage and on the passage out he had wanted to go in swimming when it was calm, but I always forbid anyone to go in at sea on account of sharks and other big fish. After breakfast this Sunday morning, as the passenger and I were getting ready to go ashore, we heard a great commotion on deck and sounds of distress. We ran on deck half-dressed to see the cabin boy bobbing up and down in the water, and each time his head came up he would say, " I can't swim." I threw him a rope and with the passenger's assistance pulled him to the gangway, none the worse for the experience. It turned out that he had never been in water over his head before, so it was lucky he did not go in at sea.

During our stay at Colombo this time in 1892 I received the bad news of my wife's death, so of course I can never think of the place without sadness. Part of our cargo was loaded here, then we sailed up to Cochin for the remainder. The latter is a very interesting place. It has been held by many nations and again and again the pirates of old times have captured it. Our cargo consisted of coconut oil in large casks, some of them weighing two tons, and black lead or plumbago. The small spaces were filled with coir mats made from the fibre of coconut husks. In the factories where the mats are made you can see thousands of women, their babies beside them, working from sunrise to sunset for five cents a day. There is a large colony of Jews at Cochin, who are the fishermen of the place. They claimed this was where the Queen of Sheba came from, and it may well have been so. We had a pleasant passage home to New York.

For the ship's twelfth voyage, which was with case oil to Batavia, Mr. Turner was back again as Mate. The run out was normal, except that when in the South Indian Ocean and carrying sail rather hard the ship gave an unexpected lurch, causing me to fall heavily against the corner of the cabin table, damaging my ribs. It took me a year to get over it completely.

We arrived at Batavia in company with the English ship *Trafalgar,* also from New York with oil. At this port the vessels lie at anchor some two miles from the shore, and crews are not allowed ashore on account of malaria, or Java fever. The Captain usually goes ashore, using a native boat, when the sea breeze sets in about ten o'clock in the morning. On the morning of our arrival I was about to go ashore with the pilot when an old bamboo raft floated by. The Mate thought he could make use of it for scrubbing around the hull so a rope was bent on it, but no sooner had a couple of men got on it than it was alive with snakes. Such a yelling those men made for ropes to climb back aboard! Needless to say, they did not care to go swimming in those waters and there was no fear of anyone swimming ashore for a lark, though I guess these snakes are harmless as I never heard of anyone being bitten.

On reaching the shore the captain takes the steam cars to the hotel, several miles away and said to be above the malaria. He remains there until the following morning, and if he has any business to attend to he takes a horse and buggy, known as a " Docedoe." In the morning, after a cup of coffee and an egg, the train takes him back to the mouth of the canal (the Dutch are fond of canals). There his native boat, or *Tambanga,* is waiting to take him off to the ship, where he can get another breakfast if he wants one. After seeing that all is in good order on board, with his cargo going out all right, and looking at the sick men if any, he goes ashore again with the sea breeze, takes the train up to the hotel or his docedoe to his agents. In any case he is back at the hotel by twelve o'clock for " tiffin ", as lunch is called. They have an appetiser composed of gin and bitters which they call a *pite.* Most people take two, and then nearly everybody has a bottle of claret. The table is set out of doors in the shelter of the hotel and is long and narrow. There is a waiter to each guest, who washes the dishes just behind him as he removes them. Of course the principal dish is curry, but it hardly seems the same dish as is called curry in America. Here at least twenty condiments and a dozen dishes of fish, meat, and fowl, all cooked in the finest style, are eaten with the rice and curry. It is certainly an ideal lunch, but this is only tiffin, at noon. Afternoon, or after a smoke, people sit on the veranda for a time, some few go to their offices for an hour or so, then everybody takes a siesta. About four they begin to come out of their nests and go for a bath.Then they sit around, or go on the veranda where all the silks and curios of India, China, and the East are spread out by the natives of the various countries, and where sleight-of-hand performances and snake charmers may be seen and watched, all free unless one cares to give them a few cents. A little later everybody puts on their best clothes, and when the sun has gone down they go to the Park, where the band is playing and the whole city goes. The ladies wear no covering for the head but dress their hair to the best advantage. About seven o'clock everyone goes home to dinner, which is the principal meal of the day. Rice and curry is still to be had, with about a dozen other courses, and the meal always ends with coffee. After dinner anything is in vogue, most people go back to the Park, and gradually about midnight everybody drifts back to their nests. Now this is good fun for a week or two, but must get monotonous after a few years.

So long as you keep your men on board in Java you will have no sickness, and it is well to keep them out of the sun as much as possible. I know some masters and mates think this is foolishness and I have known many who have lost their own lives by being so foolish as not to take proper precautions. The hotel for captains costs four guilders, or $1.60 per day. Now this time the captain of the *Trafalgar* would not employ a boat from the shore and would not go to the hotel. He said it was too expensive. He was a man as old as I was, or I would have presumed to advise him. First his crew got sick, going ashore in the boat. Then he got sick and died. The Mate took command, but died before she sailed, and a new captain took her but died before they reached Sydney. One of the apprentice boys navigated her into port, for which he received a present from the owners. Nearly all the crew died in Batavia, and all because the captain allowed the crew to go ashore and did not go up to the hotel himself. In other words, he did not take proper precautions. I have made about seven voyages to Java and never had a man die there. My cook got cholera in Surabaya once, but he died in Singapore from his own carelessness later.

We took part of our cargo to Lossum, another port on the north side of Java, and after discharging there took ballast on board and returned to Batavia. From there we were ordered to Cebu, where the only other vessel in port was the *Mary L. Stone*. George Josselyn commanded her and it seemed kind of homelike for us to be together again, as we had been together as boys in the barque *Sicilian* for a year. One day we both wrote a letter to our old captain, James H. Dawes of Kingston, Mass., who had retired for several years.

We loaded sugar for Boston and arrived in good time without incident.

At the commencement of this voyage, while we were loading in New York, John Measury came on board to see me, and of course he was glad to see the ship in which he had made a long voyage four years before. He was a doctor now, or had been studying medicine for some years, I don't know that he ever practised. Unfortunately his parents were dead and his grandfather a rich man, so I guess John felt no call to go to work. He wanted to know if I would take a boy that was wild. Well, I took him, though it was only by the skin of his teeth that he got aboard just as we were hauling out from the wharf. This boy was about sixteen and had never done anything in his life but play. His father was dead and a doting grandfather cared for him. As they came down the wharf John made him take off his gloves, telling him the sailors would laugh at him. The first work he ever tried to do was to haul in the iron mooring chains with his baby hands, a job that will test the toughest. But for all his innocent appearance he could give the sailors points on evil. Turner was a hard Mate. He taught him to furl a royal, although he had never tried to climb in his life, but unlike John Measury, he did not like the work.

When we reached Lossum he came to me and said he was not going to work any more. I told him that in that case he would have to go in irons. He replied that he had understood that if he did not like to be a sailor he could come in the cabin as a passenger (there had been some such talk). I told him I would telegraph his mother and if she said so I would take him as passenger, but he must go to work until we received a reply. As he would not work I confined him in a spare stateroom but did not put him in irons. After four days he got tired of bread and water and concluded it was easier to work on deck. In the meantime a despatch came saying that he must remain in the forecastle.

On the Sunday before we left Lossum I permitted him to go ashore with the carpenter, but I never saw him again. He must have had some money and bribed the police, for he went to Surabaya. After I got back to Batavia the police reported to me that a young man in Surabaya, who gave his name as John Measury, was on board the steamer going to Singapore. I knew it must be my boy, but as I was on the point of sailing I told them it was not, and I heard not another word of him till we reached Boston. There I happened to go on board a ship commanded by a friend of mine which had just arrived from Singapore. I asked him if he had seen my boy there. He said " No, but I had quite an experience with a young American there. He was from Surabaya too, said he was travelling with a friend who left him and went up to China, unfortunately taking his draft and leaving him destitute. I took him on board this ship and he was here for a couple of weeks, I guess. But he was not content to remain on board the ship, he wanted me to take him to the Club every day, and I could not afford that. So he went ashore, where the missionaries gave him some kind of job, but after working for them for a spell he suddenly disappeared with considerable money that belonged to the Society and they never found him. The night he left me my Chinese steward deserted, taking $75.00 of my money. I never found him and afterwards I thought it more likely this boy had taken it, for he knew where it was kept and the steward did not." " What was his name?" " John, John something, I forget now." " Was it John Measury?" " That's it, That's it. How did you know?" " Why, that was my boy. You ought to have taken him as a sailor, he could furl a royal as well as the next one."

A few days after this conversation a young man who professed to be his friend asked me about him, and I told him. Then I found this friend was his brother, so I really told him my opinion of the boy, one who would rob his best friend. He had come home in a tramp steamer from Germany, but they did not know how he had got there from Singapore. I had not heard the last of him yet. He had told the Mate he had been to Knapp's School in Duxbury, so one evening after church I asked some of the boys about him. At first they were reticent, but finally one of them told me that while he was at the school he had been the leader in a robbery of one of the houses in town, and had been forced to leave the school. Well, I am glad I have forgotten his name. He was certainly a rosy-cheeked darling who could win all hearts, and the last boy you would suspect of any offence. Is it any wonder that sea captains don't care to take boys? No one ever tells of their faults till after the voyage, then they wonder how you got along with them. It is certainly a splendid place for a bad boy, but who wants the job?

Mr. Farrell joined us as Mate for the thirteenth voyage. He was from Canada, of French descent. We loaded a part cargo of oil and filled up with general cargo for Port Elizabeth, Cape of Good Hope. A pleasant passage out was made doubly so by two young men passengers. Mr. Pray was just from Harvard College and he is now a teacher of landscape gardening there. We played a game of chess daily until he left at Port Elizabeth. The other, who was a minister's son, continued to Colombo, where he left to join his mother in the south of France. He used to entertain us with his mandolin.

While in Port Elizabeth we had a terrific South East gale. There is no harbour there and about a dozen vessels were at anchor in the open roadstead. This is my only experience of being in such a position and I thought we must go ashore, but we held on, pitching so hard that the vessels in ballast would heave their rudders completely out of water, so that you could see their keels nearly to the mizzen mast. We were all moored with both anchors, ninety fathoms of chain on each, and we also had springs on our chains made fast to our foremasts. Some even carried the hawser along to the mainmast. Of course the Harbourmaster had prepared us all for this kind of weather when we came to anchor. We also had a sixteen-inch coir hawser 120 fathoms in length bent on to our spare bower anchor in case we parted our chains. All held, though had the gale lasted another four hours all would have gone ashore, as they had several times in the past. I think this place will cease to be visited by vessels as soon as the communications ashore increase. The climate is beautiful, the finest oranges were cheap and plentiful, and I liked the people as well as the place, only I wish they might have a harbour before I go there again in a ship.

From here we went in ballast to Colombo to load a part cargo, then to Cochin, and finally to Alleppey to finish. Alleppey is some fifty miles to the south of Cochin on the west coast of India. Both ports are open roadsteads, but all the gales they get are strong monsoons. It is said of both that after a few hours of strong monsoon the sea becomes quite smooth where the vessels are at anchor, due to some oil that comes from the mud on the bottom, though farther out to sea it is rough with seas breaking. They also say that sometimes large shrimps or prawns cover the water for miles and can be baled up by the bucketful. There was only one vessel in Alleppey with us. I shall mention her master, Captain Shogren, again as he lost the *John D. Brewer* some two years later. We had a fine passage home to New York.

I now come to my fourteenth and last voyage in the *John D. Brewer*. Mr. Farrel was again the Mate, and it was my first experience of carrying lumber, which we loaded in Brooklyn for Buenos Aires.

Our passage to this port was very pleasant but rather long. Much to my surprise I found it to be a city of nearly one million inhabitants and larger than Boston. In many respects it reminded me of the Philippines, the same care being required to get along with the Customs people. Other experiences were different from those in any other port I have visited. In most ports of the world the Captain of a ship is treated with respect, but I never felt myself of so little importance as in Buenos Aires. In all my long experience as Master I never went to my consignee's office without being met by the head of the house or his representative and being invited to sit down while we had a little conversation in regard to the cargo, etc. Generally one is met by a clerk before one reaches the shore, who shows one the way to their office. But here I could find no one, and I finally hired a native to pilot me to the consignee's office, where I could not have been treated with less regard had I been a travelling salesman. Going up to a grated window I waited a long time before a clerk enquired what I wanted. I told him who I was and he replied, " All right " and disappeared. When I got tired of waiting and was seriously considering returning to my ship, to send them a written notice of my arrival and let them seek me out, another captain spoke to me. After introducing himself he said, " This is the fashion here. Don't mind it, this is the best House in Buenos Aires." So I sat down and waited, and in about an hour a gentleman came to talk to me. In spite of this same coolness all the time in the port I was well treated in other respects, and I have always wanted to go there again.

My usual good luck held, for I was the only ship in the port that was not fined. One captain was fined $100 for moving his ship without having a pilot on board. The pilot had got him aground coming into the Boca, so that he was blocking the channel and stopping vessels from going either way. When his ship floated in the night he moved her so that other ships could pass, but he was fined for it though he thought he was doing his duty. Another ship was fined because the steward threw a dead rat they had caught in a trap into the Boca. So, for one thing or another, nearly all were fined. It is a funny country. One time six captains were arrested and thrown into prison two days before anyone knew where they were. It seems they were in a horse-car and made some disparaging remarks about some soldiers they passed. There happened to be an officer in the car who understood them and he had them arrested and imprisoned. It was a serious matter too. Of course I only heard one side of the story. Since the American and British Consuls could not help them perhaps they were only getting their deserts.

After discharging our cargo of lumber we took ballast and went to Anjer, in Java, for orders, arriving there in about forty days. It was twelve years since that time I arrived here two weeks after the eruption of Krakatau in 1883. At that time there was nothing but bare rock at Anjer. Now all the thick vegetation was back, the coconut trees were bearing fruit, and from the house in which I stayed to await telegrams by day I could not see my barque at all for the tropical trees and shrubs which formed a dense jungle, except where there were roads.

After waiting several days we were ordered to Surabaya to load sugar again for Delaware Breakwater for orders. Again I was fortunate in Java and my crew escaped sickness. By the latter part of February we were nearing home, off Cape Hatteras, when we experienced a bad North East gale, carrying away our jib-boom guys and bowsprit cap and nearly losing the boom. We weathered the gale and a few days later took a tug for the Breakwater. Just as we were about to anchor there a steam launch brought off our orders for New York.

The wind had been South East but had hauled to South West and I looked for fine weather, but because my jib-boom was crippled I engaged a tug for New York. The tug captain did not know much about New York, but he too thought the weather would be fine so said he would take me if I would lend him my patent log. Hardly had we got outside when it began to blow hard from the South East, and that night at midnight off Barnegat I cast off the tug, knowing he was not acquainted with

New York, and stood out to sea. We carried sail hard for twenty-four hours and could only just hold our own in twenty fathoms of water, or twenty miles from shore. Then the South East gale died out and the wind came around to West. At Midnight on March 1st, we were close to Fire Island Light with the wind North West. It began to blow hard again and we took in all sail down to a Lower Main topsail. It did not cease blowing for three and a half days, and when it moderated at noon on the 4th, we were one hundred and fifty miles from Sandy Hook. On the first day of the gale it rained, then cleared off without a cloud in the sky. When we commenced to loose our sails they were red with mud. It must have blown off from the shore, and if they had been laid out on a ploughed field for the duration of the storm they could not have looked worse. Again we made sail, and this time reached our destination. It had taken us just a week from the Delaware Breakwater to New York, one of the hardest weeks of work and anxiety that I ever remember.

It makes me shudder now to think of it, and I must have been run down, for when we had discharged our sugar and towed down to Bayonne I was taken sick with double pneumonia. It was partly my own fault, for we hauled to Bayonne on a cold raw day and I wore a thin coat, to avoid soiling with tar a new heavy one I had. The next day I had to get a doctor to see me. When he found I had a temperature of 106F. he was worried and took me at once to hospital.

I never saw the *John D. Brewer* again. Captain Shogren, whom I had met in Alleppey a year earlier and who had lost the vessel he had at that time, was given command as he was acquainted with Zanzibar, where she was now going, but he lost her near Zanzibar. I think it was his last command.

CHAPTER EIGHT

In Seenie Hospital New York—To Glasgow for barque Highland Glen *in 1896—Renamed* Nuuanu *under Hawaiian flag—Barbados in ballast—Demerara, for sugar to New York —Honolulu—Kahului—New York—2nd voyage, Honolulu, bubonic plague outbreak and fire—3rd voyage, Honolulu, transfer to American flag—Laid up—Costal voyage to Savannah—4th voyage, Honolulu, Spanish War, back to Philadelphia—5th voyage, Honolulu, Delaware pilots, Philadelphia,* Tillie Starbuck, Thomas Lawson—6th voyage, New York, Honolulu, Turk and Lewis, Delaware pilots again, Philadelphia—7th voyage, New York, daughter Elizabeth a passenger, bad time off Cape Horn, return to New York from Honolulu, Russo-Japanese War—8th voyage, white frost, forty days rounding Cape Horn, five months in Honolulu, passengers—9th voyage, Jack Nichols, Ice off the Horn, Kanapali and Lahaina, good run home to New York—10th voyage, survey, leaking seam, fresh start, poor crew, Honolulu, schooner* Kenio—Ice again, New York.*

The period in hospital was something new to me, as I had lived for half a century in almost perfect health. I learned some wholesome lessons there, not the least of which was the ability to sympathise with the sick. For seventeen days I was kept still in bed and I think those seventeen days were longer than any year of my life. I did not worry about my ship or anything, but I wanted to be up and moving. The doctors and nurses were very good to me and I learned that I had lots of friends, more than

Captain Josselyn on board "Nuuanu" about 1910

I had ever realised. Many thought I was going to die, but I never thought so, even though they would not let me see my temperature chart or count my pulse.

Another lesson I learned was never to take advantage of a man's sickness to preach religion at him, when he can't answer back. The Seenie Hospital is also known as the Methodist Episcopal Hospital and the nurses were all members of that church, just across the street. On Sunday afternoons someone from the church used to come and preach to us, and they used to bring a number of young people to sing, with a piano kept in the ward for that purpose. I do not know how it affected the other patients but, when I was in agony with every breath I drew, it seemed like striking a man when he was down to send a company of young people in the best of health to sing to me, and a man to tell me about his ideas of religion when I could not answer.

After about a month there I was well enough to be taken to a private sanatorium, and after a further six weeks I went home to my native town to stay with my sisters. I felt well though weak, and I especially remember the day I reached home in the month of May. I spent a delightful summer out of doors, boating, driving, and fishing, and slowly regained my health, though I don't believe I was ever quite as strong as I was before being taken sick. In the meantime my barque, the *John D. Brewer* was lost at Zanzibar by the captain who took her out, so I had lost my wife, my ship, and my health, all in one year—two of them because I had not worn my new overcoat for fear of soiling it.

The summer at home passed all too quickly, and in the fall of 1896 I was called upon to go to Glasgow in Scotland to take charge of the barque *Highland Glen*, which had been bought by Brewers. Leaving the old Colonial town of Duxbury in December, I travelled on the liner *Lucania* from New York to Liverpool. We left New York one afternoon and it did seem good to get to sea again after nearly a year ashore. Our first evening at the supper table we were somewhere off Fire Island Light, and the *Lucania* was so quiet that except for a slight tremble we might have been alongside the wharf for all the motion there was. This was my first trip on an ocean liner, and always when I am in a new and unusual place I do little talking and study everybody else. No one at the table said a word, so after some time I expressed a thought that was in my mind, " Now I hope we will have a good

L

big storm." Well, there was enough talk after that. It was a long time before I could get a word in edgeways and if I'd fired a pistol they could not have looked at me in greater astonishment. At last when I got a chance I said, " I see you have all been praying for fine weather. Yet you may be making a mistake. The most dangerous thing we can have is fog, and fogs only come in the finest of weather. For over forty years I have travelled the ocean and I have seen it in all kinds of weather. But I was never on such a magnificent vessel as this, and though I can assure you no storm could harm her, and although there might be a little discomfort attached to it, I wanted to see how she would behave in rough weather." We got a storm all right, yet we made a very quick trip of only five days and some hours, and I certainly enjoyed it all. I was naturally all over the vessel and got acquainted with most people on board.

When we arrived at Liverpool I had not been there for thirty-five years, and the last time I had been Second Mate of the ship *Reynard*. On that occasion we were there only twenty-one days and it had rained all the time. When we arrived this time it was still raining, a quiet rain with little or no wind. I should have known it was Liverpool had I been brought there blindfold from the smell. I had to hunt for some time for my seven pieces of baggage but found them in time to catch the train for Glasgow. The cars could not compare with ours for comfort. Although it was winter the only heating was by iron water-bottles that were filled with hot water and occasionally changed at the different stations. I had to exert myself to make the people in the coach talk a little, but they were very kind and answered all my questions. It was a Saturday evening when I arrived in Glasgow and I stayed in the hotel at the railroad terminal. After supper I went out to buy a guide and chart of Glasgow, but did not stay out long as it was cold. The latitude of Glasgow is 56°, the same as Cape Horn. That night, and again on my way up Buchanan Street to church on Sunday morning, I was surprised to see so many of the poorer children going around barefooted in the middle of winter. At this time of year the sun does not rise until nine o'clock and there is not much daylight. That afternoon I took a trip down to the dock to see my barque, using the ferry over the little creek that is hardly worthy the name of river.

The *Highland Glen* was built by Ramage & Ferguson at Leith

in 1883. As I first saw her at a distance her appearance was not very prepossessing. Her masts were standing in all directions. I don't remember seeing any vessel in my life, especially a deep-water vessel, with masts stayed so outrageously out of place, though she was as fine an iron vessel as could be built, and of far better material than they are putting into ships at the present day. Going on board, I found her in the dirtiest condition, with no one on board but the ship-keeper, and he proved untrust-worthy. It looked a dreary prospect to get her in shape, but I had been ashore nearly a year and it was a pleasure to get back to work I was familiar with. My first job was to get a Mate, and I finally engaged a Scotsman who would have been a good man if he could have kept sober. I could have had my pick of officers if it had been for steam, no one wanted to go in a "wind-jammer". The Second Mate was also a good man but for the same failing.

It took ten days altogether to prepare the ship for sea. We were in ballast for Barbados and I took a pilot as far as Queenstown. This was my first experience of an iron vessel. I expected to find her hot in hot weather and cold in cold weather, but in practice found her no different from a wooden vessel in that respect. The greatest difference was that you did not have to keep pumping the ship out. From one year to the next there is no pumping to do, only you clean out the limbers in port once every two years or so. We had changed her name to *Nuuanu* and put her under the Hawaiian flag, registering her in Honolulu. Incidentally this was the last Hawaiian flag to be lowered, as I shall recount later. It took us about a month to reach Barbados, where we remained a week until I secured a charter to load sugar at Demerara for New York. During this time we had worked at the barque with all hands and she began to put on an appearance. I found she was a fine sailer on the wind, and now I can say I have not had a vessel beat her on the wind in thirteen years and have seen very few that could hold their own with her. The climate of Barbados was delightful, especially as we had just come from cold Scot-land. The most noticeable thing there was the excess of women to men. I was told they out-numbered the men by thirteen to one, all Negroes of course.

We took four days to Demerara, where I don't think my Mate had a sober day. For days he lay dead drunk in his room and had I been able to get anyone else I would have fired him. The

Second Mate kept sober and did all the work till towards the last, then he too was drunk.

Demerara seems to be a sailor's heaven. They were not allowed to work cargo or ballast, in fact did as they pleased, and when they were ready all but two of them took all their clothes and walked ashore. I went to the police about them but got little help. As there was no Hawaiian Consul I went to the American Consul who kindly took me under his protection and gave me a letter to the Chief of Police. I went to see him, and after waiting a long time was admitted to his presence. "Why didn't you come to me at first?" he demanded. Now if anything gets my dander up it's to have an official behind his desk and authority speak sharply to me, so I looked him in the eye and said, "I did go to the police and they told me to get a letter from my Consul, and that is the Consul's letter you have just read." When he found he could not frighten me and that my tongue was as sharp as his own, he said he would get the men for me and that I was to keep them in irons. "What! Keep the crew in irons in a British port? Just you give me that in writing and I will not trouble you again." I knew you could not put a sailor in irons in a British port, and I knew what they wanted too, an offer of a reward of $10.00 a man. But I would not give them or the sailors that satisfaction, so I let them go and shipped a new crew when the ship was loaded. I used to see some of my old crew every day, but the police said they could not find them.

Demerara reminded me very much of the East, for all the working population were from Calcutta. There is a fine museum containing some of the strangest fish I ever saw, monstrous sharks as big as a small whale. I had no idea they grew so large, but I have since read that some of the shark family grow to a length of sixty feet. As you can imagine, I did not have a very pleasant time with two drunken mates and a crew that did as they pleased. Some of them came into my cabin one night and I would have been justified in shooting them, but contented myself with firing my revolver into the air. I expected it would bring the police, but not one came. The only man in the ship I could trust was the cook.

I was glad when we got to sea and started for New York. I kept them at work all day till we arrived in twenty-one days. We had a heavy Westerly gale from the Delaware Capes to port, but carried whole topsails sharp on the wind, going ten knots and passing everything we saw till we took a pilot at Sandy Hook. He was a young man, but he handled the vessel so well that I asked him where he had learned to handle a sailing ship. He said he had spent four years whaling with his uncle, which accounted for his knowledge. Nowadays a great many of the pilots can only handle steamers. I was very pleased to pay off this crowd before the Hawaiian Consul and I have never seen one of them again although, believe it or not, that drunken Mate had the cheek to come round when we were loading to ask for another chance.

After discharging the cargo and doing some work to the barque I went home for a couple of weeks as they were not quite ready to start loading the next cargo. I had been gone just ninety days and as it was winter there was little change in the country village. In such a small town the General Store is like a Club House, where all the neighbours gather, especially on winter nights. So many people were glad to see me and asked me so many questions that I got tired of telling the story in pieces. Then we got the Minister to set an evening and I told them all the story of my trip to Glasgow, which was much enjoyed.

I returned to New York in time to get the *Nuuanu* in berth to load for Honolulu. We hauled from Brooklyn to Pier 18, East River. It was late when we came alongside, and after telling me to haul to the top of the Pier the man in charge went away. When we got to the head of the wharf I found the berth occupied by a number of lighters discharging sand. A big Irishman was in charge of the gang and he took me for an Englishman, as the vessel certainly looked English. Thinking he could bluff me, for they had no business in my berth, he told me to stop where I was. I told him politely that I was ordered to the top berth by the wharfinger, whereupon he became very abusive. I paid no attention, but hove the barque up till he had to move some of his lighters. Still taking me for the mate of an English vessel, and doubtless thinking it would amuse his gang to see an Englishman abused, his language grew worse and worse. When I was really close to him I said, "Oh, take that potato out of your mouth." For a moment he was surprised into silence, then "Pertater, pertater, pertater," each time louder and louder, "I'm an American, you come ashore and I'll lick you." I took out my watch and told him I'd be with him in ten minutes, just as soon as the ship was fast, and I was there on time, but he'd gone. Perhaps when he found he was not abusing an Englishman he thought he might be held accountable for his language, as I had plenty of witnesses.

I had a young man as Mate for two weeks, but just before we were ready to sail he had an offer to go away as Master. If he had warned me sooner I could have got another mate, but he never mentioned it until I came aboard Monday morning expecting to sail that day. Then he said he could not go and I had to take the first man that came along. He was a Mr. Martell and proved to be a very good man. He had spent several years in cable ships and could handle wire rigging fine. I think that was his last voyage to sea. He is a rigger in New York now and I always give him my work when in that port. The Second Mate was a good man too, but he only went as far as Honolulu. He was lost two years later in a ship which was on fire near San Francisco when spoken by an English ship, but never reached port as they had expected to.

We had a long passage of 152 days to Honolulu. We were loaded too stiff, and much deeper in the water than we load at present, though the ship behaved better than the one time she was too crank. Having a good crew we worked hard to make a passage, and we carried away a number of the lighter backstays and parted all the sheets except the lower topsail sheet. I could not always realise how hard I was carrying sail, for it did not affect an iron ship as it does a wooden one. I could have carried away the masts and it would not have affected the hull, apart from the falling and pounding alongside, whereas a wooden ship would wring and twist and show the strain by the pumps.

As usual in Honolulu the crew, incited by those sailor thieves ashore who make a living by preying on the poor sailors who think them their friends, wanted to leave. As I would not let them go they ran away. The police picked them up (for which they were paid) and kept them in gaol until I wanted them or they wanted to come on board. Just before Christmas about six of them returned to work, the ship lying at the reef waiting for cargo so that they could not get ashore again without a boat. On Christmas Day as I was going on board I met them all coming ashore in our scow (a scow is a little square box of a boat used in port for cleaning and painting the ship's bottom). I did not speak to them, but turned round and pulled ashore again and notified the police. The Mate was ashore at the time and only the new Second Mate, a young fellow of twenty-one, was on deck. The scow had been hanging astern, some of the crew had gone over the bows, swum astern to the scow and paddled it under the bows, then put their things in her and started for the shore just as I happened to come off. On seeing me they made for the other side of the harbour to land, but by this time the Second Mate saw them, hailed them to come back, and fired his revolver over their heads. They laughed at him, so he got into a passing steam launch and landed just behind them. He had his revolver and knew how to use it, for he had been a soldier in Honolulu for over a year and was quite a scrapper. As they refused to come back he followed them until they met the police and they went to gaol again until we sailed.

I had a good many arguments with Mr. Scott, the High School teacher, who seemed to think that sailors were abused. I admitted that they were, but not on shipboard. I told him that if I wanted their money I could easily get most of it by selling them rum at sea, just not giving them enough to make them intoxicated, but that I had only known one captain who did so, while wherever a ship goes a grog shop will be found as near to her as possible. I have many other arguments to the same effect. When he would say my ship was undermanned I would tell him that was all the more reason why I should take the best care of my men. Our very lives depend on these men and it is a master's first duty to his owners, to say nothing of the more selfish aim of his own safety, to see that they are in the highest state of efficiency. To this end they must be well cared for, kept in good spirits, fed well, and treated properly in every way. What would be thought of a carpenter who left his tools out in the rain? These sailors are our tools, without them we would be helpless. Of course, there are cases where sailors are abused, and plenty more cases where masters and owners are abused, but I think I can prove that as a class shipmasters are among the most reliable men in the world.

Another barque from New York, the *Adam M. Spies*, was also to load sugar home. She was later rigged as a schooner and lost on her first trip to the West Indies. One of us was to load in Hilo, the other in Kahului. I got my orders first and was sent to the latter place, much to the other captain's delight, for little was known of Kahului. However, I was agreeably surprised

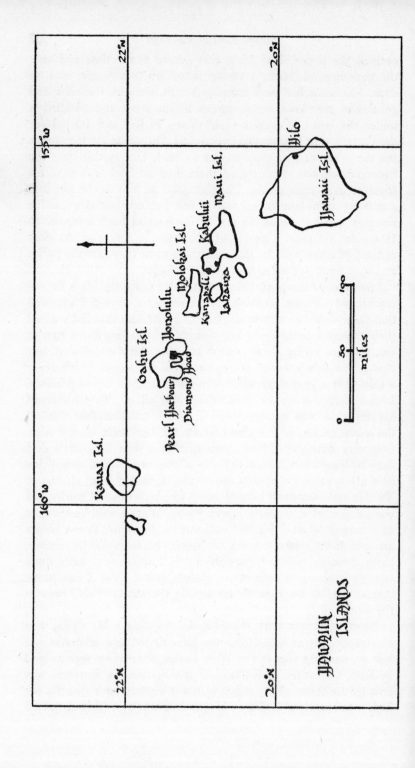

HAWAIIAN ISLANDS

Kauai Isl.

Oahu Isl.
Pearl Harbour Honolulu
Diamond Head

Molokai Isl.

Kanapali Kahului Maui Isl.
Lahaina

Hawaii Isl.
Hilo

miles
0   50   100

22°N
20°N
160°W
155°W

to find it a more desirable place than Hilo. It is on the northern, or windward side of the island of Maui, and is about sixty miles directly to windward from Honolulu. Following the advice of others I went round to leeward of Oahu, which was all wrong, as I have since beat up the other way many times. We had a fine set of sugar ballast and beat up in four days against exceptionally strong Trades. For more than two weeks the steamers could not land on the windward side of the islands and the first boat in, Captain Cameron, reporting the bad weather, said " The *Nuuanu* will be hove to under a lower main topsail." In fact I never had the upper topsails down, and furled the mainsail but twice, and in four days was safely at the buoys in Kahului. It is the only port on the north side of Maui and is connected to the sugar plantations by rail, also to the town of Wailuka. Just behind the harbour is the large extinct volcano of Halieacala and mountains rise ten thousand feet on either hand. A nice cool breeze from the North East Trades is always blowing.

You might have expected our sailors to be ugly after being so long in jail at Honolulu. On the contrary they seemed to enjoy the ship again. It was a kind of game they played, to get away from the ship. I had won the game, and they took it in good part. They made another mistake in their estimation of my boy Second Mate. To be sure he had not the experience of his predecessor and he tried to please everybody, as all new and young officers do, both at sea and ashore. Of course they took advantage of him, till one night one of the men aloft called him a bad name. When he came down on deck he took him to account for it. It was quite laughable the way the man took off his clothes, thinking to bluff the boy, but when he got down to his bare skin he did not dare to stand up to him, though he was twice the size of the Second Mate. I just happened to come on deck, and not finding the officer on the poop went forward to where he stood facing the whole crowd. The boy challenged any one of them but none cared to take him on. About a month later one of them tackled him, but got all he wanted and more. I am sorry I cannot remember his name. The last time I saw him he was editor of a newspaper in Williamsburg. He would have made a fine officer with a little more experience.

While in Kahului I wrote to Mr. Scott, the schoolmaster, telling him how happy and contented my crew had been from the time we went to sea and got away from the Land Sharks and Grog shops. We reached New York in one hundred and twenty days, and again I paid off my crew before the Hawaiian Consul.

It was not until our second voyage, that I managed to discover the meaning of the word *Nuuanu*. I knew, of course, that it was the name of what used to be the principal street in Honolulu, where all the finest houses were in the days before annexation to the United States caused the city to expand into many fine streets and buildings. I asked several residents the meaning of the word, but although they were born there and spoke the Hawaiian language they could not tell me. One day I asked a kanaka, or native, who was working in the stevedore's gang. He divided the word into two parts, one meaning *cold* and the other meaning *place,* then said " A cold place." I knew at once he was correct, for the Nuuanu Valley is the coldest place in the city, where the Trade Winds draw down between the highest mountains.

The Mate this voyage was quite an old man. It was his last trip, he has been in the Sailors' Snug Harbour ever since. It seems impossible to have a good thing without a mixture of evil. The Snug Harbour has been called one of the finest institutions in the world, yet because of it many sailors do not try to save a cent, knowing they can fall back on it in their old age. But, as I've often said, if they could take care of themselves they would not be sailors.

After a fair passage of 135 days without unusual incident we arrived in Honolulu to find that bubonic plague had just broken out. This was in 1897 or 1898. Several fires were visible ashore where they were burning houses and stables in which cases of plague had occurred. We did not pay much attention to it, and personally I did not feel the slightest fear, though I saw many men and women who were wild to get away from the town. They had to go into quarantine before they were allowed on board vessels bound for 'Frisco. All business came to a standstill in Honolulu, churches were closed and only grog shops allowed to remain open. A large part of the town was shut off and if a person happened to get into one of those streets by mistake he was arrested and placed in quarantine for a month. Everybody was on the police force and every house was visited morning and evening, all the rooms being examined to see they were kept in proper order.

On the Saturday afternoon following our arrival a building was being burned in Chinatown, when the fire got out of control and the whole of Chinatown was burned to the water's edge. The harbour was more crowded with ships than usual and it was only the lucky chance that the regular Trade Winds were blowing more from the East than the North East that saved the whole town and all the shipping. There was a great commotion on board the ships, awnings were furled, scuppers were plugged and decks flooded with water, while several vessels whose sails were bent had them on fire and had men aloft with water in the tops. When the fire broke out I was on board another ship talking to her captain. We noticed some activity on the ship next to us and saw them hurrying up the rigging, then we saw that her mainsail was on fire. We were busily watching them till someone sang out, " Our awning is on fire." Then I thought it was time to be looking out for my own ship which was only a short distance away. Arrived on board I took every precaution such as furling awnings and flooding decks, then I put on some old clothes and went up in the mizzen top to watch things. Sparks were falling all over the ship, but we were able to put them all out without damage.

The Harbourmaster came and ordered us all out into the stream. I ran lines and was all ready to slip from the wharf, but did not move. Several of the ships were in a snarl and could not clear themselves, so I decided it was better for me to remain where I was than to increase the mix-up. Before dark all danger was over, for Chinatown was all gone, and *Nuuanu* was the only vessel alongside in that part of the harbour. I had a good view of the fire from my position in the rigging, watching the merchants, some of them very wealthy, with buckets of water in their hands wetting the tops of their store-houses. Fortunately the wind hauled more to the South East and blew the fire away from us.

Up in Chinatown all the citizens had armed themselves with axe handles and joined the police in herding the Chinese like a flock of animals down to the Quarantine Station, till they were satisfied they were free from the plague. They made a strange sight, thousands of men, women and children, some with babies in their arms, some with a handful of clothes they had saved, hallooing, crying, and all destitute. Of course the city had to take care of them and pay their damages too, for it was the Fire Department that had set them afire. That little fire cost the Government some millions.

Fights were of daily occurrence ashore, and everybody was killing rats. During the night after the fire swarms of rats came aboard and many lay dead in the rooms. We knew enough not to touch them, for they were covered with fleas and one bite from one of those fleas meant death. I called on an old school-mate, Frank Porter, at his large furniture store. He was out at the back burning up trash on a big bonfire. Next door was a grocery store and they were both burning rubbish on the same fire, for the backs of the buildings joined. A young man from the grocery store caught several rats with his hands and, when warned, he only laughed at the others. But that night he was taken with the plague and was dead before morning. After that no one handled rats. Dogs and cats in the houses that had plague were killed, but horses were said to be immune. Our crew did not care to go ashore and there was no danger of their running away. I gave them five dollars each on Saturday night, but they carried it back to Philadelphia unspent.

Instead of taking sugar ballast to Kahului, where we were again ordered, I took stone ballast and before sailing we fumigated to kill any rats left on board. In spite of all the measures taken it was several years before Honolulu was free from plague, and I doubt if it is really free now. They have a case occasionally, though it is kept secret as it frightens people too much. When we reached Kahului we could not go in as the harbour was full of vessels (it could only hold four at a time). The pilot came off and told us, so I had to go to sea for a week, standing in daily to see if there was an empty berth or set of buoys. When I did eventually come in one of the clerks from the Sugar House came off in the pilot boat to tell me the pilot was in quarantine. His sister had died from plague the day before and the whole place was in quarantine. I only went up the wharf twice, and then had to dip my shoes in a tub of disinfectant. We were glad when the ship was loaded and away, this time to Philadelphia. We had a fine passage home. Although we had been four months at sea when we arrived there, every man was examined for plague symptoms. Our crew had been on board nearly a year and had not spent any money in port. They were

full of plans for spending it when we arrived, but had soon lost
it all and were hard up again.

After discharging in Philadelphia we took coal as ballast and
towed to New York, where the bottom of the barque was cleaned
and painted. All iron ships need cleaning and painting with some
kind of anti-fouling composition at least once a year, and a fortune awaits the discoverer of a paint so full of poison that nothing
will grow on it under water. Then we loaded for Honolulu again.

When we used to load in Boston for Honolulu the cargoes were
so light that we sometimes had to carry stone ballast in the
bottom. Now the reverse is usually the case and we have too
much weight. The ship will be deeply loaded, with several
hundred tons of space remaining. Where we formerly carried
furniture, carriages, crockery, matches, and light goods, we now
carry mostly iron and steel. One thing we always have, black-
smith's coal, as there seems to be none on the Pacific side of
the continent or in Australia. Sometimes the cargoes are very
dangerous and at one time or another I have had coal, kerosene,
powder, and gasoline in drums, but we have never had a fire.

Mr. Seeley, who later became Captain Seeley of the Ward
Line of steamers, was the Mate this trip and Mr. O'Neil was
the Second Mate. He is now a watchman on the piers of the
same steamer line. Nothing unusual happened on the outward
passage, which we made in our average time of 138 days.

This year the Hawaiian Government was in the throes of revolution. I suppose it was inevitable, and as it had to come sometime then the sooner the better. Of course it pleased some people,
while others were sorry, but in my opinion the natives were not
capable of governing themselves. Although they are the gentlest
people in the world they do not care to assume any responsibility. I do not know of a single full-blooded Hawaiian who is a
first-class lawyer, doctor, minister, or statesman, though there is
no lack of money or schools to educate them. They are the best
whalemen there are, even in the Arctic regions, but I never
knew of one higher than a boat-steerer. As soon as any of the
labouring class have a few dollars they have a party or picnic, to
which all their friends are welcome, and when the money is
gone they will work for more, but they cannot stand civilisation.
In another fifty years a full-blooded Kanaka will be hard to
find.

We were still under the Hawaiian flag and our crew remained on board. On the first night in port the Second Mate was so full that I had to call the police and have him taken to the police station. I paid him off the next day and I believe he was the only change in the crew. Although the plague was still not entirely subdued and we had taken all precautions to keep the rats away from the ship, including fumigation before leaving, we were able to load our ballast of four hundred tons of sugar to take us up to Kahului. There we finished loading a full sugar cargo for Delaware Breakwater for orders, and thence to Philadelphia. When we reached home we found we were not under the Hawaiian flag any more, so we hauled it down and hoisted the Stars and Stripes. This must have been the last Hawaiian flag to come down, for the American flag had gone up in the islands two months before, though being at sea we had not heard about it.

I suppose it was the political trouble in the Islands that interrupted our voyages to Honolulu at this time. After discharging our sugar the vessel was laid up, which means she is tied to a wharf in some out of the way place where the wharfage is cheap, sometimes as low as a dollar a day. With only a ship-keeper on board she waits for a paying business. Sometimes vessels are laid up for years, for various reasons such as war, or litigation, and sometimes one ship-keeper will look after several vessels. The sails are unbent, and if the lay-up is expected to be a long one the running rigging will be unrove and everything liable to be stolen placed below decks. In spite of all precautions there is always something stolen from ships every time they enter port. In a place like New York, where everybody has access to the ship, it is impossible to keep thieves away. One time in the *John D. Brewer* I was robbed of $75 in cash, a new raincoat, a box of cigars, and a revolver. The thief had spent the afternoon in the cabin while the ship-keeper was shovelling snow forward. People come on board every day, some walk into the cabin as if they were in their own houses, and are quite indignant when politely asked who they wish to see. They will say carelessly, " Just taking a look around," and seem surprised when invited to go ashore again. They would not let a stranger look around their own houses, but seem to think a ship is different somehow. Hardly ever do I come into port but I have to drive people ashore. It is the duty of an officer or a ship-keeper to meet everybody at the gangway and enquire their business, but they do not have time to watch the gangway all day.

As soon as I had laid the ship up I went down to Duxbury expecting to have a few weeks' vacation. I had engaged a boat and a horse for the season, but the day after I arrived a letter came from Brewers to say that *Nuuanu* was chartered for Savannah and Fernandina. I am used to head winds and calms, and in fact to any kind of disappointment, so I just cancelled all engagements and started for Boston. Going over on the East Boston ferry I met my old steward, who was first with me as a cabin boy when the *John D. Brewer* was new. He had been several voyages with me since, but was now married and settled down ashore, keeping an hotel. His wife was with him now, both being out on their bicycles, and they seemed pleased to see me. He asked where I was sailing now, and before we had reached East Boston I had engaged him and his wife to go as Steward and Stewardess on this short voyage. I had never been ship-mates with a stewardess before, and had heard so many cases of trouble with them that I had never taken one. But I thought this would be a good time to try one, on a short trip, so I engaged them to go on board as soon as possible, and a day or two later went myself. This was in the fall of 1900. Finding it hard to get a crew of white men for a coasting voyage I engaged a coloured crew for the first time. I have had an odd man or two since then, but will never ship a whole crew of them again if I can help it. There was scarcely a sailor among them, and a more impudent, lazy, growling crowd I never saw. I was thankful it was a short voyage. We managed to get along, but I was used to discipline and not mob law. When I first went to sea practically every American vessel had a coloured cook and steward. Now I have not seen one for a long time. At one time there were many masters who preferred a coloured crew. Nowadays I find no one who cares to have even a single coloured man aboard, though they can be had for less wages than white men, and I find the same prejudice ashore also. In my experience the coloured men are not satisfied with being as good as white men, they want to be treated better.

This being my first coastal voyage I naturally asked a lot of questions. I was told to hug the shore on my way south, not to go outside the Gulf Stream. However, when I got down to

Hatteras I let her go down south across the Gulf Stream, then with one tack made Savannah, beating some of the schooners that hugged the land by two weeks. Savannah seemed more like a foreign city than American. As it was still summer the authorities would not allow us to sleep on board on account of fever. I have learned to do as I am told, wherever I go, satisfied that local authority should know best, but the only ones who kept perfectly well were the steward and his wife, and they were never out of the ship. I must say I liked the people and found the businessmen very courteous. If I had felt well I should have enjoyed the place and I would like to go there again. At that season of the year Savannah is deserted by the wealthy, so the finest hotel was as cheap as the small ones. It was here that I heard for the only time in my life the cry, " Lynch him." One evening I was going to my hotel when a Negro stole a bicycle from outside a store and scooted up a dark alley with it. He was caught and taken by three or four police to the Station, but such a yell went up from the whites of, " Lynch him, lynch him," that I got an idea of what it really means. I have seen most things but a lynching and I have no desire to see one, I can imagine it all from that yell.

After discharging our coal we took enough railroad ties for ballast and towed to Fernandina to finish loading. We had a good deal of sickness, in fact no one felt well. On arrival at Fernandina we made fast close to the schooner *Myra B. Weaver* and I made a point of calling on her captain, as I was a stranger in a strange place and wanted to get all the points possible with regard to a cargo about which I knew nothing. The Mate told me the Captain and his two passengers, a lady and a young girl, had gone to Jacksonville. Later in the day I saw they had returned, and when I went on board the Captain introduced me to his wife. I asked her how she liked going to sea with her husband, whereupon she blushed and smiled, then said, " We have only been married three days." It seems the Captain had been a widower and this lady was his late wife's sister, the little girl being his niece. They belonged to Mobile. While we were in port I met them every day and we became very well acquainted. He asked me not to tell anyone else they had been married or the other captains would be bothering them.

Fernandina is a quiet little place at the mouth of the small St. John's River, just a loading place for lumber, more like a country

Barque "Foohng Suey"

village. It is a very bad place for mosquitoes, you could scarcely breathe without inhaling one and I used to put on my long rubber boots to protect my legs when I was writing at the cabin table. One Sunday I walked over to the hotel on the beach, where I had to fight for my life and run all the way back. It is unnecessary to state that the hotel was closed at this time of year. I suppose Florida must be delightful in winter.

Both ships finished loading about the same time, the *Myra B. Weaver* sailing for Boston the day before us. No sooner were we at sea than all hands came down with malaria. By the time we were up to Barnegat the Second Mate, carpenter, steward, and his wife and one sailor were all the crew we had on deck. I was not able to hold my head up, but had to. I had displayed signals of distress to every steamer that passed for two days but they had taken no notice of us. We were under short sail, as it was the latter part of October. I told the Second Mate to let me know if he saw a tug coming, but not to speak to it. He called me just after daylight to say one was approaching and by the time I got on deck it was alongside. There was very little wind and we talked for sometime before anything was said about towing, for I did not want him to know we were in distress. Finally he said, " Do you want a tow?" " Yes, if your charge is reasonable." " Well, what do you say to $120?" Although I would not have let him go at any price I replied, " You make it $100 and furnish the hawser and I will pay it." We had not enough men to get out our own hawser. I asked him if he was a pilot and he said, " I ought to be, I have been in the tugboats twenty-five years." He gave us his hawser, which I helped to haul on board while the stewardess held the wheel. In less than an hour it was thick fog, but I was so glad to have a tugboat fast to us that I felt almost well. Shortly afterwards we passed close to a pilot boat. I was feeling so elated that I refused his offer, though I was sorry later when I had to stand on deck all day.

We came to anchor about four in the afternoon at Liberty Island. I went ashore in the tug and was soon at our office at 18, Broadway. A doctor was sent for and he put me in the hotel where he lived, just across the street from our office, sending to the Long Island College Hospital for a nurse, and telling the owners, " He is the sickest man on board. He has brought your ship into port, you ought to be able to take care of her now." I

M

was only too glad to lay aside all care and was soon asleep.

In the meantime a tug had been sent and all the sick men taken to hospital. The nurse, Miss Grace Slingoland, took such fine care of me under the doctor's directions that I was well in a week. The next day my daughters came to see me and in a day or so I was able to look out of the window on to busy Broadway. One day there was a big Republican procession and Roosevelt sat on his horse outside my window for a long time, wearing his waterproof suit as it was a rainy day. We did not think of him as President then. Towards the end of the week I was well enough to discharge my nurse, then I went home to Philadelphia and was soon in my usual health.

Captain Mahaney looked after the *Nuuanu* while I was sick, and on the first day he came to see me as there were one or two things to tell him. I suppose he must have paid off the crew, and he had to take the barque up the Hudson River above the bridge. He had a fall on board and for several weeks after I got well he was on crutches. I think that was the last time I ever saw him, for he was lost with his wife and all hands the next voyage in the *Helen Brewer*.

On the day after I arrived home in Philadelphia there was a heavy South West gale which blew down many of the trees in Germantown. A few days later I had to go to Boston by the Old Colony boat, and as soon as I looked at the morning paper on the train I saw in big headlines, "Loss of the schooner *Myra B. Weaver* with all hands but the Mate and two men." One of the coasting steamers had nearly run down the schooner as she lay in a water-logged condition and, hearing cries, had lowered a boat and taken off survivors. Reading further I saw that tugboats had since searched for and found the schooner and were towing her to Boston. Later in the day I went to East Boston, and crossing on the ferry I saw the derelict schooner being towed to the wharf, where I went to meet her. Her foremast was standing, the mainmast pitched forward into the foremast, and the mizzen mast was broken off at the deck. The cabin was washed away, all the hatches off, and the hold full of water. The bodies of two sailors lay on deck, while in the main cross-trees was the body of the little girl I had been so well acquainted with only a few weeks before. The Mate and one of the rescued seamen were the only people on board. I went aboard and helped the Mate to take down the little girl's body and deliver it to the undertaker, who happened to be the same one that had cared for my wife a few years before. The Mate's account was that in the blow four days previously they were at anchor under Cape Cod, but parted their cables and drifted on to Handkerchief Shoal. The Captain took his lady passenger up in the main rigging but could only get her half-way up to the cross-trees. He remained with her till the vessel rolled over on the bottom and she was drowned, then came up in the main cross-trees but was washed away later. He cried a good deal when telling me how hard he had tried to save the little girl and had her covered up with the gaff topsail. No one but myself knew that the Captain was married to the lady, his wife's sister, even the Mate was surprised when I told him. It was a very sad business and I felt as badly about it as if they had been my own folk.

On our fourth voyage to Honolulu we sailed from New York on December 23rd, 1900. Mr. Seeley was again the Mate and a man well on in years was the Second Mate. He said he was a graduate of Oberline College, but he did not appear to me to be college bred, and I guess he went in one door and came out the other. He is not the only college bred man that looked and acted as though that was the only way he passed through. He left us in Honolulu. There were two passengers, the brothers George and Jack Nicholas, the former just through Harvard and the latter just ready to enter. But he was six feet three and growing so fast that the doctors told him to take a sea voyage. A long sea voyage will build up almost anyone not past repairing. Mr. and Mrs. Berry were again cook and stewardess.

The first accident that happened was on Christmas Eve. With a full Southerly gale blowing the crew were furling the upper fore topsail, I was holding the wheel and all hands were on deck. About eight o'clock in the evening I heard a sound as though someone had fallen from aloft. Any strange sound attracts my attention and I could think of nothing else that would make such a noise. It was pitch dark and raining. Presently the Mate came aft and told me one of the men had lost his hold and fallen. I went along, and sure enough he was dead. We placed his body in the boatswain's locker until the morning, by which time the gale was so bad we were hove to under the lower main topsail and the only dry place about the deck was the fore hatch. I would have carried the body aft for burial, but the two

passengers and Mrs. Berry were seasick, so without their knowledge we consigned him to the deep. They never knew about it
till we reached Honolulu. A burial at sea is sad enough under any
circumstances, but is doubly so when hove to in a gale of wind.
He was a young man of about twenty, I think a Dane. In his
sea-chest I found letters from his Minister in New York, and
although he had only been aboard about two days he appeared
such a bright young man that I felt very bad about him, and
sorry for his folks at home who would wait anxiously for his
return but would never see him again.

As a matter of fact we had an accident from that upper fore
topsail yard on four voyages in succession. The next one was on
our return passage, on a dark night off Cape Horn when a man
fell while reefing. The ship was running before a gale of wind
and he struck the fore sheet, which broke his fall and threw
him on deck. His leg was broken in three places, but he was
able to get around on crutches when we reached home. The third
man who fell from the same yard landed in the fore top, where
someone grabbed him and he was only bruised. The fourth man
had his right hand cut to pieces by holding on to the tie when the
halliards were let go. His hand went through an iron block
cutting off most of his fingers and smashing the thumb. I had a
long job on that hand, but it got well, and luckily he was left-
handed. Some people said they would change the yard, and a
reporter wrote a newspaper yarn about the *Nuuanu's* hoodoo
fore yard, but there have been no accidents since.

It is very pleasant to have a passenger if he is agreeable, and
the Nichols boys seemed to enjoy the trip although it was a long
one of 157 days. We had the usual weather to Cape Horn and
the usual fight to get round it. Off the Horn the carpenter, who
was very old, died from old age and was buried at sea. As I
could not discover that he had any relatives his wages and personal effects were turned over to the U.S. Government. They
were beginning to get anxious about us in Honolulu and the
parents of the Nichols boys had been waiting for us for some
time. They were awfully glad to see us coming round Diamond
Head and into port.

Now that we were under the American flag the crew left, of
course. You cannot keep an American seaman on board in an
American port, although they are shipped to come back to an
American port north of Cape Hatteras and you are not obliged

to pay them their wages. Those ashore who make their living out of sailors advise them to ask for their discharge, telling them stories of how they can better themselves by leaving. So it is usually better for the ship to pay them off and let them go, rather than have them around for a month doing nothing, half full most of the time and making trouble.

After discharging we took our ballast of sugar and beat up to Kahului again, with a new crew and a new Second Mate, who was a German and a very good man, named Wissel. A very nice young man called Philip Hall joined us as a passenger, also making the trip for his health. Through him I got acquainted with a lot of people in Wialuka, a town on the side of the mountain about four miles from Kahului. It is very beautiful up there and it is very pleasant to call there now and then to renew old acquaintances, while sometimes they will come down on board the barque, making a change for me.

This was the time of the Spanish American War, and while in Kahului we heard of the *Maine* being sent to Havana. I know I remarked this would be sure to bring on a war, not thinking she would be blown up but thinking her crew would make trouble ashore. On our way home we passed close to the West Indies, with no thought of war, and shortly after we arrived in Philadelphia the battle of Santiago was fought. During the following voyage I read in all the papers and reviews the opinions of the world on the Spanish War, and the best thing said about the Americans was in a Glasgow paper which said " No doubt it will be a long war, for the navies are about equally matched and it is a well-known fact that the American navy is only half-manned, though no doubt the Americans will win in the end from their great resources." I have always wanted to thank that editor for his belief in the Americans and ask him what he thinks the American navy would have done if it had been fully manned.

Again we took a ballasting of coal in Philadelphia and towed to New York to prepare for our fifth voyage to Honolulu. After cleaning and painting the bottom in dry-dock we started loading. Mr. Wissel, who had joined the last time in Honolulu, was made Mate. He had a hard job to get his Certificate, but as I had agreed to take him as Mate the examiners gave it to him and he did very well. I made him work up the ship's position every day and by the end of the voyage he was an expert navigator. The Second Mate was an Irishman from Boston, and Mr. and Mrs. Berry were still with me. I could always lean on and trust them and did not realise how much I depended on them until he died in New York on our next visit.

There was one passenger, a very quiet elderly man who was trying to keep from drinking. He spent most of his time writing, and if he had any spirits to drink I never knew it, so he was in fine condition when we reached Honolulu and he went to an hotel. After two weeks in port without seeing him I enquired for him at the hotel and found him in the bar-room quite stupid. He knew me, however, and said, " Guess I would be better off had I remained on board the ship." I have never seen him since, but I know he got home all right as I had an invitation to dine at his house and was sorry circumstances prevented me from accepting it. It's very hard for a man along in years to get rid of the drink habit.

We had the quickest passage out I ever made, being only one hundred and twelve days and taking only ten days to double Cape Horn from 50°S in the Atlantic to 50°S in the Pacific, a distance of about one thousand miles. This time we loaded in Honolulu and then made the passage home in one hundred and nine days, so the round voyage was completed in nine months and one day. I think this must be a record time with a full cargo both ways. As usual the crew left at Honolulu, for Turk and Lewis, a couple of sailor thieves, were running things to suit themselves. On the way home, down in Southern latitudes, we parted our bobstay and the bowsprit was broken nearly off. I managed to fish it and we got home all right, though we did not dare to carry sail on it very hard. I suppose it increased the length of the passage by about a week.

On arriving off the Capes of Delaware I engaged a tug, telling him I did not require a pilot as I had held a Coasting Licence. As we neared the pilot grounds about eleven o'clock at night the steam pilot boat came around us, read our name with his searchlight, then came alongside and hailed us, saying, " I will send a pilot on board you." " I don't require one," I replied. " You are subject to pilotage," he said, and immediately blew his siren. Our tug stopped towing, and he kept us waiting half an hour. I could have ordered the tug to proceed, but I thought it might be as well to have a pilot for nothing, and anyway I could have blamed the pilot boat for stopping me and claimed damages had any accident occurred. The pilots were evidently all asleep, but when one eventually came on board I said, " Are you not making a mistake? I have a Coasting Licence and I am from an American port. I am not subject to pilotage." They had not yet found out that Honolulu was an American port. The pilot hailed his boat and told them, then they talked of sending him back, but I said, " No, you can't go now until the doctor comes and examines us, and if we have to go into quarantine you will have to go with us." I knew there was no chance of this, for we were all well, but I wanted to frighten him all I could, and I never saw a man so provoked. It was his own fault, he had no right to stop my ship. I was the captain, and am not obliged to take a pilot if I don't want one.

In the meantime we were waiting for orders to proceed and the pilot said, " Well you had better tell the tug to go ahead." I said, " No, you stopped the ship and can take charge of her now till we come to anchor inside the breakwater." So while I had nothing to do he took her to anchor. Afterwards he talked with one of the crew, wanting to know where Honolulu was. The doctor came off at noon the next day and the pilot went ashore, but he had his trouble for nothing, they never sent in a bill.

After discharging in Philadelphia we again towed to New York to load for Honolulu. When we were ready we had to wait four days for a tug, they were all working on the *Thomas Lawson*, the largest schooner built with seven masts. She was aground in the river and about stopped all traffic up and down. Later, at home in Duxbury an old friend, Charlie Clapp, asked if I had seen " our schooner " in Philadelphia. I told him I had, and had felt her too, having to wait four days for a tug on her account. " What do they say of her?" he asked. " Well, I don't know much about schooners, but I heard it said that if she had been built as two schooners she would have been much more profitable." Charlie then told me all about her, what she had cost, and what she was earning, and called her a very good investment. Then I found he was one of Tom Lawson's employees and had a lot to do with her, since then I have been watching Tom Lawson and all his doings with greater interest. That schooner came to grief on her first trip abroad. I don't know the particulars, whether it was the fault of the schooner, the master, or the weather. Probably it was just the dangers of the sea. I notice, however, that schooners on long voyages seldom succeed, they seem to be out of their element, which is the coast.

While the ship was loading at Pier 9 in New York my Mate, Mr. Wissel, was on board, and I was very surprised when he told me he was leaving to go in the *Tillie Starbuck,* a larger ship, forgetting all the trouble I had taken in getting him his licence. He is not the first man I have helped to a position who, as soon as he was competent, has taken the first chance to better himself. The ship he went to was one of the worst iron ships that ever sailed and she was always in trouble. I wonder how he got along, and if he was still in her on her subsequent voyage when Captain Wynn abandoned her at sea. I imagine he had had enough of her after one trip and had already left her, but I have never met Captain Wynn to ask him, as he has never come into our office again after he lost the ship. I have had three Mates that have been in the *Tillie Starbuck* and they all pronounced her a brute in heavy weather.

A few days after this my old steward Stephen Berry died. He had been with me nearly every voyage for twenty years and was going again, but was taken ill on board at Pier 9 and only lived a few days in hospital. I arrived at the hospital almost too late to see him alive, with his last breath he was calling for me. His wife was nearly crazy and they were very glad at the hospital when I arrived and took her away, as they could do nothing with her.

For the sixth voyage I had a new Mate, Mr. Knight, who had sailed with me as Second Mate of the *John D. Brewer* before I was ill with pneumonia. He only joined a few days before Stephen Berry died and had the duty of attending the cremation of his remains. Mr. Nelson was the Second Mate, while the new steward was only with us temporarily, being replaced by a Chinese at Honolulu.

When we were loaded and ready to sail, a long-distance telephone call from Duxbury informed me of the death of my sister. As the wind was East and it was a poor sailing day I went home for the funeral, returning the same night.

This was a very uneventful voyage, which usually means a pleasant one. A young American boy, who said he was from Pennsylvania, asked for a chance to go out and I agreed to take him. He proved a good worker, but was a great liar and simply could not tell the truth, even when it would have served him much better. On the passage home I took him as cabin boy and he did well, but lying and stealing go together. He stole my clothes and curios and tried to steal the silver spoons belonging to the ship, but did not quite get away with them. I have often wondered how he could have been brought up.

Of course our crew left in Honolulu. Turk and Lewis had both got into trouble and were over on the reef in prison, while Mrs. Turk was shipping crews to keep up her husband's business. She was the only woman I ever heard of as a sailors' shipping master. This suggests that she was a very masculine woman. On the contrary, anyone meeting her and not knowing her reputation would have thought her a perfect lady, while those captains who did business with her all spoke well of her. I was able to get my own crew so did not have that experience, but she told me that she was only trying to keep her husband's business together until he was released from confinement where his enemies had put him, so did not mind my getting my own crew as long as no one else did it for me. Consequently I was greatly surprised when I next arrived to find that she had become notorious, had separated from her husband and had, in fact, shot him but not killed him, and was now keeping a disorderly house.

At this same time I nearly got myself a bad reputation. Captain Calhorn of the ship *George Curtiss* was in port with me and I knew him and his wife very well. She was an artist and was always painting. One day, when he was busy, I took her and their two nieces to Nuuanu Valley to see the tombs of the old kings, and while going up the valley in one of the horse-cars we met one of the prominent church members. Mrs. Calhorn and Mrs. Turk looked very much alike, both being handsome women and both wearing glasses. It turned out later that this man spread a story that I had been taking round the notorious Mrs. Turk and her companions in broad daylight. I still see this man every voyage and I don't think he likes me very well, but he was hardly to be blamed, anyone might have made the same mistake.

This time we loaded in Honolulu and had a quick trip home. We had a miserable crew, but coming home round the Horn is not like going out and in spite of some trouble with the parral of that same fore topsail yard we arrived safely. Our Chinese steward was a poor cook and had no idea of taking care of the stores, so I had to do it all. When we arrived at the Delaware

Breakwater I took a pilot, for I was sailing in with a fair wind and needed no tug. A stranger never knows what may have happened in a year's absence, no matter how well acquainted he may be with a place. After we had come to an anchor the pilot said, " Captain, I will tell you our rules. If you tow to Philadelphia you will have to pay pilotage whether you have a pilot or not. If I remained on board we charge three dollars a day for my time, or you can let us know when you want to go and we will send you a pilot." I listened to him patiently, then told him, " I guess not, Pilot. I shall not require a pilot when I get a tug." " Oh yes, you will. I know the rules." It was a long time before I could convince him that I was not obliged to take a pilot, but at last he tumbled to it. We did go to Philadelphia, but I took no pilot, though it kept me on deck all the way up the river.

Mr. Knight left us at Philadelphia, though I have heard from him several times since. He was the only man I ever met who would not meet his mother. She tried hard to get in touch with him, but he went to great lengths to avoid meeting her and I have often wondered what the reason was.

On November 20th, 1903, we left Erie Basin, New York, and were towed to sea by the tug *Charm*. By 2.00 p.m. all sail was set and Sandy Hook Lightship was NW$\frac{1}{2}$N 14 miles. This voyage my younger daughter Elizabeth was with us. Mr. E. P. Richards of Portland, Maine, was the Mate, Mr. Nelson was Second Mate, and an Englishman called Bush was a very good steward. I tried to get Mrs. Berry to go with us, but she wrote she would go in any ship but the *Nuuana* as she thought she would miss her husband too much after so many voyages in the ship with him.

This turned out to be the longest passage I ever made at sea. We crossed the Line on December 24th, thirty-five days out, the winds and weather being as usual, and having a fair crew. On January 21st, in latitude 52°S one of the sailors named Martin caught his hand in a block when turning a reef out of the upper topsail. It was terribly mangled and I had to amputate one finger with Elizabeth's assistance. The steward, though an embalmer by trade, was too faint to help. Had Martin been a good sailor he would not have taken hold of the chain which led through the block. I see sailors every day going up and down the rigging holding on to the ratlines instead of the shrouds. Some day a ratline will break and overboard they will go. I think this was the last accident with that hoodooed fore topsail yard. We made a creditable job of Martin's hand and it healed up remarkably quickly.

On Sunday, January 24th, we made *Staten Island. Sixty-six days out, not a bad passage so far. It was here our bad time began, and until March 3rd we were fighting against head winds and gales, only making about a thousand miles in forty-three days. It would be tedious to describe all our manoeuvres off the Horn, but twice we went back under the lee of Staten Island I think the thing that keeps our courage up under these circumstances is the air we breathe, which seems so stimulating that we laugh at our troubles. Once round the Cape all is pleasant and an almost continual fair wind to Honolulu makes everyone happy. We passed in sight of Mas A Fuera Island, a bleak barren rock some six thousand feet high with hardly a sign of vegetation on it. Still, it was land, and only the hungry eyes of a sailor who has been two months off Cape Horn amid mountains of water can appreciate mountains of land. At one time this island was a great resort for seal, but they have been killed off or driven away.

It was not until daylight on April 24th, that we made the island of Maui, and the next morning we passed by Diamond Head, the whole view of the Paradise of the Pacific bursting upon us, the island of Oahu surmounted by its mountains with their tops in the clouds. To really enjoy such a sight you must come around the Horn on a 156-day passage as we had just done.

The time in Honolulu passed quickly as Elizabeth was with me. Loading our homeward cargo there too, we were soon ready for sea again. She was very happy at Mr. Hall's nice home up the valley, where there were two daughters about her age. I thought it would be a terrible strain for her to leave her new friends just as she was getting acquainted with them and to undertake another long trip. She was delighted to remain for a time, to return home overland or to wait until I returned to Honolulu on the next voyage. So on June 6th, after thirty-seven days in port, I sailed for New York without her. Little did we think that it would be several years before she left the Islands and that when she did return to Philadelphia it would be by steamer and train as a married woman with her baby. No more Cape Horn for her. Such is life.

* Not to be confused with Staten Island in New York Bay—W.J.M.

We had a fair passage home, arriving late in October 1904. The owners decided to load the ship *Henry Villard* first, so the *Nuuanu* was laid up until March, and a long cold dreary winter it was. The ship was frozen into the dry-dock, where she was being cleaned and painted, and we were several days getting her out although they worked night and day with steam trying to melt the ice. If it had not been for the constant passing of steamers the harbour would have been solid, and on several days we could not pass from Brooklyn to New York by the ferry boats but had to take the bridge.

This was the time of the Russian-Japanese War. Off the Delaware Capes on the way in a Philadelphia tug spoke us and gave us the papers. The first thing I read was that Mr. Carnegie had replied to questioners that, "Of course Russia would win, because of her great resources." I thought of the time when Europe was going to conquer the French Revolutionaries but France defeated them all, and I thought this a parallel case. Japan was a unit, and Russia was not.

Probably Mr. Richards would have continued in the ship, but she was laid up so long we lost all our officers. When we came to load again I had to find a new crowd. It is always better to keep old hands if they are satisfactory as it takes a year for men to get used to a ship.

On March 16th, 1905, we sailed on our eighth voyage for Honolulu. Following the long lay-up in South Brooklyn we had found it hard work to get through the ice to Pier 9, East River, to load. On the morning we sailed the old sailor I stay with in Brooklyn rose early to make the fires and said to me, "Don't get up, there is another North-easter coming." I looked out of the window and saw the street covered with white frost. Now I had been taught as a boy that a white frost meant a South-west wind (an old Indian sign) so I hurried off to the ship. When I passed the tugboat office they said, "You will not sail today, the Herald says there is another North-easter coming." "I guess not, send the tug."

When I reached the barque the pilot was there, also the shipping master, and both were delighted when I told them I was going. In the owners' office they said, in a mournful tone, "Well, there is not much chance today." "Why not?" Then, more brightly, "Why, do you think you can go?" "Sure." So I got

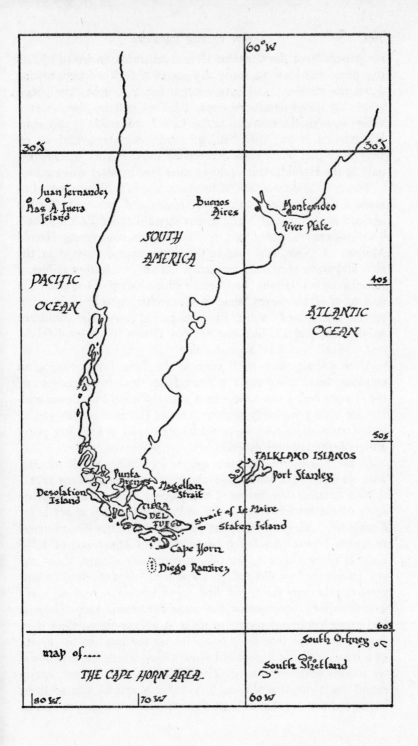

60°W

30°S   30°S

Juan Fernandez
Mas A Fuera
Island

Buenos
Aires   Montevideo
                         River Plate

SOUTH
AMERICA

PACIFIC   40S

OCEAN   ATLANTIC
                                          OCEAN

                                                    50S

                         FALKLAND ISLANDS
                         Port Stanley

           Punta
           Arenas   Magellan
Desolation   Strait
Island   TIERRA
                DEL   Strait of Le Maire
                FUEGO   Staten Island

                Cape Horn

                Diego Ramirez

                                                    60S

map of....   South Orkney

    THE CAPE HORN AREA.   South Shetland

80 W   70 W   60 W

my papers from the Customs House, returning on board to find tug, pilot, and crew all ready. By eleven o'clock we were towing down the harbour, and sure enough found a light South-west wind that lasted us several days. Then we got the North-easter, which gave us the best run to the Line I ever made in any ship. We crossed it on April 6th, in twenty-one days, and all on account of that white frost. Everybody in New York was looking only at the Herald, which said another North-easter was coming.

The new Mate was Mr. Knutson, while Mr. Nelson, who had made a short voyage to the West Indies and was ready for me again, was the Second Mate. A new steward called Parker joined. Two passengers, Mr. Grant of Philadelphia, and young Harold Morgan of New York, made the entire round voyage in the ship and were very good company. One of my former sailors, a Kanaka called Hiram, had remained on board all winter. He sent most of his wages home to his mother, who lived in a hut on the outskirts of Lahina. She was an old crone who could not speak a word of English, but her boy Hiram was a good fellow and, like all Kanakas, a good sailor.

After making such good time to the Line I was hoping to continue, but we got stuck at Cape Horn, mainly on account of the barque being too crank. In a gale she would lie down with her lee side completely under, even as far as the fifth ratline in the main rigging, so we could not carry sail to keep her going although she lay very quietly.

So much nonsense has been written by authors and journalists with no first-hand knowledge about rounding the Horn that I think a detailed description of this passage may serve to explode some of the myths. I can claim to know something about it for I am now making my fifty-first passage round, the largest vessel in which I have rounded it being the ship *Matchless,* of 1,198 tons. It often seems to me that any rubbish written about the sea, no matter how absurd from a sailor's point of view, or how far from the true facts, will find a publisher and readers, while a true sailor's yarn seems too tame for them. Cape Horn is bad enough without trying to make it appear worse than it is, but we all know that forty feet is about the limit to the height of a wave and that it does not always blow a gale here. If it did we should never get round. There is a constant current setting round the Horn, from West to East, at a rate of one to three knots, and but for that current there would be nothing to it. The weather is no worse than in the Atlantic between Europe and America and there is never a hurricane in this area. All a man wants is a good ship, properly loaded, with a good average crew of seamen.

On this occasion we took forty days to cover the thousand miles from 50°S in the Atlantic to 50°S in the Pacific in the middle of winter. Quoting from the Mate's Log, on Tuesday *May 9th* lat. 49° 40′ S long. 64° 00′ W Moderate breeze from WNW and fine weather. *May 10th*. Same weather, made 126 miles. *May 11th* SW gale. Hove to under Lower topsails and fore topmast staysail, made 90 miles. *May 12th*. Strong SW gale, heavy cross seas. *May 13th*. Gale increasing, with snow squalls. Wore ship to WNW and hove to under a goose-winged main topsail. Now our trouble began. Being loaded too crank the vessel lay over on her side till the water was up to the main hatch and the lee side was completely submerged. *May 14th*. Gale continued, ship on her side. *May 15th*. Weather moderated. From this date until the 21st, we continued fighting the weather, sometimes with whole sail and then down to lower topsails. On the night of the 21st, we made the light on New Year's Island. This is a small island just off the north side of Staten Island, where there is a company of sealers. We went close to it, within two miles, and how cheerful it was to see a light and the signs of habitation. If we had remained there for the next two weeks while the SW gales lasted we should have been just as far ahead. But I passed out by Cape Saint John and down into the Easterly current, which no sailing vessel can beat against under short sail. *May 22nd*. Light breeze from SW which hauled to the Westward and freshened up. Reduced sail to lower topsails. *May 23rd*. Wind NW, blowing hard, barque under reefed topsails and reefed courses. As we have a leading wind we are carrying all the sail we can, the barque plunging into a heavy head sea. We know the wind will come ahead soon. 8.00 p.m. Wind shifted to SW in a heavy squall of hail, lightning, and thunder. Hove to under lower main topsail, heading South-east and, of course, drifting back to the Eastward. *May 24th*. 4.00 a.m. Moderating, made sail. Noon. Still blowing hard from SW. *May 25th*. 2.00 a.m. Calm. 8.00 a.m. Light breeze from South. All sail set. Noon. Light breeze from West. 6.00 p.m. Fresh gale. Reduced sail. *May 26th*. 8.00 a.m. Clearing again. Made sail. Noon. Blowing hard from South. Hove to under a lower main topsail. Ter-

rible sea, ship labouring heavily. *May 27th.* Wind hauled to ESE
and moderated, but such a heavy head sea we can do nothing but
pitch our jib-boom under. Staten Island in sight to the Northward so for all our work we have gained nothing in six days.
May 28th. Wind back to the Westward again. Made sail. PM.
Wind backed to South and increased to a heavy gale. *May 29th.*
Heavy SW gale, barque under lower main topsail, lee side completely under. *May 30th.* Continued terrific gale from SW. 4.00
p.m. Moderating, made sail. *May 31st.* Moderate Northerly
winds and fine clear weather. We are getting back what we have
lost these last two weeks. At 4.00 p.m. could just see Cape Horn
from the mizzen rigging, and my two passengers went up six
ratlines to have a look at it, the only time they were in the rigging during the voyage.

June 1st Moderate breeze from WNW. 4.00 p.m. calm, then
came out from SW full force. Reduced to lower topsails. *June
2nd.* 4.00 a.m. Hove to under a goose-winged main topsail. Terrific gale. Lee side under. We are drifting back again. 7.00 a.m. Just
as daylight began to break a large four-masted ship came up
astern carrying a whole main topsail and a whole foresail. We
hung a light over the stern but they did not see it, then we got
out the fog horn, but they still came directly for us, straight for
our stern. We called all hands, for we expected to be run down.
It was awful to see that towering mass of iron coming on to us.
Her great jib-boom swinging in the air rose up above our mast-
heads as we were lying down so far. I expected when it fell it
would crash into our little vessel, so I dropped the fog horn,
threw aside my oilskin coat and was ready to jump on board
her if possible. Fortunately the next sea threw her head to leeward. Those on board her had just discovered us and their helm
was hard up. Just by accident she cleared us and went off to leeward, while above the shrieking of the gale we could hear the
yelling on board her. As soon as they had cleared us they took in
full sail and remained about a mile from us all day, probably
thinking we were sinking as we lay so low in the water.

June 3rd. The same howling gale. Drifting back. *June 4th.* I
had almost decided to give it up and go round Australia, getting
out my charts for that way, but when daylight came the gale
moderated and there was our big ship, ten miles to the Eastward
of us. I thought that if we could hold on as well as he then we
would keep her going. We were now in longitude 61°W, eighty

miles to the Eastward of Cape Saint John, or eighty miles worse off than we were fifteen days previously. How much better to have remained under the lee of Staten Island. *June 5th*. Wind came out SE. Made sail, but at 6.00 p.m. it hauled to SW, heavy gale, down to lower topsails again. *June 6th*. Heavy snow squalls and SW gale. *June 7th* Moderated. Made all sail, but head wind continues. *June 8th*. Moderate breeze and fine weather. 8.00 p.m. Heavy snow squalls from the SW. *June 9th*. Snow squalls. Wind hauling to West. *June 10th*. West wind, thick snow storm. *June 11th*. Hip, hip, hurrah. An East wind at last. Thick snow, but we made one hundred and sixty miles on our course to the westward. *June 12th*. SE wind, hauling to WSW but we made one hundred and fifty seven miles to the westward.

We were now north and west of Cape Horn and could laugh at gales from the SW, for now we had two legs because we could go north as well as west.

After seven more days of fighting we were in 49°29′S. 80°12′W on June 18th, round Cape Horn, clear of the current. To recount all the times we wore ship and took in sail would be tedious, but we were glad it was over, with each day growing warmer. No one was hurt or injured, and no man was laid up during those forty days, and all did their duty. We lost one or two sails. Our crew consisted of as many as ten nationalities, and I was the only American born. One of those men sailed with me again. His name was James Steel, and I can see him now as he saved a lower top-sail they were trying to goose-wing. He took a gasket round and really saved the sail, but did not think he had done anything extra. In spite of our long time off the Horn we were only 145 days to Honolulu.

Much to our surprise when we got there the *Henry Villard* that sailed six weeks before us had not arrived. She went round Australia, in fact put into Melbourne leaking, discharged part of her cargo and repaired, and arrived in Honolulu some two months after us. However, our long wait in New York had caused us to lose our charter home from Hawaii, so now we had to wait for the next year's sugar crop. I supposed that the owners would send us to Australia for coal, but they did not think it would pay as freights were so low and ordered me to lay the *Nuuanu* up. She remained tied up to Hackfield's Wharf for five months.

This time passed very quickly and pleasantly and I had a chance to do a lot of work to the barque. My daughter Elizabeth

N

was one of the first to come on board from a launch outside the harbour and through her I made many new friends and had the unusual experience for a shipmaster of attending a cookery school. This started as a joke, but it did make a difference with my cook, for he ever after stood in fear of my knowledge of cooking, though coming home round the Horn he did say, " I'd like to see your cooking schoolteacher off here trying to cook without eggs or milk or fresh meat, and the galley washed out every day by a wave." At this time too I sold my first story for money, and told the story of my shipwreck to a large audience at Punahoe College for the benefit of the Girl's Rowing Club, having the satisfaction of raising a good sum towards the building of their fine new boat-house at the entrance of Honolulu harbour.

I had some trouble with the sailors after they left the ship. They came on board and assaulted Mr. Knutson, the Mate, and when I tried to get the police to arrest them they said they could not find them. As usual they wanted a reward, then they would have found them in half an hour. Finally I did get one of the men arrested, but when he was brought to trial he was fined the immense sum of one dollar and costs. And they say sailors are abused! The Second Mate, Mr. Nelson, was suspected of stealing some money, and he showed up so badly during the trial that I gave him his discharge, keeping only the Mate, Steward, and Carpenter with me.

Eventually our pleasant time came to an end. We took our ballast of sugar at Honolulu, then sailed to Kanapali, on the south side of Maui, to finish loading. From there we made an uneventful passage home to Philadelphia in 130 days, where I landed my passengers in good health.

Returning to the subject of last voyage's passengers, these two men proved excellent comrades, only neither of them did any work except occasionally to steer. Grant was trying to keep away from liquor and Morgan was sent by his family, who seemed to think he was lacking in something. If I were to guess what had made them failures I would say that it was because their parents were rich and they had been brought up to be gentlemen. This was apparent at my first meeting with Morgan in our New York office, for I am always consulted with regard to passengers. As there is generally something the matter with a person that wants to take a sea voyage I usually ask, " What does he want to go to sea for?" He had worked for a bank, it seemed, and got into trouble through losing a document. He caused me no trouble and I did my best to look after him in Honolulu. When we returned to New York he went to work in our office for two years, where he gave complete satisfaction. Then he went out to the Islands and the last I heard of him he was in a bank there. The family seemed to think I had performed a miracle with this boy and wrote me many kind letters.

Grant was a different person. He was about forty-five, was a man of many friends, and he could not say No. In Honolulu he lived ashore, where he became frendly with many officers of the Army and Navy and lots of the people in the place. When I learned he could not pay his bills I telegraphed to his family for money for him and they sent me a sum to pay his debts. He returned to Philadelphia with us, with never a sick day and apparently no desire for liquor. With his abilities and the manufacturing business with which he was familiar, he could have made a fortune in Honolulu, but for rum. When he left me I gave him good advice and he said he would drink no more, but his friends were too much for him. I have never seen him since, though I heard he drank himself to death in a few years.

On August 7th, 1906, we sailed from Pier 9, East River, on our ninth voyage for Honolulu. Mr. Knutson said he would never go round Cape Horn again, so I shipped Mr. Sam Latham as Mate. He hailed from New Jersey, though I was told he was an Englishman, and but for drink he would have been a very good man. Mr. Werner, a German, was the Second Mate and Parker was again the Steward. Jack Nichols, who was with me five years before and had been at Harvard since, was again a passenger. As he was studying birds and fish he had all the nets and lines to catch them and he certainly was an enthusiast at his work, always up at first call whenever a strange bird or fish was around. He was as good as an extra hand in working the ship and was at the top of the masts every day. I was sorry when he left us to return home overland, though I did worry sometimes because he would sit on the martingale for hours with a scoop net watching for fish or weeds. I was afraid it would breeze up and plunge him under and overboard, for he did not understand the danger.

On the second day out we had a tempest and there was lightning in some part of the horizon for the next twenty-one days until we were in the NE Trades. We crossed the Line thirty days out, then had to beat down the Brazilian Coast, as often happens. We frequently sail in among the fishermen, on catamarans. These do not seem like boats, just two or three logs lashed together, but they can sail very fast. They would never come on board, though we would have liked to buy some fish if they would sell them.

On October 12th, in 47° 00′ S. 55° 00′ W. I saw my first iceberg. Though I had spent many anxious nights on the lookout for them I had more or less decided that I should never see one. The unexpected often happens and here, more than 200 miles north of where they are shown on the charts, we fell in with them. As dawn approached I noticed some unusual white clouds to the westward, and looking to leeward saw an island some five miles away. There being no land in the vicinity I knew at once that we were among icebergs, and when full daylight came we counted as many as forty large bergs to the south of us. We were heading SW with a northerly wind, but at 7.00 a.m. the wind came out of the SW and we tacked away to the WNW I had always supposed that an old berg would look like a barren mountain, covered with pinnacles and points, but these were like square blocks of marble, as white and clear as crystal. We judged the largest to be from five hundred to nine hundred feet high, and one of the smallest, which we measured by sextant, was two hundred feet. We were passing them all day, going about six knots, and they were a magnificent sight on such a bright clear day. While we were pitching and tumbling about in the sea they were as immovable as rocks. All day long we were passing through Oregon lumber, so some vessel had evidently been wrecked among them. We kept a lookout from aloft for a boat with men in it, but saw nothing but lumber. We passed the last berg about dusk, but kept on steering west until morning, when there being no berg in sight we kept away to SW again.

This time we were only thirteen days from fifty to fifty, and made the passage in 134 days, arriving on December 19th. Honolulu grew more lovely each voyage. The harbour had been much improved and enlarged since the U.S. Government took over, and there at the entrance was the Girls' Boat House, very ornamental with its oriental architecture. And there too was my daughter, awaiting my arrival. When I come to New York, Boston, or Philadelphia, I never see my own people on the wharf, but here I know nearly everybody I see, and it seems like home.

A lot of bad weather delayed the discharging, then the volcano on Hawaii erupted and when we were ready to go to Kanapali to load we could not see Diamond Head from the harbour for smoke, so we towed up. The distance is only sixty miles, and leaving in the afternoon we were there before daylight. Again we had a lot of the SW gales called *Konas,* and lay with one hundred and thirty fathoms of chain out on both anchors, our stern being just clear of the breakers for nearly a week, during which time we did no loading. Last year it was worse and we lost ten days in this way. Kanapali is only a loading port for the Pioneer Plantation, which belongs to Hackfield & Co. The nearest town is Lahaina, which used to be the capital in the old days, when there was always a fleet of whalers there. Now there is little left of its old glory. It is always sad to look upon an old town gone to decay, with all its houses rotting away, but Lahaina is an interesting place in which to spend a day. Nowadays it all seems to belong to the Pioneer Mill and Plantation. They own the hotel and the store and there is a fine school or college on the side of the mountain four or five miles behind the town. It would be ideal if we could only load our ship here instead of at Kanapali, from which place I have to cross the island to the Custom House at Kahului when the loading is completed. It takes all day and is a nuisance, although the journey is delightful, with fine views as we drive round the ends of precipices hundreds of feet in height. Far below are the great waves coming in from the sea and dashing themselves at the feet of the cliffs. In the distance you may see a sail or two and twice I have seen whales spouting, for whales still frequent the islands.

The passage home was uneventful. Sailing from Kanapali on February 7th, 1907, we arrived at Delaware Breakwater on May 27th, in one hundred and nine days, the second time I have made the passage in that time. Two half-Kanaka boys shipped with us, Martin Mett and Lawrence Row. The former was so fat he could not go aloft, but when we returned home he could furl a royal. The other was tall and slim and a fine sailor. These Kanaka boys remain by the ship in New York, and being such honest faithful boys they are very desirable crew members. One very pleasant thing happened on the way up the Brazilian coast in the SE Trades. We were doing about eight knots, with all sail set, when a large German steamer passed close to us. I hoisted our ensign and dipped it to her when she was close, and to our delighted surprise her band struck up the Star Spangled Banner and played it until they were out of hearing. All our sailors ran up the rigging waving their hats, and I never heard music sound so sweet.

This time at home the *Nuuanu* had to undergo a complete survey, rigging as well as hull, for she was twenty-four years old. All the ceiling was taken up and several hundred holes were drilled through the plates to see if they had deteriorated or not. They only found one place where the plate was not equal to its original thickness and pronounced the ship better than the new vessels at present building.

In August we sailed for Honolulu, again with Mr. Richards as Mate and Mr. Werner as Second Mate. Parker, the steward, had to leave on account of his eyes, so I shipped a Japanese steward and a new carpenter. The latter could do a heavy job as well as the finest and was the best man at handling sails in the ship but he could not keep away from the rum in port and was usually unfit for duty on sailing day. We started off under favourable circumstances, with a good crew and fine weather, making 150 miles on the first day and 130 on the second. That day the carpenter reported twelve inches of water in the hold. The ship had never leaked and never needed pumping, so I thought there must be some mistake, but when I sounded and found thirteen inches I reluctantly turned back for New York. After rigging the pumps I soon found I could relieve her, so turned back again to continue the voyage. After only a few hours on the other tack she was leaking as badly as ever, so I again turned back for New York, the pumps going all the time, and arrived at Staten Island after being gone just a week. I know of nothing more annoying than having to turn back from a voyage after going through all the trouble to get away. We found there was a steady leak of one inch an hour while at anchor, but it was more at sea and was worse on one tack than on the other.

Mr. Noble, the head of our House in New York, was most surprised to see me. "Where on earth have you come from?" I soon told him, and we commenced our work to find the leak. First we towed to Erie Basin, and after discharging cargo for half a day found the leak on the starboard side amidships, about six inches under water. As we had received several smart raps from steamers on that side I think one of them must have started the plate. For a distance of six inches you could insert the blade of a sheath knife, but when the ship was at sea and heeling over the water must have squirted a long way, for the cargo was wet half-way across the 'tween deck. We had the place riveted up, then reloaded the cargo, and on August 31st, resumed our journey, having lost eighteen days.

As soon as the ship was fast in Erie Basin all but one of the crew took their belongings and left. A couple of days later the steward and the remaining man also cleared out. Each man had received a month's advance for which he had only worked a week. One would think they would consider it their duty to work off their obligation. Legally this allotment is not payable until the ship has been a month at sea, but the shipowners pay it on the day after she has sailed, and by law I believe they could be fined for doing so. The Second Mate Werner also left, but the Mate and the carpenter and the two Kanaka boys remained by the vessel. We shipped a Mr. Edwards, an Austrian, as Second Mate, but men were very scarce and instead of our good crew we had a miserable crowd. When it came to choosing watches on the first night out it was discovered that five out of the ten sailors could not steer. As I had done before in the *Reynard* during the Rebellion in 1864 I just drilled them until off Cape Horn, by which time we had a reasonable crowd for handling sails and the ship, if not for sailorising. The Line was crossed thirty-five days out, and on November 11th, we passed through the Straits of Le Maire. Taking twenty-four days to double the Horn, a little longer than my average, we arrived in Honolulu on January 22nd, and made fast to Bishop's Wharf. Of course Elizabeth was waiting for me, and as her husband had to go to Europe I spent all my spare time with her and her baby son.

This time we loaded in Honolulu, sailing on February 15th, for New York direct after being in port just twenty-four days. The new crew was rather poor, but better than the one coming out, and we made the passage in 123 days. I had shipped another Japanese steward in place of the one who deserted in New York and he proved one of the best I have ever had, remaining with me several years. Off the Delaware Capes we were in company with a large five-masted schooner, the *Kenio*, Captain Patten, both of Bath, Maine. A few years previously this schooner had made a trip round the world and the papers in Philadelphia had made much of a story that the captain's daughter had steered the ship for days during a hurricane. It was obviously a lot of journalistic nonsense, not for sailors to read, but this time we lay next to the *Kenio* at Staten Island in New York so I had a chance to meet this girl. I was surprised to find she was only a schoolgirl of thirteen and had been only nine at the time of the voyage round the world. The story had started as a joke in Manila with a friend of her father's, but some reporter had got hold of it and had blown it up out of all recognition. which just shows that any story about a ship is all right with the public if only it is impossible.

On the passage home we again encountered ice, on April 16th, in latitude 51°S. to the eastward of the Falkland Islands, or about 200 miles south and east of where we saw it the previous voyage. We sighted a number of bergs and it took us two days to get clear of them, but the weather was dark and gloomy so there was no romance in the sight, only dread and danger.

CHAPTER NINE

Nuuanu 11th voyage—Crew changes—story of the loss of the barque Prussia *in June 1907—Cape Horn—Fort George —Honolulu—Kanapali—Trinidad Island—New York—12th voyage, Officers hard to find, sailed July 1909, struggle off the Horn, Honolulu, Kanapali, crew troubles—13th voyage, sailed August 1910, grandson William Miller Reed, drunken crew, Cape Horn, Honolulu, more crew troubles, odd story of the loss of the ship* Arabia *in 1895, New York—14th voyage, sailed August 1911, crew list, brig* Fleetwing, *severe gale off Cape Horn, vessel damaged, return to Port Stanley in distress, crew troubles, life in the Falkland Islands, Hulks at Port Stanley, mails, Berkley Sound, penguins, funeral, first W/T mast in the Falklands, sailed and returned, voyage resumed, Honolulu at last.*

Most of the narrative up to this point has been written from memory. Though I may have made a few mistakes with regard to dates, and perhaps have got an incident in the wrong place, it is in the main correct. Looking back over all those voyages I remember what happened fifty years ago better than the events of five years ago. As far as I know I am the only survivor of those eight years in the *Reynard*—Captains, Mates, and Second Mates are all dead, though of course I know nothing of the crews. When I think how those men used to worry and fret over little troubles like head winds or unruly sailors I have to smile, and I try to take the lesson to heart that " Man is nothing but vanity."

Mr. Richards, the Mate, did not go with us this time, having had a drunken row with the Japanese carpenter in which his arm was broken, so I was obliged to ship a Mr. Granzo. A first voyage officer, Mr. Lensen, was the Second Mate and he did very well. Both officers were of German descent. The carpenter proved a very indifferent fellow and I was glad to change him for a green hand jack-of-all-trades, George S. Conrado, when we reached Honolulu. By way of contrast we had a very fine crew, with not one poor man. I think we could make a new topsail in a day, for each one could use a palm and needle and in bad weather could do anything in reason with the sails.

Sailing from New York on Tuesday, August 4th, 1908, in the Atlantic we experienced the hottest weather I ever remember at sea. Off the River Plate we passed the schooner *Alice Davenport*, bound from Winsor, Nova Scotia, to Bahia in Argentina. We had beaten her by twenty days, and had crossed the Line thirty-four days out. Nothing much of interest happened until we were approaching Staten Island, nearly down to the Horn. The day before we expected to sight the island the Mate told me that among the crew was a survivor from the ill-fated barque (formerly ship) *Prussia*. His name was Stanislas Pothin and he was French, a native of Mauritius. I called him into the cabin and this is the account he gave me of the disaster : —

" It was a thick stormy night, June 19th, 1907, with the wind NE and snow squalls when we ran ashore on Staten Island. When I came on deck at midnight the barque was running SSW under topsails and foresail. The lookout was at the pumps, for we had to pump out every hour in bad weather, with the windmill going too. Looking around I saw land ahead, so sang out ' Land ahead ' and ran into the forecastle to get on my clothes, having been called twenty minutes before twelve to get our coffee before relieving the wheel. The barque was brought to the wind on the port tack and braced up sharp. The Mate sent the watch below and I relieved the wheel. Still I could see the land and told Captain Johnson, ' Sir, I can see the land ahead on the lee bow.' ' Mind your steering,' said the Captain, then went below, probably to look at the chart. The Mate came along, and the Captain coming up at the same time asked him if that was the land, or clouds. He replied, ' Yes, Sir, it's land.' I then got orders to hard up the wheel and all hands were called to wear ship, but when we got round we were still unable to weather it and were close to the reef. Then we kept off and ran straight ashore. As soon as we struck, the sea boarded us on the starboard quarter, tearing the wheel away and washing me on to the top of the house. I met the Captain, who said, ' Go back to your wheel.' I replied, ' The wheel is gone, Sir, and the ship is aground.' He seemed to be dazed and was standing to leeward of the mizzen mast. I took him into the cabin. Then all the hands got into the boat on the forward house, after collecting life preservers and provisions. In the meantime the barque turned broadside to the reef. In twenty minutes the masts were over the side and the crew washing ashore on the rocks in all kinds of ways. At last we were all there except the cook and one man, Harry Hammond, of Atlanta, Georgia. The Captain and three others were badly injured, while all were more or less bruised and nearly frozen to death in the cold water, for it was dead of winter. At daylight we mustered together and crawled round the rocks to look for anything that had washed ashore, since it was then low water and we had come ashore at high water. Among other things we found a tin of matches, but they were all wet so we did not get a fire for three days. We made a hut out of wreckage. At ten o'clock the Captain died, and we were obliged to take his clothes for we had none. We rolled his body in a flag and left it under some bushes on the rocks. Five days later we buried him on top of the rock, laying a cross on his grave on our last day there. After climbing the mountain for a day and finding nothing there, we returned after one night to the first place. Then the carpenter and others started to build a boat, while a Norwegian seaman called Hoirten Hoseth and myself set out on an exploring expedition. We were living on seal, of which there were plenty. We started on the tenth day, and three evenings later we saw the light on New Year's Island. Returning with the report my companion froze to death, but I reached the camp in two days. When the boat was finished on the 4th July, John Hunter, the Mate, with the Second Mate and two men, took her away, reaching New Year's Island in seven days. From there they had to go to Saint John's harbour for a larger boat and then back. The lighthouse folk then sent a crew up and took us all there. We had been ashore forty-nine days, living on seal until they became scarce or frightened away, after which we lived on kelp. We spent seven days at New Year's Island, waiting for the steam tender of fifty tons to call. There we also found the crew of the British ship

Indore, wrecked the same time as ourselves. We were all taken to Punta Arenas, in the Straits of Magellan."

After I had heard this account the weather thickened up and it blew a gale from the North with driving rain, much the same kind of weather the *Prussia* had when she went ashore. Although I felt sure of my position I could not get out of my head the terrible experience of that vessel, and I gave the land such a wide berth that when it cleared up the next day we could not see it. So for the first time I passed Cape Horn going to the westward without sighting Staten Island. The following night was so beautiful I shall always remember it. After a period of rainy and unpleasant weather all the clouds had disappeared. With a full moon almost overhead the wind died away to a gentle breeze from the NE. I never felt happier as we made all sail and were going along at about seven knots from midnight till three. Then a cloud came out from the West and it took all hands to shorten sail. By 4.00 a.m. we were under lower topsails with a head wind and cloudy weather again, but I am so used to this sort of thing at Cape Horn that I took the disappointment cheerfully. Having a good crew we drove the barque to the Westward and in a few days had worked up to Diego Ramirez, with Cape Horn visible in the distance. We were twenty-six days "rounding" this time.

On the evening of October 19th, a large ship passed us, bound East under short sail. I thought it strange, for she could have carried all sail, until we could see she had a signal flying "Look out for ice". We had only time to hoist the Answering Pendant before it was dark and she was away in the gloom. We kept a good lookout for ice but did not see any, perhaps because I kept away to the north more than I would have done. However, there were many reports of ice this year off the Horn. Passing in sight of Mas A Fuera Island we had a fine run to the Line, and on October 27th spoke an English barque one hundred days from Liverpool when we were but eighty-four from New York. From the Line to Honolulu we had a poor run, so the whole passage took 131 days.

Coming home on our previous voyage the ship *Erskin M. Phelps* made the passage to Delaware Breakwater in 100 days and the *Fort George* took 101 to New York while I was 123 days. I had lost two days in the ice and had a miserable crew, but both these ships were much faster than the *Nuuanu.* Our firm had expected to load the *Fort George* out, but the Honolulu Iron

Works got her and she sailed ten days before us. For some reason or other they felt sore because they did not get her to load and the last words spoken to me were, " We hope you will beat the *Fort George*. As we took 131 days on the outward passage I was quite surprised when the tug came out to us at Honolulu and her captain shouted, " Where is the *Fort George*?" She had not arrived, although she was reported in latitude 10°N. at the same time as we were there. I thought she must have gone round Australia as I understood her Captain Fullerton had a great dread of Cape Horn and had never been round it to the westward in his life. Once when he was first at sea and was a sailor the ship he was in was lost with only two survivors and since then he had a dread of the place. She still had not arrived when we sailed for home, and in fact she never did arrive, so it remains one of the mysteries of the sea where she went down.

My daughter and grandson were on the wharf to meet me, having returned from a visit home where I had also seen them. How little I thought fifty years ago that I should one day find my grandson waiting for me at Honolulu! The *Nuuanu* is quite a nice little vessel to look at when painted up and one morning on my way up town I stopped at the head of the wharf to have a good look at her. Everybody knows that a captain always falls in love with his ship, and it is not so strange. This one, for instance, has been my home for twelve years and has carried me safely round the Horn twenty-two times. People ashore become attached to a house, but a ship is a thing of life, so it is not surprising that her master falls in love with her when she has carried him safely for so long. Perhaps that is the reason a ship is referred to as " she ", I know of no other. Anyhow, as I was admiring my sweetheart, a couple of man-of-war's men came along in their jaunty suits, and standing beside me one of them said, " I wonder what that bloody old hulk is putting out." Just fancy hearing your sweetheart spoken of in such terms! I turned to him and said, " That bloody old hulk is putting out general cargo from New York." " What, has she come all the way round Cape Horn?" Neither of these men had ever been round the Cape, and so I told them all about it. They were quite surprised to learn I was her Master, but perhaps I don't look like a sailor. At all events I do not roll in walking, as these two men did. I walked up the street with them, telling them how Honolulu looked fifty years

before, and when I finally said good morning to them, off came
their hats with the greatest respect.

After only twenty-three days in port we towed to Kanapali.
I enjoyed being back there and meeting old acquaintances. Sailing from there on January 20th, for New York we crossed the
Line on the ninth day and passed the Horn on the forty-eighth
day out. By March 26th, we were in latitude 26° 42′S., four days
ahead of our best passage. We thought we had the SE Trades,
but instead found weather more disagreeable than off the Horn,
rain and variable wind, a day of calm, then a gale from the North.
Finally came a spell of doldrums, which means the winds are not
steady in force or direction, with calms perhaps for a day perhaps
for an hour. The wind shifting from side to side makes it necessary for us to brace round the yards continually, and it rains in
torrents now and then, perhaps for hours, perhaps for five
minutes. The ropes and braces are swollen with water and everyone aboard is disagreeable. Between the showers the sun comes
out hot and stifling. I always pray on such a day that I may make
it as pleasant for everybody as possible and under no circumstances lose my temper.

On April 1st, after seven days of averaging only 50 miles a
day, we were close to *Trinidad Island and Martin Vas Rocks,
which I had not sighted for more than twenty years, though
passing near them twice a year. Trinidad used to be a penal
settlement for Brazil, I believe, and it must be horrible to wear
out a lifetime there, especially if one were accustomed to society,
as most political prisoners have been. A man might have been
there the last time I saw the place and still be there. It is particularly interesting to me as my mother's uncle, Captain Amasa
Delano of Duxbury, gave the earliest account of it. He was in
the ship *Perseverance* and landed there to get water for his ship
in 1805, finding goats, pigs, and cats. Trinidad is three miles long
and 2,000 feet high. Martin Vas is 300 feet in height, and they are
twenty-six miles apart, both barren-looking rocks. I expect there
is good fishing and I saw plenty of tropical birds about as well
as petrel which are found in all oceans. By the 14th April, we
were passing Fernando Noronha, which we see almost every passage. This island is much finer, extending some six miles with its
highest peak 1,000 feet high, in the shape of a pyramid. Although
this too is a Brazilian convict station and penal settlement and

* Not to be confused with Trinidad in the West Indies—W.J.M.

there is a large number of people on it, the climate cannot be equal to Trinidad's, for in the dry season it is too dry and in the rainy season it is too wet. It is directly on the track of vessels both ways and ought to have a telegraph station on it. We sighted several vessels in the vicinity and set our signal letters for a German steamer that passed close to us on her way towards Europe, hoping she would report us.

We were only 800 miles from New York on May 4th, and still hopeful of equalling our best passage, having gained considerably during the previous twenty days in very pleasant NE Trades. This crew were really the best workers I ever saw, they seemed to take as much interest in the vessel as the officers did. On several mornings I had flying-fish for breakfast, but Tom the cat got most of them. He can smell them as soon as they come on board.

On May 10th, I completed fifty-three years at sea, and I had hoped to be in by then. But we still had 400 miles to go, having had the most beautiful weather possible—for yachting, not for making a passage. We finally reached port on the 13th May. Two of my good crew I particularly remember when paying off. One of them was half full and he had some two hundred dollars he had worked a year for. The Commissioner tried to get him to look at his accounts, but he said they must be all right if I said they were, and he went away with all his money in his hand, swinging it around as though it was only a bundle of grass. The other man was just the reverse. He argued for a long time with the Commissioner over fifteen cents. Had he been sober he would have been perfectly satisfied, but he insisted that fifteen cents would get him a good meal. I saw him the next day, money all gone, wanting to know if he could go in the ship next voyage. I told him he could, but he was probably many miles away when we got ready to ship another crew.

Each voyage it seems harder to find officers as there are no young men available. This time I had to take two old fellows who, no doubt, were very good men twenty years before. The Second Mate had been very ill with beri-beri and seemed stupid. One could not get any information out of him. I have often noticed that people who have had that complaint never seem to be quite themselves again afterwards.

We left New York on July 17th, 1909, and had pleasant

weather to the Equator, which we crossed in longitude 25°W.
on August 21st. This weather continued to Staten Island, which
we sighted on September 20th. A moderate gale from the SW
drove us back behind the island, where we spent a delightful day
in smooth water only five miles from the land, for though the
mountains were covered with snow any land looks good after
two months of water only. My intention was to take the Straits
of Le Maire as usual, but when a breeze came from the North it
was so foggy that I went round the island. When we got to leeward of it the fog cleared and we had a lovely sail to Cape Horn,
with all sail set and the water as smooth as a pond. We passed the
Cape on September 23rd, only sixty-eight days out, passing five
or six miles off with the wind still northerly. A large full-rigged
ship was in company, but she steered away to the south and east
of Diego Ramirez Islands while I hugged the coast as long as I
could, until the wind came out from the NW and headed us off.
By then I was one hundred and thirty miles to the westward of
Cape Horn and thought all my troubles were over, even beginning to think of a quick passage and a pleasant surprise for my
friends at home. They had all bid me good-bye as though it might
be for the last time, for they all knew I had a hard cargo to handle.
They did not know what I knew, that it was impossible to stow
it without having the vessel too stiff. Only the stevedore and myself knew that, but as the ship was not full it was difficult to
secure the cargo, and they had lost so many friends in the last
few years off Cape Horn, also many good ships had disappeared
lately.

On the day we passed the Cape two large steamers passed us
bound East. I had never met one off Cape Horn before, and with
fine weather, smooth water, and steamers, it was like a yachting
cruise. But old Neptune was only fooling. The next day there
was a howling gale from the NW and all we could show was
lower topsails. We passed an English barque eighty days out from
the Tyne for Callao and signalled to her all the forenoon. Our
name seemed to puzzle them, they could not believe that
N U U A N U would spell anything, said they could read the flags
but could not make out what they meant. Evidently they had not
been to Honolulu. Then it really came on to blow, and continued
from September 25th, until October 3rd. We should have been
under a goose-winged topsail only, but rolled so fearfully I was
afraid the masts would go over the side, so kept both topsails

and the fore topmast staysail on her until the latter blew away. We shipped one sea that filled the decks, washing away the tanks and ladders, while all that kept the main topsail from blowing away was its being a hemp sail. By this time we had drifted down to latitude 61°S. and it was cold, freezing. We carried away the truss of the foreyard, having great difficulty in securing it with chains and tackles in the violent rolling.

Finally on October 10th, it moderated, the sea went down and the sun came out. But we were a sight. The whole ship was coated with ice from truck to deck and we had a bad list to port, for the cargo had shifted. We could scarcely stand on deck the ice made it so slippery. We made sail as fast as we could under the conditions, and by ten o'clock the sun melted the ice on deck so we could stand, then we got all sail on her. Neptune was not yet through with us, however, and by two o'clock the wind was back to NW and blowing a gale again. This continued for another three days, though not so hard as before, so we could carry sail and hold our own. One day at the height of these gales a large four-masted ship passed us on the other tack, heading north. Two weeks later we were again in company, but had reversed our positions. She was now five miles to leeward. We had a hard fight till October 27th, when we passed the island of Mas A Fuera and had another good look at the land. Then Neptune let up on us, the wind came SE and for four weeks we never braced a yard, until we crossed the Line in longitude 125°W, 127 days out and from there to port had fresh NE Trades.

Honolulu is always pleasant, yet each year now I find one or more of my old friends have passed on. Nothing unusual happened there on this visit, except that I enjoyed the company of my little grandson, Billy Moore, and we had great times together. We had rather a long time in Honolulu, waiting for the steam tug. In the end she could not tow us, but as I had expected to tow to Kanapali I had not placed my sugar ballast as low as I should have done. As a result the vessel was rather crank, so it took us a long time to beat up. It is not normally a bad job, being a kind of yachting trip, and gets the men into shape, especially such a miserable new crowd as I had this time. The mates had no control over them, although some of them were disposed to do right.

I was glad when we reached Kanapali, and even more so

o

when we got away, for most of the crowd were trying to get ashore all the time. When I had to leave the barque for two days to go across to Kahului to clear her I hardly expected to find all the crew on board on my return. I arrived back on board about 4.00 p.m. on Friday, intending to sail the next morning, but learned from the boatman that the men were trying to get ashore. Neither of the mates said a word about it to me, although they knew about it and it was their duty to warn me. So soon after I got on board I ordered the anchors hove up and the ship made ready for sea. The crew came aft and wanted to know what I was going to do about a man who had been discharged sick, one Englishman saying the Articles called for ten men, as though I did not know it. I pretended not to know that they had been trying to get away, and told them the carpenter would stand a watch and make the tenth man. They went to work heaving up the anchors, and when we cast off from the buoy I said to myself, " Now you are master of your own ship again." I was fully prepared to get the anchors up without their assistance if necessary, and to take them to sea whether they wanted to go or not. It was a Friday too, but I don't worry about " unlucky days " or ghosts, as I've remarked before.

The passage home was rather long, 141 days, but not as long as some we had made. I found my friends at home in New York were worrying about me, for an unknown barque had been run down and sunk with all hands off the coast of Brazil about where we ought to have been. One of my friends who is a dreamer had seen me in one of his dreams struggling in the water. He was quite surprised when I came in all right, in fact almost disappointed that his dream was not true!

Among the crew was a soldier who had had little or no sea experience, but he was a willing and able fellow and I took pains to teach him, so that by the time we reached home he could " hand, reef, and steer " as well as most of them, though that was not saying much. The only first-class sailor among them was old Ranzie, a Scot, and I made him the sailmaker. He had lost the forefinger on his right hand, but managed to sew with his middle finger. I had found a splendid carpenter, so managed to get a lot of work out of the crew and the barque looked as well as usual arriving at home. But I had to do it myself, as though the two mates had little control over the crew the men would do anything for me. The lime-juicer who made the complaint about leaving

with one man short was a real sea lawyer and at the start was
the leader of all the mischief. But I am quite a sea lawyer too,
and put my wits against his. He was impudent to the officers and
he was lazy, and therein lay my opportunity. I kept calling the
attention of all the crew to the fact that this man was letting
them do all the work, and it was not long before they were all
down on him. First an American sailor gave him a good thrash-
ing on deck, while I stood by to see the fun and fair play. Then
the soldier found fault in him and gave him a trouncing in the
forecastle. By the time the ship reached New York all the conceit
was taken out of him. So much for management. Most captains
and mates would have taken the conceit out of him themselves,
but the world ashore would have fined them hundreds of dollars
for " abuse of seamen." I must say it's much more satisfactory, if
rather expensive.

Our thirteenth voyage commenced on Friday, August 5th, 1910,
from New York, and this time I took my grandson William Miller
Reed with me. He was a very nervous boy and it was thought
the trip would be good for his health, though in my ignorance I
had an idea that all he wanted was to be out of doors, at work
on a farm, or anything away from school. He was just thirteen
years old.

Such a drunken crowd I never started to sea with, though I
have heard of them. Five of these had been with me before. The
Second Mate, carpenter, Ranzie, and half the crew were stupid.
We waited several hours for them to come aboard and the Mate
took several bottles of whisky from them or they would have
been worse. I was thinking of coming to anchor at *Staten Island,
but just then they all came down but one A.B., so we proceeded
to sea. As it was summertime I did not care so much. After a
while we managed to get some sail on, and with a light wind
from the SW were soon outside the light-ship. On the first night
out only one half the crew were on deck, but the winds were
light and the weather fine until we crossed the Line on September 22nd, 48 days out, the longest I ever took in getting to
the Line. From there to Cape Horn the weather was ideal, not
a gale of wind until we reached Staten Island, then a moderate
SW gale while we were behind the land. Another ideal day

* Staten Island in New York harbour.

followed as we lay becalmed about three miles from it, looking at the snow-capped mountains with the seals and penguins playing around us.

Then towards night a Northerly breeze sprang up and we sailed down through the Straits of Le Maire. With the sea almost as smooth as on the previous voyage, but going much faster, we passed within five miles of Cape Horn and away to the west of it until in latitude 56°27'S. longitude 75°15'W., just twenty-eight miles south of the Cape, we stopped. I was afraid of a repetition of last voyage, but we were able to hold our own and on November 1st, were in latitude 54°S. Then for ten days, by carrying sail hard and having a good crew, for they had proved good men when sober, we managed to keep off Desolation Island. It was in sight for a week, each day a little nearer, and we began to get anxious. It would have been a horrible place to be ship-wrecked, but there was a last resort. If necessary we could go East and drift along the land as long as we could carry a little sail. However, on the afternoon of the 12th, when we were close enough to see the breakers, the wind shifted to the northward, we wore ship to the west, and by morning were well clear of the shore.

In the SE Trades we passed a four-masted barquentine bound towards the Chilean coast, the first sailing vessel we had sighted since passing the River Plate. I don't remember ever rounding the Horn before without seeing a sail. Altogether we had the finest weather, except for that ten days struggle off the west coast of Tierra del Fuego. One has to come round the Horn and watch the weather for weeks to properly appreciate the fine settled weather of the Trades and the Tropics. I felt as though I had nothing to do now until we reached Cape Horn again on the way home, for the mates could attend to the work, the wind was nearly aft, just enough on the side to make the head sails draw, and we were travelling over the same ground which I had already covered twelve times in the *Nuuanu*. Off Cape Horn I hardly sleep, and never trust to anybody, but am always ready for an emergency. As I pass over these old tracks I think of the old shipmates that have passed away, many of them long ago.

Crossing the Line on December 9th, we had hopes of being in Honolulu by Christmas, but for the rest of the way had almost constant rain and squalls. On January 2nd, we made the island of Hawaii, but the wind was NW so we passed between the islands and beat up in smooth water. On the morning of the 3rd, we were off Diamond Head and, as the wind was still ahead, glad to get a tugboat and be towed into port. This was my second-longest passage in the *Nuuanu*, 151 days. My younger daughter and her husband and little boy were on the wharf to welcome me, and of course I knew everybody on the waterfront. This time Captain Fuller, the Harbourmaster, had passed on and the place did not seem the same without him, though he had contracted leprosy and was probably glad to go.

As usual the " land sharks " enticed my crew ashore, and the Mate, Mr. Lenard, practically drove the Second Mate and the carpenter out of the ship. Had I known him as well as I do now I would have sent him away and kept them. He is a man of great experience, but he is certainly the most disagreeable man to me that I was ever shipmates with. Sometimes I think he is a little out of his mind, he will go for a week without speaking and then the next week will talk non-stop until he is very tiresome. But he is getting old, and to be Mate for all one's life is enough to make a man crazy. The Second Mate, Mr. Moore, was from Maine, an excellent man but for rum. Both officers had done well on the way out. I have often noticed that the sailors work much better for American officers than they do for foreigners, especially Dutch or Scandinavian.

When paying off my crew at the Commissioners' a man spoke to me. He was dressed in a naval rig and at first I did not recognise him. He was the man I had discharged sick at Kanapali the previous voyage. The next morning I was surprised and hurt to receive a lawyer's letter claiming a year's wages for him, saying I had thrown him ashore without money, etc. Now I had taken him ashore, hired a carriage to take him to Lahaina, had him examined by a doctor who diagnosed appendicitis, and put him on the boat for Honolulu, all against the wishes of the officers and crew, who maintained he was only shamming. I had not paid him off because no money was due to him and it was essential to get him to hospital quickly. According to his own story I had saved his life, and now he was perfectly well, with a good job on the *Thetis* at forty dollars a month. I thought he had come to thank me for my kindness, instead of which he claimed I had thrown him on the beach. Well, after telegraphing to Boston and London (for the barque is insured against such troubles) I received orders to settle the claim for $200. I would rather have fought it out in court and pleaded my own case, and am pretty sure I would have won it.

The new crew were a miserable lot. I took one of the old sailors as carpenter and a young fellow called Heimenn as Second Mate, and when we left in tow for Kanapali had six white sailors and four Kanakas. These native boys had never been to sea and were entirely ignorant of seamanship. Ranzie, who had spent all his time in port drunk, was the only one of the last good crew left. He was not sober enough to appear on deck until after we reached Kanapali, and a few days later he was taken ill and had to be sent to hospital in Honolulu. But this time I was careful to sign him off the Articles and to send his receipts and the news of his coming to the agents at Honolulu, so I don't think there will be any kick coming when we get back next time. In his place I took another Kanaka boy, making five, so that my crew now consisted of four white men (of whom only one was worthy of being called an A.B.), one German boy born in the islands, and my grandson Miller, who is on the Articles as a Sailor Boy and in fact taught the Kanaka boys to hand, reef, and steer (which makes them A.B.s). They are very strong fellows and I would rather have them now than white men.

We passed Cape Horn sixty-eight days out, going close to Diego Ramirez Islands. This small group lies some sixty miles South West of the Cape and is only about two hundred feet high. Though I have seen them a great many times, sailed round them, and of course had to keep a lookout for them, I shall always connect them with the loss of the ship *Arabia,* of Bath, Maine, Captain MacLoon. She sailed from New York for San Francisco on March 4th, 1895 and ran ashore on these islands on May 25th. Her crew numbered twenty-eight all told, including the captain's wife and small son. Mr. Lenard, my present Mate, was the mate of her at the time and he tells a very strange story about her loss. He says she was reported by her captain as having foundered at sea, the crew watching her go down from the boats and later being picked up by the English barque *Achilles,* Captain Dunbar, and taken to Montevideo. But his own version is entirely different, and he has it all typewritten and signed by nearly all the crew. In it he says they had been beating back and forth off Cape Horn and in one of the gales their bulwarks had been partially washed away. At last, with a fine

East wind but thick weather, they were steering to the West with all sail set. Just as he came on deck at 8.00 p.m. they saw the islands right ahead, close aboard. The helm was put down and an attempt made to brace up the yards, but before they could clear them the ship piled up on a rock on the north side of the east island. It must have been in a smooth place or a kind of cove, for they took to their boats and landed, finding a house or hut left by sealers in 1855 which the captain, his wife, and little son occupied, while the crew lived under tents. They were able to go back and forth to the ship and had plenty of provisions after the first day or two, also a barrel of whisky. Eight days later this English ship came close to the islands so the Mate went off to her in one of their three good boats, then came back and got the others. It seems from this account that the Captain and Mate were at loggerheads, and the Mate says he had hard work to persuade the Captain to leave the islands and that he would do nothing to help the crew throughout. Altogether it is a very strange story and I hope some day I shall meet the Captain and hear his version of it. He, the Captain, was afterwards master of the *Martha Davis* at the time she was burned in Hilo. Actually, one of the worst points against the Mate in this story is the fact that he lost the ship's log book, although all their effects were saved. I think he would be apt to be a mutinous fellow. His whole life, and he is quite an old man, is a volume of shipwrecks, fires, and mutinies. He scarcely tells of a voyage free from trouble. No wonder he is so nervous and always worrying about something going to happen.

From Trinidad in the South Atlantic to New York we had normal weather and had a good run of thirty-six days, anchoring off Staten Island on a Saturday evening as on the previous voyage. Next morning my grandson and I went up to New York and across to Brooklyn, then, as we had plenty of time we took the afternoon train to Philadelphia, where it was fun for me to see him greeting his friends and his mother. The following day he returned to New York with me, and quite a crowd of relatives and friends went down with us on the tug to Staten Island to bring the *Nuuanu* up to Jersey City to discharge. The voyage had been a great experience for the boy and he was the life of the ship, after getting over a little homesickness and seasickness the first week. His nervousness had gone, he no longer had to wear glasses, had grown several inches in height, gained twenty pounds in weight, and earned $47 besides his board for ten months. He had seen whales, porpoises, dolphins, Albacore, and flying-fish, and had caught sharks, albatross, and Cape pigeons. In geography and arithmetic he had gained more than he would have at school, for he became quite a navigator, while in seamanship he could hand, reef and steer, and was like a monkey aloft. While we were towing up harbour he dressed himself in a sort of pirate's rig of his own and mounted the rigging at a dog's trot, not stoping until he had reached the head of the royal mast. Then he seized the royal backstay with both hands and slid down to the deck almost as quick as falling, by which time his relatives were about ready to faint. He came down so rapidly that I could not help cautioning him, for though he had done the same thing almost daily I feared that in his endeavour to show off he might meet with an accident.

On Saturday, August 12th, 1911, we started on our fourteenth voyage with everything propitious. The barque was in fine condition, having gone through extensive repairs on deck and had her hold ceiling renewed. For the first time in my life I shipped a crew without the aid of a shipping master, the men coming on board by themselves, most of them without any advance. As we were to have so many experiences involving various individuals I will mention all their names here: —

Mate—J. B. Monteith, of Nova Scotia
2nd Mate—James McCauley, of Ireland
Steward—Yejiro Soneda, Japanese
Carpenter—John Stram, Russian Finn
Cabin Boy—Hendrik Vlietstra, Holland
A.B.—Louis Andrawson, Norwegian
    „   Peter Anderson, Norwegian
    „   Rathor Rasmussen, Norwegian
    „   Joseph Guillau, French
    „   Louis Mayvan, Norwegian
    „   Henry Banter, German
    „   F. Flebbe, German
    „   Anthony Punis, Russian
    „   Kurata Nurata, Japanese
Boy—George F. Rush, American

This list gives an idea of the different nationalities forming an American crew at this time, and shows clearly that Americans have ceased to become sailors. The only one on board, apart from myself, being a simple-minded boy whose father hoped that a sea voyage might improve him. His health was good but his mind was weak.

Our passage to the Line was one of the pleasantest I ever had and I even hoped to put it on record when I arrived at Honolulu that I had the ideal crew. This illusion was soon to be shattered and six months later I could truthfully say that I had never had so much trouble with a crew in all my thirty-nine years as Master. Crossing the Line on the forty-second day out we proceeded with pleasant SE Trades until, just south of Rio, we had one of the worst squalls I ever experienced in that part of the world. It came from the NW and luckily we had all our new sails bent or we would have lost most of them. The gale only lasted four hours, then we had ideal weather again till we neared Staten Island. On Sunday, October 15th, we sighted a sail ahead, coming up with her about 4.00 p.m. She proved to be the full-rigged brig *Fleet Wing*, 80 days out from Liverpool, bound for Port Stanley to become a hulk. We exchanged longitudes, and the wind being light she was still in sight next morning. Off Staten Island we met variable winds and weather, and after a day or two looking at the hills we passed down by Cape Saint John and got within forty miles of Cape Horn. That morning we passed a small iceberg to the north of us not far from the land. The Second Mate did not report it to me and we were past it when I came on deck at 5.00 a.m. He is certainly a most stupid officer, if there is anything you might call the captain for it is an iceberg, and off the Horn I sleep with both ears open.

On the evening of November 3rd, in 55°28'S. 64°00'W. we met the worst gale I ever saw at Cape Horn. It not only blew with hurricane force but it was freezing. The ship was as snug as possible, with all sail securely furled and only a goose-winged main topsail on the ship. Our royal yards were on deck and all their gear was unrove. During the afternoon the Mate got rolled across the deck, injuring his knee, and the carpenter was also washed across the deck and injured. The gale commenced at NW then hauled around to SW and South. When it got to West we tried our best to wear ship, but did not succeed and blew away our new foresail in the attempt. Had we succeeded we should have luffed up to the sea and all the subsequent trouble and damage would have been avoided. We lay over on our side and our lee, or port, bulwarks began to wash away, so I let go the lower main topsail sheet, letting the sail blow away, and cut the weather topgallant backstays to let the topgallant masts go over the side. They would not go, the topgallant rigging held them and no man could go aloft. The thermometer stood at 27°F., our rigging, masts, and sails were covered with ice. The lee forecastle door was smashed and the forecastle washed out, the sailors losing all their clothes except those they were wearing. They had to come into the cabin to live, sleeping on the deck in their oilskins, and we tommed the cabin door on the inside to prevent its being stove in. All night we lay in this condition, and I must give credit to Louis Mayvan and Joe Guillau, for they worked harder than the Second Mate did to batten the fore hatch and the forecastle scuttle, succeeding so well that very little water got down them. The galley was gutted and the stove broken, so we could only boil water in the cabin, but we had plenty of tea and coffee, and canned meats and hard tack to eat.

On the morning of the 4th, it moderated a little, though still blowing a living gale from the South clear and cold, with our masts iced from truck to deck. Sixty feet or more of our port bulwarks were gone and water was leaking into the hold through the bolt holes of the broken stanchions. We could not sound, but the ship had a bad list to port and we knew there was more or less water in the hold. Towards noon we were able to get the vessel off before the wind and ran to the north under the lower fore topsail and upper main topsail. It was easier for us then and all day we ran before the wind. I expected we would see Staten Island, but the current had taken us to the eastward and on the morning of the 5th, we made the west end of the Falkland Islands. As I could not weather it, the wind having hauled to the SW and having no braces on the port side of the fore yards, I kept away round the islands from headland to headland, keeping as close in as I could so as not to miss the entrance to Port Stanley and passing through miles and miles of kelp. It was worrying, but the chart did not show any dangers and we had to keep her going. There must have been a very strong current with us for we came the whole distance of 450 miles in two days with only two pieces of canvas on us. But it was blowing, our brand new upper main topsail was blown from the rope in places.

At noon on the 6th, we made the lighthouse at the entrance
to Port Stanley, and passed close to the Billey Rocks where three
vessels have been lost coming in without pilots in recent years.
Then bracing up as sharp as possible, for we had braces on the
starboard side, we set all the sail we could fore and aft, reached
in as far as we could go, then anchored in 15 fathoms of water.
Of course we commenced to get up chain as soon as we saw the

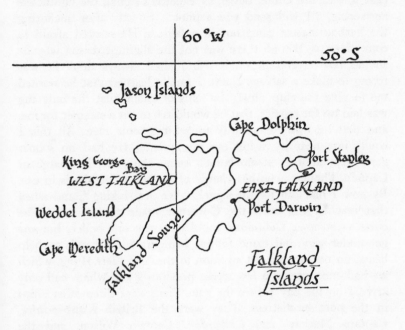

lighthouse but there was only time to bend one before we came
to anchor. Fortunately the Mate had been able to limp forward
and attend the bending of the chains, or we might not have got
so far in or might have drifted away again, for it took all my
time to navigate the ship between the rocks and breakers. I had
scarcely slept for four days and nights. The water was now quite
smooth and after hauling down the fore and aft sails I let go the
anchor. By rights I should have lowered the upper main topsail,
but I forget all about it till I sent the men aloft to furl it. By
then the tide had swung the ship so that the sail had come aback,
and the man Louis Mayvan used some very insulting language
to me. When he had had his say I told him I was so thankful

all our lives were saved that he could have the privilege of calling me anything he cared to. When he would not keep quiet I told him he should have the benefit of the law and that he could consider himself in irons until the magistrate had decided on his case.

We sounded the pumps and found 28 inches of water in the hold. I had already set our signal for a pilot and hoisted the ensign with the Union down, as a distress signal, the lighthouse answering, " I will send you a pilot ". Shortly after anchoring the harbourmaster came out in a launch. He seemed afraid to come near us, though there was not the slightest reason why he should not have come on board. I shall always think he was trying to make a salvage claim. I finally learned that he wanted me to give the ship ninety fathoms of chain, that the only tug was laid up for repairs, that he would try to get a steamer for me, and that he was going away to get me some men. All this I could just hear by using my megaphone. He had no sooner gone than another steam launch came alongside, in charge of Captain Thomas, who has charge of the tug when she is in use. By now I had run up the signal, " We are sinking ", and when that reached the town the Governor made them hustle. The coasting steamer *Columbus* could only use one boiler, but she got under way and came for us, bringing some hands to help heave up our anchor. In addition to the brig *Fleet Wing*, which we had encountered a few weeks previously and which had only arrived on the day before the gale, there were three other ships in the port in distress. They were the British *Kinross-shire*, Captain Mackay, and *Claverdon*, Captain Wilson, and the Russian four-masted barque *Albyn*, Captain Karlson. All four of these captains came on board, and while one of them took the wheel the others helped to man the windlass. By 9.00 p.m. we were safely moored with two anchors inside Port Stanley.

There we remained for five months, in the course of which I came to know the town and islands and their people very well. We lay at the top of the bay, the town within hailing distance and the opposite shore about half a mile away. The harbour is full of sea gulls that are very tame, and wild duck of some description are always swimming round. The shores are barren, not a single tree to be seen and I believe there is not one on the islands, only piles of rock and rocky hills between which a scanty vegetation grows which will support sheep and a limited number of cattle. The cattle and most of the horses looked wild and have long uncombed hair and tails, but the sheep look fine and sheep-raising is the principal occupation. The population of the islands at this time was about two thousand three hundred, of which eight hundred lived in Stanley, the chief town and port. The Falkland Island Company owns nearly everything and does all the repairing to the vessels that come here, but the number of workmen is limited, just about enough to repair one vessel at a time. I was given to understand that each man could do all parts of the work—wood, iron, caulking, and even rigging. With three ships ahead of us in need of repairs it was obvious that our stay would be a long one.

On November 8th, we surveyed the damage to the ship, estimating from her draught of nineteen feet that about 120 tons of water were in the hold. There was no American Consul with whom I could consult, but Lloyd's Agent, Mr. Gerling, was most helpful and the Governor, Mr. W. L. Allardyce, C.M.G., who had formerly been at Fiji and had visited Honolulu more than once, was also very kind to me. We found the ship's hull to be perfectly sound and did not anticipate much damage to cargo as no water had gone down the main or mizzen hatches and very little down the forehatch. The damage was all where the port bulwarks had been torn away, and of course some sails and stores had been lost. Cost of repairs was estimated at $10,000 or thereabouts, apart from a salvage claim made by the steamer *Columbus* and one by the launch *Plym*, which it was agreed should be settled by arbitration in London. We started work on the rigging and some of the carpentry ourselves, and it looked as though we might even make the new sails before any shore labour became available.

Crew troubles took up a fair amount of my time. Most of them were due to drink ashore, but I discovered that the Irish Second Mate McCauley was a very disloyal fellow and had been running me down to the crew in the forecastle for some time before we came to grief. On November 11th, for the sake of discipline, I brought the mutinous sailor Mayvan before the magistrate, and although he did not put him in gaol he gave him a hard talking to and advised me to get rid of him. I decided I would also be better off without the Second Mate. On Dec. 8th, we had the second trial of Louis Andrawson before a Superior Court, the Governor presiding. He was charged with cutting Henry Banter in a drunken brawl with knives, and I was counsel for the prisoner. We were all day taking evidence, and next day the jury found him guilty. He was sentenced to hard labour for one year. I thought he would be cleared, for all said that I made a splendid defence, on which the Governor publicly complimented me, and the evidence was entirely circumstantial. No one saw him do it, and there were three others drunk, two of them with pointed knives, only this man's knife was found on the spot covered with blood. I hope they got the right man, but no one is sure, so perhaps he will be pardoned when we are ready to sail. In any case it was a good lesson for the sailors in port, though in my view the man or government that sold them the liquor is the true guilty party. Afterwards I saw the prisoner every day, painting fences and government property.

For many years I had passed by the Falkland Islands on my voyages back and forth around Cape Horn. I had never known much about them and had thought of them as being populated by some kind of South American race, so it was a surprise to find a regular English people with such institutions as churches, schools, and public houses. There is no communication with the outside world except by steamer once a fortnight, and there are no places of amusement, so the public houses are naturally well patronised. When I consider how easy it would be to have a Temperance Colony I am surprised they do not make it so. It is not known for certain who discovered the islands. Although neither Vespucci nor Magellan mention them in the accounts of their voyages they appear in the charts of 1527 under the name of the Ascension Islands. Later they appeared as the Simpson Group, and as Maiden Land. The first authentic account of their discovery was given by Captain Davis of the British *Desire,* but they have been claimed by many nations and given a variety of names, such as Davis Southern Islands, Hawkins Maiden Islands, Isles of Sebold de Weert or Sebaldian Islands, Nova Belgia, Ancien Islands, Isles Nouvelles, Les Malouines, and Isles Malvernus. French, Portuguese, Spanish, English, and others have all laid claim to them. In 1833 the British flag was hoisted by H.M.S. *Clio,* and for some years the place was in charge of the naval officers engaged in surveying. In 1842 a Colonel Moody took charge and a British Civil Administration was formed, the islands being named after Lord Falkland, the Treasurer of the Navy. I find very few people in the town that have any love for the place, the talk is usually of other

countries as though they are exiles in a foreign land. I was struck
by their poor teeth, not a dentist in the place and only one
doctor. Amusements being totally lacking and news scarce, people
have to entertain each other, while tales and rumours spread
quickly as in all small places. The streets are stony and everyone
wears thick-soled Congress boots.

The houses are very small and most people in comfortable
circumstances have a flower garden on the north side, with the
entrance through a conservatory. The Governor has a large hot-
house, heated by steam pipes, and even attempts to raise grapes,
peaches, pears and other fruits. I think I missed the morning
papers and magazines more than anything else. One little monthly
publication contains all the news of the islands. I read Captain
Snow's account of his coming to the islands fifty-five years
previously to establish a Missionary depot for the conversion
of the Fuegans, finding it of interest because of its survey of the
islands. Evidently the same rapid changes of weather were pre-
valent then as in 1911. One day early in December I walked
across the island with a party of ladies and gentlemen. They
said it would not rain, but I thought it would. We got all the
rain we wanted and more, as we walked about five miles each
way, through bogs and over rocks and up and down hills.
Certainly the English ladies are great walkers. In some places
the peat was ten feet thick. It is used in every house, making a
slow but pleasant fire, and seemed to be free for the gathering.
At one point of this walk we saw a schooner ashore. She had
been wrecked in the same gale that damaged us, and preparations were in hand to refloat her. A few days later they were
successful and she was towed round to Port Stanley by her
owners, the Falkland Island Company.

With the approach of the Christmas holidays all the talk was
of the coming sports and people began to come in from the
Camp, as they called it. Anything outside the town is called the
Camp, and for a long time I thought they were referring to some
village of tents or huts. The only transport on the islands is the
horse and people ride in from a considerable distance, a hundred
miles or more. On Christmas Day most people went to church,
and put in a little practice on the racecourse. Boxing Day was
devoted to horse-racing, and on the third day of the holidays
there was every kind of race for men, women, girls, and boys—
Throwing the Hammer, Putting the Shot, Obstacle Race, High

Jump, Long Jump, etc. My crew were third in the Boat Race
and got no prize, nor did my boys win in their races, so it was
left for me to win the Veteran's Race. I had rigged up a tent
for some friends, and taking it all round we had a jolly good
time at the sports. At the end of the day the Governor distributed
the prizes and the holidays concluded with a ball in the school-
house, which was the only hall available, everyone turning up in
their dress suits and evening dresses.

From the number of hulks in Port Stanley the place might
appropriately be named the Cape Horn Mausoleum. In any
direction one looked could be seen the hull of some old vessel,
or perhaps just a stern post, or a stern, or a few ribs only visible
at the low water. Each old bone could tell a story could one but
follow it from the first home where it grew before being taken
to the shipyard, a story of the young men and boys who helped
to shape it for its place in the construction of a ship, of the cheers
and good wishes at her launching, of her first voyage bright with
paint and varnish and with her brasswork shining. Then the
good-byes, many of them for ever, the arrival at a foreign port,
the years of sailing through seas hot and cold, boys growing into
men on board and men growing old, still she ploughed the ocean
until Neptune in one of his fiercer moods said, " You have done
your duty and I will send you to your last resting place in Stanley,
to keep company with ships from all parts of the world."

One day I looked over the old East Indiaman *Jehlum* as she
lay across the landing stage of one of the richest men in the
Falklands, Mr. Vere Packe, used as a store-house and carpenter's
shop. She had laid there forty years. What a magnificent ship
she must have been and how proud her captains must have been
of her. Her very beams were of mahogany. At the West Jetty
lay the *Charles Cooper*, of Boston, Mass. Very likely my father
helped to build her, perhaps some of her timber came from the
woods where I played as a boy, and now we have met briefly
again. Although her decks were leaky they stored such cargo as
coal in her hold. Her bottom was a mass of barnacles around
which waterfowl fed at low water. She was rudderless and mooring chains were passed up through her rudder post. Housed over
and with seven windows on each side of the sloping roof the
deck was used as a warehouse for cargoes from the coastal
steamers of light draft. One wonders who Charles Cooper was.
Lying against her were the ribs and lower deck of the *Bacton*,

which had been there for sixty years. At the end of the East Jetty was the *Egerie,* a St. John's built ship, and supporting the jetty was the *William Shand* which had been there thirteen years, only the lower deck remaining. Then there was the once famous clipper ship *Snow Squall,* which they say was running away from the *Alabama* when she ran ashore on Staten Island, but got off in a sinking condition and made Stanley.

There was the *Great Britain,* the first vessel to cross the Atlantic with a screw. She has the lines of an extreme clipper, and a picture of her when she was built in 1841 which is in the Governor's house shows her beautiful qualities, with six masts, one or more of which were square rigged. Nearby lay the schooner *Farie,* formerly an American slaver, and the older inhabitants who remembered her coming told of the immense spars she had. Of course she was built for speed, not only to save her live cargo but to escape the men-of-war that were looking for slavers. She could probably tell a terrible story of misery. Close to her was the hull of the American whaler *Rosie Baker.* A sad story was told me of the American ship *Philadelphia* lost on the Billey Rocks at the entrance of the harbour. She had been seen for some time, some said three days, before she attempted to come in without a pilot and struck about seven in the evening, sinking with all hands. Perhaps the captain had no chart, and the rock she struck is covered at high water.

On Wednesday every second week the mail arrives from England, and on the alternate weeks it comes from Valparaiso via the Straits of Magellan. It is looked forward to as an incident in the life of the place, not only because it brings later news from the Earth (for this seems like a separate planet) but because if the day is fine most of the passengers come ashore to see the town and the museum, to buy souvenirs, and to have a look at the *natives.* On one of these occasions we had the largest steamer of the company, a vessel of some 8,000 tons. She was too large to enter the harbour so anchored outside, while about one hundred passengers came on shore. I found several Americans trying to get something to eat and was able to help them to get lunch as, not knowing if there would be any, the hotels had made no provision for them. Later I went on board their ship and spent a delightful afternoon with my new-found countrymen. As there were about fifty of the Stanley people on board too, we had a jolly time until they sailed at five o'clock.

P

One day during our stay the ship *British Isles* arrived with her master, Captain Anderson, sick. When he had recovered sufficiently to see visitors I called on him at the hospital. I had heard rumours that he knew me and I go about the world almost looking for men I have met before who are liable at any moment to cross my path again. I was not surprised, therefore, to find that we had indeed met and had been together sixteen years before in the port of Buenos Aires. We had time to recall all the old friends who had been in that port with us and to follow their later adventures. At least half of them had gone to the Home Port, there to await our arrival.

The brig *Fleet Wing*, which we had overtaken off the River Plate in September on our way out to Cape Horn, was now a dismantled hulk and was hauled alongside *Nuuanu* to take a portion of our cargo temporarily so that the workmen could get at the damaged part of the ship to repair it. By late January the weather had improved very much and some days were quite warm. The *Kinross-shire, Albyn,* and *Claverdon* had gone their respective ways, leaving *Nuuanu* as the only vessel repairing. We hoped to be finished in another two months. I began to feel as though I belonged to the place, for although I now had a little mail from some of my relations I'd still had no word from the owners or from my own folks. My sailors were making a little extra money by working on the local steamers that came for cargo. In that way they could get back some of their clothing lost at the time of our disaster.

On January 16th, a number of us had a trip to Berkley Sound on the tug *Sampson*. She was chartered by a Mrs. Smith, who had just returned from a European visit and was on her way to her home at Johnson's Harbour at the head of the Sound. I went along at the Captain's invitation, to enjoy the sail and see the country, and although there seemed to be some heart-burning due to differences between the captain's other guests and Mrs. Smith's party, I was innocent and it only made me smile. As I have remarked, Stanley is a small place and little things often loom large in such communities.

Mrs. Smith was a wealthy widow with five sons and two daughters. Both daughters were married and living on their farms, two of the sons kept hotels in Stanley, the other three running their father's farm which consisted of thousands of acres and supported many thousands of sheep. Sheep are raised here mainly for wool and skins, most of the carcases being thrown away. They take about three minutes to shear a sheep and this was the busy season for four months. The rest of the year they have a lazy time. One very fine sight was to see a flock of sheep being driven by dogs on the side of a mountain or hill. They look like a stream of running water and the dogs seem as intelligent as humans in their care of them.

The land up Berkley Sound is much more free from stone and rock than it is around Stanley, reminding me of the New England hills where there are no trees. I am told that the climate is much milder in the West Falklands than in the East. Leaving Port Stanley at 11.00 a.m. we were back at 7.00 p.m. after waiting two hours at Johnson's Harbour. During our wait there we shot three wild geese. We only saw six, but sometimes the pastures are covered and a bounty is offered for their heads. They eat so much grass it interferes with the sheep raising. I was surprised to learn that on these islands our New England strawberries grow in great profusion.

One of the most interesting sights in the Falklands is the penguin rookeries, where these curious birds congregate in vast numbers and march like regiments of soldiers. All the rookeries I saw were about a mile from the water, which seemed strange because penguins are such slow walkers, waddling along like a duck but upright like a man. Perhaps the reason is that if the young took to the water too early some fish or animal would devour them. As we passed from point to point we came to the different rookeries—the Jackass, Gentu, Rockey, Macharone, and King. Each is different in looks and habits and the separate varieties keep to themselves. The Gentu are here all the time, but the Rockeys leave for parts unknown, returning every year almost to the day. As we passed a small island called Couchant, a pile of uneven rocks about eighty feet high and a mile in circumference, it was covered with Rockeys like flies on a molasses cask. They did not move or flutter a wing when we blew the whistle, though when we passed Kidney Island the tremendous sea lions that looked as black as ink against the yellow beach immediately took to the water.

The British cruiser *Glasgow* visited Port Stanley about this time for a stay of three weeks. I have never seen a more quiet set of men from a man-of-war and I did not see one of them under the influence of liquor. Captain Hill, his officers and men, looked as though they could give a good account of themselves if called upon, and every one seemed to be an Englishman, not as ours used to be, a mixture of all nations. One evening her crew gave a concert in the Parish Room, which was far too small for it, and it really was very fine. As everybody knows everybody else at any such event in Stanley it is lots of fun. It made me smile to hear them just as pronounced in their praise of England as we are in the U.S. in praise of our own country. Later the ship went to Lively Island for a couple of days' target practice, then returned for a further short stay. The Captain was said to be very strict with his men, perhaps that is the reason they kept so sober.

Another very pleasant annual event took place on February 23rd, during the man-of-war's visit. This was the Flower Show, or Fair, when prizes were given for every form of husbandry—vegetables, flowers, cooking, needlework, carpentry, and harness for horses made by hand, even for shoe repairing. The principal exhibit was wool and about twenty or thirty bundles were on show, each bundle being the amount taken from one sheep. Although there were not less than a dozen different kinds they all looked the same to me, unless some were cleaner than others, but even the best of it did not look very clean. After the prizes had been distributed in the evening the Governor made a short speech, as did the Captain of the *Glasgow*. After the latter had praised the Girls and Boy Scouts he went on to describe the glories of his country and I never heard a Fourth of July orator that could surpass him. You would have thought England was on the verge of war and that it needed every man, woman, and child to preserve her. Afterwards the Governor advised him to buy the fresh vegetables for his ship, and then we had an auction of the fruits, at which I actually bought three peaches for nine shillings. Many a time at home I have bought a whole basketful for a quarter of that price, which only goes to show what an effort people will make to keep up appearances. Yet here they have one fruit that cannot be beaten anywhere, and that is the greatest fruit of all—children. In numbers, beauty, and behaviour the children of Port Stanley cannot be surpassed in this world.

On March 24th I attended the funeral of the young wife of the Rev. Mr. Johnson, who had died in childbirth. It was a very large funeral as both the deceased and her husband were popular and well-known and the weather was fine. It surprised me to find that the town did not possess a hearse. The coffin had to be carried a distance of something like two miles by eight bearers who relieved each other about every two hundred paces. A service was conducted in the Tabernacle by the Dean of the Cathedral (this was considered by many to be a great concession), then we continued our slow and solemn march to the burial ground. After the coffin had been lowered into the grave, amid many groans, sobs, and tears, a strange thing happened. The bereaved husband pointed at it and said, for all to hear, " Behold the handwork of Doctor —", and repeated it a second time. To me it seemed wicked, especially from a minister of the Gospel. At such a time one should forgive one's enemies, but I gathered that for some time there had been an element of dissatisfaction with this doctor among the public and shortly after this a rather scurrilous handbill attacking him was scattered around the town. Eventually the doctor, who is the only one in the islands, had to stand trial and was acquitted.

At noon on March 27th, 1912 the foundation of the first wireless telegraph tower in the Falklands was ceremonially laid. The weather was most disagreeable, with a howling NW gale, and I had no intention of going along until the Governor sent me a request the night before to be present. The party was taken down to the mouth of the harbour in two launches, the *Penguin* and *Plym*. About one hundred of Stanley's leading men were present, and some twenty ladies headed by the Governor's wife, who goes along with her active husband whenever and wherever there is aught to be done. A more bleak place could not be imagined. To the east was the cold sea lashed into white waves by the fierce wind, to the west nothing but bare rocky hills and mountains. We looked like marooned people on some desert island, raising this tower as our last hope of getting assistance.

After landing from the launches we walked a third of a mile over bogs and rocks, boards having been laid at the worst places. On the way I noticed plenty of Malvena or Tea Berries growing on a kind of vine. These red berries are very sweet and about the size of huckleberries. On fine days the children gather them, while the vines on which they grow are used by the sealers when dried for making tea.

Arrived at the site for the tower over which flags were waving, we found a large hole ten feet deep and twenty feet wide had been dug and cemented inside. After depositing a box containing all our signatures and some coins in the hole and covering it with an iron plate and cement the Governor read a speech. He said it was only since his arrival that the telephone had been introduced, though it and the wireless had been talked of for twenty years, and that the position of this tower would give a clear passage for the wireless waves to Buenos Aires to the north and to the Strait of Magellan to the west. Then he spoke of the benefits it would bring to the islanders in disposing of their produce, but he did not mention that in case of a war the colony could be notified in time for them to make preparations for it. There is no doubt it will dispel to a certain extent the feeling of isolation one has here. He went on to say that future generations might dig up our names and smile at our having lived at a time when men had to depend on such a poor instrument as the wireless. Then, after drinking success to the wireless and to the Falkland Islands, we gave three cheers, before wending our way back to the boats. But for the strong gale blowing it would have been a picnic. As it was, the cabin was the best place to keep away from the showers of spray blowing over the launch so I lost the view of the land which I had not seen before, the latter part of which was up a narrow passage forming a natural dry-dock where they have careened vessels in old times.

Two new sailors arrived from Montevideo to make up my crew, one of them an Irishman named John Dunlea hailing from Cambridge, Mass. On April 7th, the British ship *Wiscomb Park,* Captain William Griffiths, arrived from Cape Horn in a leaking condition. I had met the captain two years before in Honolulu, just after he had lost his ship at Kahului. This time he was outward bound from England with a cargo of cement, had been run down in the English Channel, and had beached his ship at Southampton to keep her from sinking, and she was now leaking around the place where she was repaired. He seemed to think the leaks were below the waterline, but I thought they were above it, as his stanchions were loose on the port side and the bulwarks would soon have gone if he had not made port or met fine weather. He had already jettisoned 152 barrels of cement in the North Atlantic. This was the fifth survey I had been called upon to do, they seemed to like me for it, perhaps because I typed out the reports and gave copies to the captains for their guidance. I enjoyed doing it in Mr. Harding's office. He said I did all the work, but I told him he was giving me an education and perhaps some day I could set up as a surveyor in New York.

By this time we were bending sails again, and on Saturday, April 20th, *Nuuanu* sailed from Port Stanley to resume her voyage to Honolulu, after five and a half months in port. In spite of the unpleasant climate I had become very attached to the people, if not to the place, I had become so intimate with all their lives that I felt like one of the family. Then there was the dread of Cape Horn before us, and I knew every man on board would have gladly got clear of the ship and joined one bound north, even if he went for no wages. Many of the people were disappointed that it was foggy when we left and they could not wave good-bye to us from their doors and windows as we towed out, but could only see the tops of our masts. However, on Tuesday morning we were back again. We had set out with a fair East wind, then it had hauled to the SW and blown a gale off the western end of the island, and we had broken the fore yard truss. When they sighted us from the lighthouse the whole town was agog to know what was the matter. The lighthouse hoisted the signal, "Why have you returned?" I had hardly slept since leaving, what with the fog and the gale, and was busy beating into the harbour with short tacks so did not reply, but if there had been time I would have replied, "Another sheep." We had lived on mutton all the time we were there and never got tired of it. The wind dying away, we came to anchor in the outer harbour. I must say it was one of the unexpected pleasures of my life to come back, though we lost a fine East wind while we were there. Soon I was back in my room at the Stanley Arms, with my good friends around me. The truss was brought ashore and they went to work on it immediately. But some of the ladies were not pleased that we did not come into the Inner harbour, so on Thursday I took three of them to see their friends on board and it was a lovely day.

On Friday morning I left the shore early, scarcely saying good-bye to anyone. We got to sea by late afternoon, and though many urged me not to sail on a Friday, there was still an East wind. After a hard time down to the Horn we found favourable winds there and made good progress. Thirty-five days out we were nearly in the SE Trades, with all our troubles over. Those two days in Stanley on our return were among the happiest I ever spent, seeing again so soon people I thought I had said good-bye to for ever. I sometimes wonder now if I will ever go there again. The rest of the voyage to Honolulu was uneventful and we arrived on July 25th, 1912.

POSTSCRIPT

With the arrival of *Nuuanu* at Honolulu on July 25th, 1912, Captain Josselyn's account of his adventures ends. The opening of the Panama Canal caused Charles Brewer & Co. to go out of business and the barque was sold at Honolulu, to become the schooner *Hai Hong* and trade around the Philippines for some years. The last time I saw her she was a rusty hulk laid up in Manila harbour in January, 1926, the old Hawaiian name cut into her stern still clearly legible.

The old Captain returned to the eastern States as a passenger, not to retire as might have been expected, but to take command of the barque *Foohng Suey* for her new owners, the Texas Company of New York. Though still hale and hearty when he took over, it was not many months before his old enemy pneumonia caught up with him for the last time and he was landed dangerously ill at the end of a voyage in New York, dying a few days later. He is buried in his old home town of Duxbury, Mass.

W. J. MOORE.

To W.L.J.

The Old Man's hair was marked by Winter's snows
His furrowed face as brown as walrus hide
His eyes gave back the blue of many seas
But the same old youthful roll was in his stride
The same old boyish swagger met life's blows.

The iron square-rigged ship he used to drive
Against the winds and current past the Horn
Is now rigged fore and aft in coastwise trade
Or else a helpless lighter, masts all gone
A ship perhaps, no more a ship alive.

The ship whose quarterdeck he now commands
Is sailing seas beyond those mortals know
A fairer ship than his first clipper was
Flung by a hurricane long, long ago
And lost, a wreck, upon Far Eastern sands.

The course he sails will never more make port
But far from coastwise lights when gales are high
Through wind and sleet and roll we still may catch
The Admiral's signals in the distant sky
A hull down lighthouse flash just faintly caught.

From Sea-Rimes, by John T. Nichols, 1921

234

INDEX OF SHIP NAMES

INDEX OF PLACE NAMES

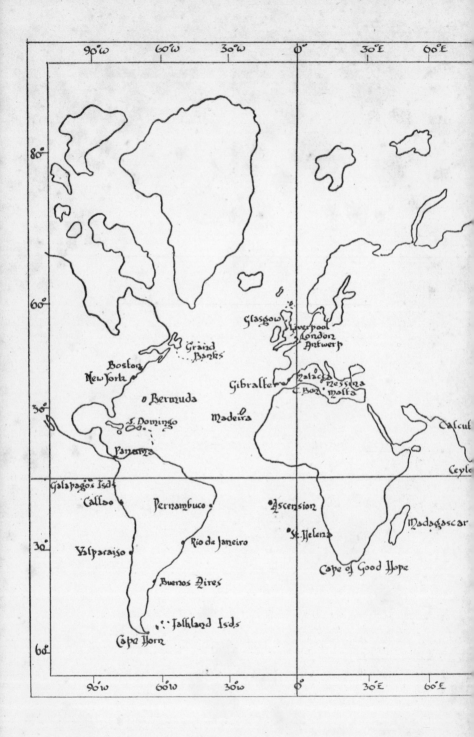